SMALL STEPS

Shortlisted for the

2018 City of Fremantle Hungerford Award

Julie Sprigg is a Perth-based author whose debut book, *Small Steps: A Physio in Ethiopia*, was shortlisted for the 2018 City of Fremantle Hungerford Award. She worked as a physiotherapist for ten years before switching to a career in foreign aid with programs improving human rights of people with disabilities. After years of regular travel to China, India, Bangladesh, Cambodia, Vietnam, Vanuatu and Ethiopia, Julie returned to Perth and now evaluates government programs to overcome social disadvantage. When not writing or working she can be found reading a picture book atlas with her young son and delighting in domestic adventures.

Published with support from the Dorothy and Bill Irwin Charitable Trust

JULIE SPRIGG

SMALL STEPS

This is a work of creative non-fiction. All character names and identifying characteristics have been changed, with the exception of Tadesse and Marieke who agreed to appear as themselves. To former colleagues and students of University of Gondar, I wish there was space to write about all of you and your dedication to your work.

Chapter 1

To eat: መብላት /*meblat*/

My first patient arrived tied to his mother's back like an overgrown baby. The mother panted from the effort of carrying him on her back up the hill to the clinic and looked relieved to untie him. She crouched as she loosened the torn strips of cotton and the child gently slid to the mat.

Set high in the mountainous outskirts of Ethiopia's capital city Addis Ababa, the clinic was inside a converted shipping container with a door and windows cut into the metal walls. It was just big enough to fit a desk, a low plinth, a bench and a blue floor mat. Physio equipment was crammed into any remaining space. Although it was still early on that morning in October 2004, the street outside was busy. Road workers clinked pickaxes on rocks, pedestrians called out to each other and donkeys brayed.

I hovered in the doorway while the head sister directed the mother to sit on the mat next to her son, then she waved me over. The head sister wore a blue uniform, the same shade of blue as the nuns had worn at my Catholic primary school in Western Australia. Strands of white hair poked from beneath her blue veil, her face was pink and she puffed as she spoke.

'Meet Yeshe. She is the team leader for community-based rehabilitation workers. You will work together.'

Yeshe was tall and very thin. She might have been older than me but her skin was free of wrinkles. She was striking, with high cheekbones and a delicate, pointed chin.

'Yeshe speaks the best English; most of the other rehabilitation workers speak none.' The head sister snapped her wrist to summon the staff chatting under blue gums outside. They hurried inside and she addressed them in the staccato sounds of the Amharic language. I recognised the greeting from the lessons given to me by an Ethiopian family a sister in Perth had introduced me to. The final lesson had been just last week.

The head sister turned to me, her face stern. 'I told them you were the new physiotherapist from Australia. If you want to communicate with them, you better talk through Yeshe.'

When she gave a sharp nod to the closest man, he shot his hand out to shake mine, then each of the ten others did the same. Each person pumped my hand and announced names so unfamiliar and long that by the time I'd been around the circle I couldn't remember any of them.

The head sister looked at me. 'Well?' she said, then gestured with her chin at the child.

'Yes. Okay. Well. Righto. Thank you, Sister Starling.'

As she walked out, I cleared my throat and turned to Yeshe. 'Let's begin?'

'He name is Teferi. Eight years old, mental retardation case,' Yeshe said.

I cringed, but said nothing. The child's face showed the characteristic features of Down syndrome.

'Could you please walk with him to the other side of the room, so I can assess his walking?' I asked Yeshe, hoping I sounded more confident than I felt. Even though I'd been a practising physiotherapist for seven years, at that moment I didn't feel at all confident.

The ten rehabilitation workers gathered around me in a circle. The child walked with his legs widened and knees out straight as if they were tethered to sticks. When Yeshe let go of his hand, he tottered on the spot for a minute, unable to balance without support. He wore no shoes, the sleeves on his jumper were shredded from the elbow and the patched knees on his green trousers were worn through. Both inner leg seams had unravelled and his trousers hung around his waist, leaving most of his lower body exposed. Although Sister Starling had told me in the car that the clinic was in one of the poorest areas of Addis Ababa, I was still shocked to see such poverty up close for the first time.

Too disconcerted to focus properly on a physiotherapy assessment, I asked Yeshe, 'Is his mum so poor she can't afford to buy cotton to fix his trousers?'

'Oh no, is important like that. Infection in the ... how you say?' Yeshe screwed her nose up as if it might help her think of a translation. 'Ureen. Doctor told mother fresh air for healing.'

I carried out a full physiotherapy assessment and when I asked Teferi to stand, he peed on the lino. His legs wobbled until they gave out and he fell to the floor, his bottom exposed amidst footmarks in the layer of dust on the floor. The area around the clinic was unsealed and even with the first patient for the day, the staff had tracked dust and gravel in on their shoes.

With the assessment over, I demonstrated some simple exercises to help Teferi's walking. His mother, who had a narrow face and a white headscarf pulled tight over braids, looked as if she was in her mid-twenties, like me.

When I asked Yeshe if she could translate 'Let's practise the exercises now', Teferi's mum removed his threadbare trousers so now he left a trail of splotches that turned the dust to mud.

No-one seemed worried about the mess, and when I asked Yeshe if we had anything to clean the floor with, she shook her head.

I asked two other rehabilitation workers whose names I'd forgotten, 'What can we use to clean this?'

'No have for cleaning,' one of them said, and both looked at me with kind expressions.

'Okay. Do we have a towel?'

'No have towel,' the other said.

I asked about every cleaning material I could think of. Did we have tissues? Did we have toilet paper? Any paper?

But no-one understood me and Teferi continued his exercises with a puddle between his feet. Then Yeshe opened the plywood wardrobe in the corner and took out a roll of toilet paper. She pulled off a few sheets and blew her nose.

'*There*!' I almost yelled it. 'What do you call that?'

The rehabilitation workers all nodded and two said in unison, 'Aahh. *Soft*.'

'We call it *soft*,' Yeshe said as she replaced the roll and closed the cupboard.

'Can I please use some?' I asked.

'Oh, you need toilet?' Yeshe looked surprised and pulled the door open again.

After Teferi left, I squatted with the toilet roll, smearing black marks where the wee mixed with the dirt. I wondered if I was offending my new colleagues, or if they would think me helpful.

Fortunately, Sister Starling appeared at the door and provided an excuse to stop. 'It's time for prayers.'

I looked over at Yeshe. 'Yes, prayers every Monday.'

When we gathered in the central office, instead of bowing my head and closing my eyes, I waited until everyone else's eyes were closed and peeked around the room. I studied my new colleagues, the crucifix on the wall and the statuette of the Blessed Virgin Mary beside a portrait of the order's founding sister. I took in the mismatched wooden furniture, sagging ceiling, and the whirr of the ceiling fan.

At my going-away party the week before, my sister Michelle said, 'Will you need to go to church every day and say prayers from the Bible?'

I sipped Margaret River cabernet sauvignon, saying, 'I won't be a real nun. I'll volunteer as a physiotherapist with the nuns' clinic, and I'll get my food and accommodation in the convent.

It's just logistical.'

My friend Andrew asked, 'If you live in a convent will you need to wear Clarks lace-ups and scratchy underwear?'

'I'll wear normal knickers, but I'll cultivate my latent spiritual side,' I said through a mouthful of brie cheese. 'I'm looking forward to being a volunteer and living a simple life. You know, putting aside my earthly desires for a year, at least until I turn twenty-eight.'

It was midday by the time we'd finished prayers and I was relieved when we broke for lunch. I was almost light-headed with hunger. I had taken a meagre scoop of porridge from the communal serving bowl at breakfast as I hadn't known the correct amount to serve oneself in a convent in Ethiopia and didn't want the sisters to think I was greedy.

Yeshe and the rehab workers headed towards the corrugated-iron shed for lunch. But when I followed them, Sister Meaza, a young sister, beckoned me from the open door of an office. I had met her at breakfast, where she told me that as a novice sister, she was still in training and spent part of her day carrying out duties for the senior sisters.

She said, 'Sister Starling said you'd better not eat there.'

'Why is that?'

'You won't like it. You better eat at the head office. That's where the *ferenjis* should eat.'

I knew *ferenji* meant 'foreigner' from the Ethiopian family in my street. They had taught me Amharic pleasantries and I supplemented their tuition with furious independent study. I'd completed the homework up to chapter five from *Teach Yourself Amharic* and made notes in my copy of the Lonely Planet Amharic phrasebook, which fit in the pocket of my jeans.

In the head office, I realised I hadn't met any of these staff members, and that I was the only female. Too intimidated to start a conversation, I sat in silence, willing everyone to start eating so I could too. But no-one else at the circle of desks took out their lunches, so I took out the phrasebook and studied the section on 'meals' instead of opening my bag.

It seemed the men were all waiting for a catered lunch. An old lady with no front teeth stood on tiptoes to lean over the garden and pass enamel pots through an open window. With equally flagrant disregard for occupational safety, the office workers stooped to a knee-high table to serve their lunch. My stomach rumbled as I smelt garlic and spices and watched my new colleagues dish up a variety of stews from the enamel pots. I wished I could substitute my lunch for this spread but I didn't know what the etiquette was, how I should pay, or if the sisters would allow it, since they'd sent me with a packed lunch.

Earlier that morning at breakfast Sister Meaza asked what I'd like for lunch. I replied, 'Just whatever everyone else has.'

She had replied, 'Oh no, you won't like it. You better have what *ferenjis* eat.'

So without knowing what it was, I agreed not to eat it. Now I untied the blue plastic bag Sister Meaza packed for me and took out a boiled egg and a wedge of plain homemade bread wrapped in alfoil.

My fingers trembled from low blood sugar and my stomach rumbled as I tried to shell the egg. I wished I'd eaten more at breakfast, or packed some morning tea, and wished it even more when I had to stop peeling as everyone said grace. For a minute the room hummed as the diners mumbled prayers in Amharic and repeated the sign of the cross three times above their plates. I was thrilled when the prayers stopped so I could recommence preparing my lunch.

'Are you new?' The man sitting next to me spoke. He had silver-speckled curls and a kind face.

'Yes, I am the new physiotherapist.'

'Aha. We are lucky to have a physiotherapist. There are not so many physiotherapists in Ethiopia, you know. There is no university course for studying physiotherapy in this country yet.'

'Yes, Sister Starling told me.'

The man looked as if he would take a mouthful but spoke again. 'Just there were a few trained, in Cuba ... was it Cuba? Or Russia? I forget.' He clicked his tongue against his teeth as he tried to remember. 'After the war. Just a few. The government sent them for training. Just for treating the soldiers though. Not really for the civilians.'

I couldn't get the shell off my egg and I was too hungry to think of a reply, so instead I smiled. The cook with the missing teeth moved around the room, serving tea. She set a glass of black tea in front of me and I took a sip before trying again to peel my egg.

The man tore off a piece of flatbread and used it to scoop his stew. He paused with it midway to his mouth. 'How do you see *injera*?'

'I'm sorry?' I asked, wishing I could just eat instead of talk.

'How do you see *injera*?' He still held the flatbread by his mouth.

I'd read about *injera*, Ethiopia's staple food, but I didn't understand his question. I paused as I tried to guess, before I offered, 'It looks delicious?'

He beamed at me, and I beamed back, wondering if *injera* was what the sisters had insisted I wouldn't like.

I ate half my boiled egg and a mouthful of bread, but it was so dry my saliva vanished at once. I took another sip of tea and tried to swallow both together. The man continued to scoop his meat, potatoes and rice. It smelt so good. With an insufficient breakfast and now a lunch I couldn't swallow, I felt more than envious. I felt *starving*. Then I felt guilty, remembering the coins we used to collect at school for the nuns to send bread to the starving children of Ethiopia.

In grade one at my Catholic school in the farming community of Boyup Brook, we had a missions box just inside the door of the classroom. The money box had a slot in the top and the photos printed on it showed African children with swollen bellies and flies on their noses. The children looked morose beside the beatific statuette of the Virgin Mary and the blooms in a vase that always flanked the box.

'Donate your money for the missions,' my teacher Sister Brendan advised us. 'Those children are starving. Bring coins from home to feed the Ethiopians.'

My classmates and I proudly dispatched our pocket money into the missions box, but in catechism class, Sister Brendan tapped her cane on the front desk and said, 'God likes the silent giver. Give when no-one is looking.' We all nodded but only pretended to wait until no-one could see before clinking in our contribution as loudly as possible.

Once a term, we had missions day at school where each classroom set up a stall and we spent our pocket money buying delicious things each other's mums had baked. Our bellies ached from mixing Mrs Piper's chocolate crackles with Mrs Hester's curried egg sandwiches and two wedges of Mrs Lane's coconut ice. We sat on the floor and, with legs prickling from the sisal carpet, piled the five-cent coins, ten cents and twenty cents to tally our takings. We were excited, knowing the money would help those children on the missions box whom Sister Brendan said didn't even get to eat bread, let alone Mrs Coole's lamingtons.

Now here I was in Ethiopia, eating *ferenji* bread.

The man next to me spoke again. 'Is this your first time to Ethiopia?'

The tea softened the bread so I could swallow and say, 'My first day.'

'How do you see Ethiopia?' He gestured with his hands around the room, at the window with its shutters falling off, the banana palm outside, the lunch lady standing back in the garden, resting her elbow on the windowsill to chat. I thought about my first patient here and the morning so unlike any other first day on a job.

I leafed to the back of the phrasebook and pointed to the word I wanted. The phonetic script was set out next to the Amharic script, but I couldn't pronounce it, so instead I held my finger under it.

'*Aw-od-arl-ehu*,' he pronounced for me. 'I love it.'

Chapter 2

To walk: በግርመሄድ፡ */be-eger mehed/*

The next morning's patient was already there when I got to work. I sat next to him where he lay on the thick vinyl mat on the floor. Yeshe slipped off her mules and sat cross-legged next to me, arranging her long skirt over her bare legs. The other ten workers formed a circle.

'He name Ammanuel. Four years old,' Yeshe translated from the boy's mother, who perched on the edge of a chair.

I tried hard not to look surprised. This four-year-old was the size of an eighteen-month-old, with an enlarged head and emaciated, flaccid limbs. He didn't look at me when I picked him up, instead his eyes glazed. He wore no nappy, only a shirt I guessed had once been white but was now brown and stiff with dirt and urine. When I picked him up to sit him in my lap, the shirt lifted to reveal a tiny withered body with legs dangling from soft hips. His mother's outfit was speckled with holes and the neckline of her shirt had disintegrated and split in two. The skin on her face and hands was dirty, dry and cracked.

The child and his mother smelt so strongly of rotten vegetables that I felt nauseous and while they explained their situation I pretended to scratch under my nose so I could block the smell.

Yeshe translated that Ammanuel had spent the first four years of his life tied to his mother's back, whenever she was at home or walking somewhere. She always tied him to look over her right shoulder. Now I saw how the muscles on one side of his back had shortened and stiffened, which had caused a lopsided curve in his spine.

'Has she ever taken him for physio?'

Yeshe translated for us. 'Never. There is no place for physiotherapy. Just to come to small clinics like this one.'

I asked if he ever lay on his tummy.

'Not ever lying on stomach. Only lying on back. When she wanting for resting her back, she is lying him on the bed,' Yeshe translated and then asked, 'Do you think he'll learn to walk?'

Ten rehabilitation workers peered in to hear my answer. Having never seen a child in such a state before, I was overwhelmed and didn't know how to answer. Instead I said, 'Let's do an assessment and discuss what we find.'

I tried standard paediatric physio assessments and saw that when I rattled a toy in front of him he wasn't able to focus his eyes on it. He couldn't turn his head to follow the toy when I shook it at the side. Although old enough to be a preschooler, he had the development skills of an infant. When I put him on his tummy he lay there motionless, not making a sound. As I picked him up, a trickle of his urine went onto the treatment mat.

'*Yikerta*, *yikerta*, excuse me, excuse me.' His mum dabbed at the puddle with his knitted hat.

'No matter,' Yeshe said in English and repeated the message to his mum in Amharic.

When I sat Ammanuel on my knee, his head sank as if too heavy for his little body. As his head lolled to one side, saliva dripped from the corner of his mouth. His mum dabbed at it with the hat, the same hat she would later put on his head when it was time to go. I was appalled but, taking my cue from the workers, I kept quiet.

Therapy for a child with this degree of disability would be a challenge anywhere, but here it seemed impossible. My first thought was that he should receive a wheelchair so his mum needn't carry him everywhere.

‘Does anyone use a wheelchair here?’ I asked Yeshe.

She replied, ‘It is difficult, who can push a wheelchair up these roads?’

The roads were so rocky and on such impossible gradients that a wheelchair would be of little use. I put the idea of a wheelchair aside and showed his mum some exercises to do. She said they would come again the next day.

Ammanuel’s mum brought him in for treatment again the next day and every day that week. By the Thursday of the second week, he focused his eyes on a rattle when I shook it above him and began to be more responsive. It was a good sign – developing control of the eyes is the first developmental stage. As I waved goodbye to Ammanuel, who looked snug tied to his mother’s back, I wondered: if he could develop control of his eyes within a week, what other improvements might he make?

As he left, another mother arrived. She extended her hand to shake mine, bending forwards from the weight of her child strapped to her back. Teferi popped his head over her shoulder and beamed at me and I recognised him from the floor-cleaning incident of my first day. When his mother had untied the child from her back I asked him to sit on a low stool.

‘Does she carry him everywhere on her back?’ I asked Yeshe.

‘Not everywhere. Sometimes he is walking, even though he is a bit slow at it.’

I rummaged in the toy box and pulled out a toy maraca while Yeshe translated for me. ‘Her home is too far from here, forty-five minutes. He cannot walking so far, and he is so slow.’

I shook the toy up high and as Teferi stretched up to reach for it, he splayed his legs wide for balance. His thighs wobbled, too weak for the weight of his body.

‘Could we visit him at home? We can show his mum exercises to make his legs stronger day to day. So she doesn’t need to come for therapy every day.’

Teferi's mum looked thrilled when Yeshe translated my offer and invited us to come the next day.

'Do we need to organise for a car? Maybe Sister Starling could drive us there?' I asked.

Yeshe looked surprised. 'No, Julie, no car can driving there. *Be-eger mehed,*' she said in Amharic and when I looked confused she slipped her arm in mine. 'We go by walking.'

That night, in my room at the convent, I studied the copy of *Disabled Village Children* that I'd borrowed from the physio office. I pored over its pages, which gave therapy ideas for places with few resources. I made notes about the exercises Teferi might do and drew stick figures performing the exercises on a small handout for his mum and folded it inside my diary.

To get to Teferi's home from the clinic the next morning, we crossed a bridge where the land fell away in a deep cleft and a creek trickled through umbrella palm leaves. The morning light caught in the dew of winding foliage, making the leaves shine an almost pearlescent blue. The mountain air still held its overnight chill so our breath fogged as we walked and I pulled my headscarf around my neck and over my nose for warmth.

We picked our way across a low creek. I followed Yeshe as she leapt from a stepping stone to the bank. Plastic bags and household refuse dotted the riverbed and I wondered what happened to the rubbish when the river rose. On the other side of the river, rubbish overflowed from two skips piled twice as high again, with children clambering on top picking through the refuse. The surrounding area was littered with detritus. An old man hobbled from the top of the skip, carrying a full plastic bag.

I was sweating by the time we'd reached Teferi's house, almost an hour's walk from the clinic. The morning fog in the foothills of Mount Entoto had burned away and I unzipped my jacket and unwound my headscarf from around my neck and wore it like Yeshe, pulling the front of the stiff cotton out to shade my forehead from the burning sun. Outside the house, a group of women sat on low stools, peeling onions and garlic, dropping the peeled cloves into piles on the ground. Teferi threw his arms in the air and yelped with delight on our arrival and held both our hands to lead us inside.

The one-roomed house was dark and cold, with the only light and heat coming from a single window. An iron bedstead with rusting legs sat against the wall beneath the window, lined with rags in place of a mattress. Another bed on the opposite wall had a mattress with hair stuffing poking through a split along its length. Teferi fossicked under the bed then careened across to us, first holding onto the sideboard, then the knee-high table, then wobbling towards me with a huge smile, holding out two ankle splints and two socks as an offering.

He almost reached me before falling backwards and landing on his backside with legs splayed, but he still looked elated.

'He is very proud of his socks.' Yeshe translated when he spoke. 'These are his only socks.'

I helped Teferi with his socks. The black sock was so big it almost reached Teferi's knee, with the heel flapping halfway up his calf. The green sock was better, fitting his own heel. I slid on the ankle splints made from moulded plastic that fit from the soles of his feet up to the back of his knees, then I wedged his sneakers on over the top.

'Let's think of exercises Teferi can do around the house to strengthen his legs, now that he is wearing his splints,' I said to Yeshe. I took the folded handout from my diary and pointed to my diagrams.

'For example, maybe Teferi can carry his own plates to the table at dinnertime.' I was proud of the culturally appropriate exercise using locally available materials, as per the *Disabled Village Children* textbook, chapter one.

Yeshe translated for us. 'They have only one plate, they all eat from the same one. His mother says can he carry a cup instead.'

Teferi's mother took three cups out of the small kitchen area.

'This the whole family can drink from,' Yeshe said.

Picturing the family of six taking it in turns to sip from a cup shared between two, I realised my exercises were less culturally appropriate than I had imagined.

Teferi clutched a cup between his hands and staggered across to the small table. With his ankle splints on, he wobbled less, and could walk further before lurching for the furniture.

'Where did he get the splints from?' I asked Yeshe.

'From the clinic in the city centre. They are giving many of splints and things. Sister Starling she already organised it.'

'Why doesn't he wear his splints all the time?' I asked Yeshe. I wondered why his mum hadn't brought his splints to physio any of the days this week.

'His socks were dirty. And then drying,' Yeshe explained.

I hadn't considered the logistics of being able to afford only one pair of socks that weren't a pair anyway, and how cold his little feet would be with no socks on in this chilly house on a mountainside, and felt a sudden outrage. This family just had one plate to share between six people, and only two socks for their son, while everyone I knew at home had more than enough plates and socks, and no-one lived near mounds of uncollected rubbish.

Teferi's mum spoke to Yeshe, who translated. 'Julie, his mum wants to know. If he walking every day with splints on, will his walking become stronger?'

'Yes, it will. He needs to walk every single day.'

The convent held a silent retreat day that weekend. No-one spoke, except for whispered essentials. Calm settled over the convent and the pacifying effect of mutual quiet was more intense than the silence of solitude. Tranquillity pervaded when everyone tried to minimise sound, to watch how they placed their feet, the speed at which they walked, or the way they placed a cup and saucer or a plate in a pile.

It was a stillness I'd never experienced in my hectic, share-house lifestyle in Australia. The sun was out, so I spread an old blanket on the grass within the convent grounds to read a book. It was such a treat to have time to read a book in the sun, with only the sounds of prayer chants drifting over from a nearby Ethiopian Orthodox church, along with birdsong and the rustle of leaves in the breeze. On Sundays at home in Perth I was usually hungover, or at committee meetings organising pro-refugee rallies. Back there I combined a job, postgraduate study and social activism with a hectic social calendar.

But this morning I marvelled at how much I had enjoyed handwashing my clothes. Timesaving devices like washing machines don't actually save time, I reasoned. They only allow us to reapportion time to fit more tasks into our lives. Now I had few tasks, and only a backpack's worth of clothes to wash.

The book shaded my face as I lay on my back and, instead of reading, imagined what I might learn from the sisters. These women had devoted their lives to helping the poor, the sick and the needy. They had turned their backs on a conventional life to achieve purity through scarcity. Perhaps I should become a nun as well? I fantasised about living a life of impressive purity and calm.

I had considered becoming a nun before. Admittedly it was in grade two, when we were visited by a nun from Thailand who was nothing like the nuns I knew. She looked no older than my cousin in grade twelve, and while my teacher Sister Brendan had wrinkles and a tuft of spiky hairs poking from her chin, Sister Theresa's face was smooth and hairfree. Instead of walloping her cane to bellow about purgatory and scrubbing the stain of original sin from our souls, Sister Theresa sat us on her knee at lunchtime and sang songs in Thai about mud crabs.

Sister Theresa was captivating when she stood in front of the blackboard to talk about her work in Thailand, helping orphans and children too poor for shoes and food, or even school. I adored this soft, fun sister and decided I wanted to be just like her.

Maybe that's why I paid attention when, not long after, Mum and I watched *The Bert Newton Show*. Dad had just installed our colour TV and Olivia Newton-John scissor-kicked in hot-pink lycra leggings and blue top to 'Physical'. We were both still spellbound when Bert announced that the next segment would be about a nun, Mother Teresa.

'Is it my Sister Theresa?' I asked, overjoyed to think of my Sister Theresa singing about mud crabs on the colour TV. But this sister on the TV looked more like the nuns I was familiar with. Her face was craggy and wrinkled. As we watched, she handed out bread to beggars and kissed a dirty baby.

'I want to do that,' I said to Mum, and I remember her looking at me with surprise. Twenty-one years later, before I left for Ethiopia, I asked Mum if she had cherished that memory, being proud of my showing such vocation at an early age. Mum looked blank and said she had too many other important things to remember and had I packed my malaria tablets?

As I became a teenager, I put aside my yearning to become a nun, but the feeling of a vocation never left me.

In grade twelve at my all-girls Catholic boarding school, I became missions coordinator with my friend Angela. Every week, we collected the missions boxes from next to the plastic statuettes of the Blessed Virgin Mary just inside the door of each classroom. We emptied the cardboard coin-boxes and counted up the change. Every week we wrote encouraging snippets for the school newsletter, imploring our fellow pupils to be generous for those in faraway places less fortunate than we. We wrote earnest editorials about the countries donations went to. Most of the time I needed to look up these places in the *World Book Encyclopedia*, and daydreamed while I researched, looking at the photos, imagining myself one day working somewhere like that.

Outside the career counsellor's office, I picked up a pamphlet about physiotherapy. I skimmed until my eye was caught by the section reading: 'Physiotherapists' skills are needed in developing countries to assist in rehabilitation of serious injuries.' A year later, when I was accepted into physiotherapy at university, my parents prudently enrolled me in St Thomas More Residential College. 'St Thomas More College adheres to Catholic principles,' read the promotional pamphlet, clearly intended to reassure devout parents of the safety of their children. 'The rules of the College forbid boys in girls wings after 12 p.m. and vice versa ... St Thomas More College encourages the responsible consumption of alcohol.'

On my first Saturday night at college, drunk in the boys wing at 2.30 a.m., I realised I didn't have to go to church in the morning. There was no-one to make me go, only a nagging sensation. I'd been to mass every Sunday for the last eighteen years. That first Sunday of university, I went to mass, then for a couple of Sundays after that, until a new place of weekly devotion called. They both had wine, you could attend on a Saturday night, but one was more fun. My love affair with the pub continued for the duration of my physiotherapy degree until long after I had graduated and set off travelling.

In England, I worked as a physiotherapist and sometimes went to church on a Sunday morning, providing I wasn't hungover, or indeed, still drunk. The need for spiritual satiety bubbled out of nowhere amongst new friends, new nightclubs, historical monuments and monumental homesickness. In church, for that hour, I knew who I was. I knew when to stand, when to sit, when to kneel, what to say and when to say it. I prayed to God to forgive my sins, which transgressed a wider spectrum of the Ten Commandments the longer I travelled. I prayed for God to keep my family safe; to please let me get this new locum job; to please let my visa for my Russia trip come through on time. Spiritual refreshment achieved, I'd delay for months before the feeling crept up again and I'd need another hit of familiarity.

Then I discovered socialism. I had never heard of the May Day protests, but travelling the Big Wide World™ had given me a new perspective on capitalism. At a tube station one frosty morning, a guy in a red bandana handed me a thin newspaper. Squashed against the other commuters, I unfolded my copy of *Socialist Worker*. Inside, articles explained how corporations exploited consumers, how consumer greed leads to poverty and how our government was complicit in keeping bad governments in power. I had an epiphany on the road to Bethnal Green. I realised, after devouring the article on corporate profit from war, that I was now a socialist.

It was socialist Julie who worked as a paediatric physiotherapist in a mostly Muslim suburb of London. Anti-capitalist Julie learnt about Muslim cultures and acquired a rudimentary Arabic vocabulary. This was before September 11, before Islam became synonymous with terrorism, and I wrote home long emails about onyx-eyed toddlers from Oman, and Saudi mothers who fed me rosewater sweets.

When my visa for England expired, it was collectivist Julie who backpacked through South America, witnessing Peruvian *campesinos* queuing by the roadside for a chance of a day's paid work on the land. My red socialist hair dried in the sun after a swim on Copacabana beach on the day I saw shanties lining the hills above glittering condominiums in Rio de Janeiro. In La Paz, I discussed left-wing politics with my Bolivian Spanish teacher, and the world made so much more sense. Until September 11 happened, and I was in Bolivia with a connecting flight through New York airport that I couldn't take. I was tired of the Big Wide World™ and couldn't wait to get to safe, predictable Home.

But home wasn't predictable anymore. Only a few months later, I was back at my parents' house and spreading Vegemite on toast in front of morning television.

'We will decide who comes to this country and the circumstances in which they come!' Prime Minister John Howard announced to the country. The TV flashed footage of Muslim people alleged to be ruthless enough to throw their own children into the water.

'They're all like that,' people said. 'They should go back where they came from.'

But this didn't fit with the Muslim people I had known just months earlier. No-one wanted to hear stories from the physio work I'd done, of my cute paediatric patients. No-one was interested to hear about a heartbroken Muslim father from Kuwait cradling his terminally ill baby. Or about the Muslim father who asked after my family's health while recuperating from donating a third of his own liver to his son.

What had I come home to? I didn't recognise my country anymore. Its people seemed selfish and mean.

We incarcerated refugees from the same countries we had bombed in the name of liberation. We kept toddlers in maximum-security institutions. It seemed so *wrong*. The more I read articles and listened to those who'd seen behind the razor wire, the less I could ignore this incredible injustice.

Before long, I joined organising committees for pro-refugee protests and got arrested at a demonstration outside a detention centre in the South Australian desert. Letters to detainees soon became telephone calls, which led to visits to a detention centre in the hostile heat of Australia's north-west.

I moved to Port Hedland to be near the centre and got a part-time job at a university health centre. In between visits, I was a political activist. I wrote to my comrades in Perth and organised information for media releases regarding the latest detainees attempting suicide or facing deportation.

In Port Hedland I met Sister Maeve, a Catholic nun who devoted herself to supporting the asylum seekers. Like the nuns of my youth, she had wiry hair and a maternal air. She didn't wear the veil, but she wore the uniform of blue cardigans with navy skirts and Clarks lace-up shoes.

I went to church with Sister Maeve the first week I lived in Port Hedland, but it was a long time since I'd been a regular congregant. I couldn't go to church every weekend and sing hymns beside the comfortable piety of those happy to talk about injustice yet take no action. Standing against unfairness was the way I now expressed my vocation. Religious life had two elements, I reasoned: being and doing. I was a *doer*.

Over lunch in the convent guesthouse, I told Sister Maeve my feelings about talking versus *doing things*.

She knew injustice, she murmured with appropriate sympathetic sounds. She had worked for twenty years in Africa.

'Julie,' she swallowed a mouthful of cucumber. 'What do you think about doing things with my order of sisters in Ethiopia?'

'Do you mean working with orphans and people in poverty?' I was so excited I had to put down my salad sandwich. I could leave Australia and go somewhere to make a real difference.

My heart beat a little faster and I waited to catch her eye but Sister Maeve didn't look up. She simply rearranged her sandwich so the tomatoes didn't fall out, as if we were discussing an everyday matter, not the very thing I'd waited a lifetime for.

'Yes, you would work with the poor. Be prepared though, the poverty and sickness will be like nothing you've ever seen. You will never be the same again.'

A week later at a protest rally, an onlooker in stubbies shorts and a bluey singlet caught my eye and scoffed 'do-gooder'. I'd never heard the term, but I understood his tone and wondered how it was an insult. I stood taller. I raised my placard higher and rejoined the chants.

He's right, I thought. I *am* a do-gooder. I'm going to Ethiopia to do good things!

And now here I was, taking a rest from doing good things. I settled into reading my book in the late afternoon convent sunshine until a stream of ladies in blue heading to the chapel disturbed me. Oh dammit, it was 5.30 p.m. already, time for mass, and I'd wanted to finish the chapter.

It was possibly the first time in my life that I had willed the weekend over so I could get back to work. I was eager to see Ammanuel, the little boy who looked more like a baby.

On the Monday morning I demonstrated new exercises for Ammanuel. I laid him on his tummy on the blue therapy mat and rolled a small towel to go beneath his armpits. When I propped his elbows in front of him, his head drooped heavy onto the mat. Saliva trickled from his mouth and this time I whipped toilet paper from my pocket and wiped his face before his mum used his hat, and she looked grateful.

'If you make a stroking motion on the back of his neck it can help to stimulate the neck muscles,' I explained to the observing workers. I put pressure through Ammanuel's shoulders to stabilise, and stroked the back of his neck. Yeshe gave instructions to his mum, who then stretched out across the mat in front of him and called his name, and with that Ammanuel lifted his head off the mat. He tried to look at his mum, and we all cheered. His mum looked joyous and Ammanuel looked a different child to the unresponsive boy who had lain here just a few days ago.

'Let's make a plan for his mum's aims in therapy,' I said to Yeshe.

Yeshe spoke with the mother then translated, 'She says she wants him to go somewhere so she can work.'

When I looked confused she continued.

'She cannot working with Ammanuel like this.' Yeshe translated the mother's story for me. She was twenty-five years old. She had brought Ammanuel to Addis Ababa from the countryside, hoping to find work as a weaver, sitting at the loom with Ammanuel tied to her back.

'But the people, they didn't to like Ammanuel. He make ureen, so he smells, and, how do you call it ... stigma? The people they felt some stigma for him.'

Stigmatised by this baby who never learnt to walk or talk or become a toddler, she lived a transient lifestyle, getting work where she could, but evicted each month because she didn't make enough money to pay her rent of twenty birr, less than three Australian dollars. Over the weekend I'd spent twenty birr on an hour's access at an internet cafe.

At least feeding Ammanuel was free, his mum explained to Yeshe. She breastfed him even when she didn't have money to feed herself. As she talked, she leaned forward and kissed Ammanuel's forehead then tickled his armpits. His giggle was precious, mischievous and raucous all at the same time. It was the first time we had heard him laugh, and everyone in the physiotherapy room turned to look at him, all of us surprised and charmed.

His mum flipped him into standing and propped him beneath his shoulders, speaking in Amharic.

I turned to Yeshe. 'What is she saying?'

'*Be-eger mehed*,' Yeshe said, then followed in English, 'To walking. His mum is saying, look, he wants to walking.'

The mother dangled Ammanuel until the soles of his feet hit the floor and his stepping reflex activated. In the same way that very young babies will look as if they are walking when their feet are placed on the ground, Ammanuel's legs jerked and he tiptoed across the room hanging from his mother's hands. His head lolled backwards like a disjointed doll's and a string of saliva hung from the corner of his mouth. His mother repeated the phrase, looking hopeful.

Ammanuel wasn't walking; it was a primitive reflex that should have faded away when he was six months old, about the time he was learning to roll and later crawl. I felt so glad no-one asked me to comment, as I didn't want to say, he's not walking, he's probably never going to walk. Instead, I supported his flopping head and asked, 'Can she come again tomorrow, in the morning?'

'She will coming every day, until Ammanuel is walking,' Yeshe translated.

In a move she must have perfected over four years, his mum

flipped Ammanuel onto her back, tied a cloth around him and over his head and fastened it under her bust. Ammanuel made happy noises from his cloth cocoon while his mum slipped her feet back into her cracked plastic shoes. At the doorway she turned to smile and wave goodbye.

In my bed in the convent that night, I compared myself to Ammanuel's mum. We were similar in age, but otherwise worlds apart. Before my going-away party in Perth, I had treated myself to a spray tan. Instead of the instant transformation into a runway model as I expected, it peeled off at inopportune moments and ruined my clothes. The money from that spray tan could pay Ammanuel's rent for one year.

It seemed unlikely that Ammanuel's mum analysed failed love interests over cups of tea and Ethiopian Tim Tams. I wondered, if she could read, would she read self-help books about unlocking the hidden potential within, like I did? Or would she read *Green Left Weekly*? Or maybe she was just consumed from dawn to dusk with the task of surviving.

I felt excited Ammanuel was showing so much promise. He had already improved in just two weeks of therapy. As I drifted off to sleep, I made therapy treatment plans in my head.

But the next day, Tuesday, Ammanuel and his mum didn't arrive. They didn't have an appointment as there was no appointment book in the clinic. The closest we had to appointments was asking someone to come morning or afternoon, but patients only followed that sometimes and would arrive for therapy at random times. None of the patients seemed to wear watches, and no-one seemed to mind waiting half an hour for treatment if the therapy room was full. On Wednesday I looked up every time someone entered the physio room, but still there was no sign of Ammanuel and his mum.

By Thursday afternoon Yeshe and one of the other workers walked to the address Ammanuel's mum had given. When they returned, too soon, Yeshe reported the pair was evicted because she couldn't pay $3.50 rent for the month.

'Where have they gone? Can we find them?'

'No, Julie. It is impossible.' Yeshe shook her head.

I had grown fond of Ammanuel in just a short time, and he had shown such potential. With the pace of his improvement, it might only have taken one month's rehab until he could sit in a special chair and his mum might get work. Without Ammanuel tied to her back she might weave enough to make over twenty birr in the month and stay in her lodgings.

The next morning I paid extra attention out the back window of the Land Cruiser as Sister Starling sped along the main road to work. Beggars usually lined the roads by the churches. Each was a pile of dirty blankets with heads down and a hand out, palm moving up and down for alms. It was difficult to tell if they were old men or young women with children tied to their backs as we drove past them. Ammanuel's mum wasn't amongst these avenues of beggars, so I looked out, hoping I might see her walking by the roadside. But she wasn't near the church, or on the crowded streets of the Shiro Meda weavers market where crowds milled around the stalls and spilled onto the streets. I looked from the car every morning and every afternoon, for two weeks, hoping Ammanuel might return for more therapy. After two weeks I stopped looking and just hoped instead.

Chapter 3

To give: መስጠት /*mestet*/

Danyel was fifteen years old, and walked by steadying himself with a pole that reached his shoulders. His t-shirt was sodden from the effort of walking and smelt of stale sweat. He put all his weight through the big toe on his left foot and the ball of his right. With each step his knees bumped and his muscles spasmed, jerking his legs up and down.

'What's his diagnosis?' I asked Yeshe.

She crinkled her nose to think. 'Tiptoe.'

'Why does he tiptoe?' Walking on the toes could indicate a diagnosis of cerebral palsy, autism, muscular dystrophy or another pathology in a child.

'Because his foot will not go flat,' Yeshe replied.

'Thanks, but what is the reason?'

Yeshe looked at me as if I was simple. 'Tiptoe.'

'It might be cerebral palsy? Can you ask him to lie on his back so I can examine his muscles?'

Danyel's muscles were so tight on examination, it was hard to get his legs moving. I marvelled to Yeshe that he could get around like this since birth.

'Not since born,' Yeshe translated for Danyel. 'Since twelve years old.'

'That can't be right,' I said.

Danyel was solemn and whispered into his chest.

'Cultural leg problems,' Yeshe translated. 'Actually, it's from eating. He is from the countryside, in the south. He tell it came after he ate from the countryside bean.'

It seemed superstitious to think eating a bean caused such paralysis, and I wondered if I should correct them, but I held my tongue until dinner that night. Then I asked permission from the sisters and dialled up on the holy convent internet.

The grass pea, *guaya*, I read, is one of the hardiest plants, able to withstand drought conditions, so is often the last available food source during famine. The boiling process denatures the toxic proteins so the pea poses no threat when cooked with adequate water. However, when roasted over the fire without water, as necessary during drought and famine, the toxins in the pea accumulate to create dangerous side effects in the body. Symptoms include degeneration in the nervous system of the legs.

With my belly full from the nuns' dinner, I raged at the injustice of a double evil, that the only thing to eat when food was short could paralyse a person.

When Danyel came for physio over the next few days, Yeshe and I noted down a problem list. It was clear how much energy it took just to walk. When he lurched on his walking stick I saw the sweat stain on his back, the beads of sweat across his forehead. The back of his thigh had stiffened so he could no longer move his knee, and his calf muscles had tightened so his feet were almost fused into position. I demonstrated stretches for Yeshe to trial on Danyel's legs.

I talked about it with Sister Starling as she drove us home after work that night.

'Sister, I saw plaster of Paris in the cupboard. Do you think I could use some to make a cast for Danyel's leg? It would stretch his leg into the flattest position and hold it there. Like a sustained stretch over days.'

Sister Starling slowed down to veer around a lamb suckling from a ewe at an intersection. 'Plaster of Paris is very expensive.

Are you sure it will work?'

'Oh sure! I've done serial casting before,' I said. 'Sometimes, with the kids with cerebral palsy, we used to take them to Princess Margaret Hospital in Perth, and in the physio department there, I mean they were the experts, but I assisted, we would make plaster casts, and repeat the casts every couple of –'

Sister Starling interrupted. 'How many rolls of plaster? It's very hard to get.' She jammed her horn at the sheep until they moved.

I hesitated then guessed. 'Probably only two?'

She gave a sharp nod. 'Okay.' She said it like a warning.

It took seven rolls of plaster of Paris to make a plaster cast for Danyel's whole leg. It took a lot of energy to position his leg, roll the wet bandage soaked in plaster around it and hold it still until the cast set. After two hours Danyel was ready to go home.

I rummaged in the pile of donated medical equipment in the corner until I found a set of crutches. 'Yeshe, can you please translate? He needs to keep this cast on for one week. Then next week we will stretch his leg more and make a new cast. We will need to make six casts before his leg can go straight.' We would need to order in more plaster of Paris, but we had time.

Yeshe explained to Danyel, who gave a solemn nod.

Danyel limped out of the clinic. He was less mobile than usual, as he had to swing himself through the crutches, but I was pleased to help someone with disability resulting from grand-scale injustice. The damage to his nerves from the toxins in the *guaya* pea was irreversible, but at least if we stretched the muscles on his legs he might hobble rather than lurch on his stick.

The next day, Yeshe led the way to Danyel's home for us to check up on him. It took thirty minutes to get there from the clinic, but it was a picturesque walk by streams and past boys playing football in the field, and the light through the pine and eucalyptus trees was gentle.

Danyel's home was an adobe of cow manure, straw and dark

earth. Inside the hut, the air was moist, and the only light came through a square hole high in the wall.

Danyel sat on hessian sacks in the corner with his plastered leg straight out in front of him on the earthen floor.

I squatted next to him and asked, 'How does your leg feel?' for Yeshe to translate.

Danyel shrugged his shoulders with a wordless reply and kept his eyes downcast.

We asked if he had any pain and Danyel shook his head.

A few fleas jumped onto my ankles and I wondered if they were also biting Danyel's legs.

'Why is he on the floor?' I asked Yeshe, looking around for a chair, but the room was empty save for a cast-iron bedstead, with a thin mat and a kitten sleeping atop two folded blankets. 'Can't he sit on his bed?'

'Not his bed.' Yeshe whispered, although we didn't need to whisper as no-one else spoke English.

'How many people live here?'

Yeshe whispered back that seven people shared the three rooms. I wondered where Danyel slept and if he had a bed of his own.

'These people have nothing!' I whispered, but before she could answer, Danyel's elderly dad took both of Yeshe's hands in his. He shook her hands over and over, saying, '*Egziabher yimesgen*. Thanks to God.' When he repeated it, raising his hands to heaven and bowing, I saw that his right eye was completely clouded with cataracts. I wondered how much extra stigma this family might face, having two people with disabilities.

Together we showed Danyel how to squeeze his thigh and lift his outstretched leg to strengthen his leg muscles and helped him to stand up. Yeshe and I flanked him to hobble out and do a lap of the housing compound on his crutches. Once back inside, I encouraged him to walk a little with the crutches each day to maintain his existing movement, and Danyel agreed, as he handed the crutches to his father and eased himself back to sitting on the floor with legs outstretched again. His father clasped Yeshe's hands, then mine, all over again until we were out of the compound.

As we walked back to the clinic, Yeshe explained Danyel's family was from the countryside, and they shared those lodgings with other families because it was cheap.

'How do they get enough money to eat?' I asked.

'Begging. They sit outside the church. Both can beg.'

We visited Danyel's house again the next morning. He was still sitting on the floor although this time his leg was bare.

Yeshe asked him why he had taken the cast off and translated his answer, 'Because it was like this.' She demonstrated with exaggerated scratching on her forearm.

'You mean itchy?'

'Yes!' Yeshe clapped once.

I had forgotten to tell him it would be itchy, that plaster always was. 'No problem.' I did my best to look cheery. 'We'll just bandage it back on again; it can still stretch the muscles. Where is it?'

Yeshe translated, 'He threw it in the river.'

I imagined the leg-shaped cast bobbing down the river, past women collecting water, past donkeys submerged to their shins, past kids splashing while their mums washed clothes. I also imagined Sister Starling's reaction on hearing I just wasted seven packets of plaster of Paris.

'What should we do? Should we make another cast?' I dreaded asking Sister Starling for more plaster.

Yeshe asked Danyel, who said he didn't want another cast, it was too itchy, he wanted 'just to continue as before'. I hoped at least it meant continue with stretching as before.

I was working with another patient the next day when Yeshe returned distressed from a home visit. She had gone with Sister

Meaza and they had found Ammanuel's mother begging on the road.

'Ooh, she is in a bad,' Sister Meaza said, wiping away tears.

'Julie, oh she is have terrible problem,' said Yeshe. 'She crying, she crying. Nothing she has.' Their distress seemed to make both of them forget their English.

Yeshe plonked herself into a chair and looked out the window of the office, leaning her chin on her hand. 'They have no money for eating.'

'Shall I give you some money for her?' I said.

'No, no,' both of them said.

'It's not good for *ferenji* to give money. If you give her money, always she will ask you for money,' Sister Meaza said.

Yeshe nodded in agreement.

'How about if I give it to you, and you pretend it's not from me?' I tried again with Yeshe.

'No Julie, it's not necessary,' Yeshe said.

Ten minutes later, though, I noticed two of the other rehabilitation workers slip a wad of birr from their coat pockets, and look over their shoulders before passing it to Yeshe.

'What's going on?' I asked another of the workers, who replied, 'We all giving money for Ammanuel's mother, she very terrible condition.'

Sister Starling told me the week before that community rehabilitation workers earned about thirty dollars a month, about two hundred birr. They were happy to give away some of that small amount, yet they insisted I shouldn't give. Before I came to Ethiopia I had wondered if living in abject poverty inured people to others' suffering, but here it seemed to heighten their sensitivity.

In the car on the way home from the clinic that afternoon, I told Sister Starling about Ammanuel and his mum, hoping to fill the time so she couldn't ask about the cast. I asked if we had any donated clothes to use for Ammanuel.

'It's better not to give things away, it encourages a handout mentality.' She looked over her shoulder, checking the road was clear before overtaking a man rolling seven barrels down the hill.

'But Yeshe said they have *nothing*.'

'Yes, yes, very distressing.' Sister Starling acknowledged my emotional response as if we were discussing logistics. She slowed down outside the high school as the road thronged with students in black and red uniforms. 'But the fact is, if you give them things, they will always expect handouts. I've seen it many times, and it always ruins them. Don't give your money to the clients, that's what I tell the staff – but who knows if they listen to me.'

Sister Starling stared out the windscreen with her lips pursed. I wondered if she'd always been this detached, or if she had hardened over twenty years in Africa.

So the next day, when Yeshe unlocked the wardrobe in the physio clinic and rummaged in the box of donated clothes for jocks, trousers and knitted hat for Ammanuel, I got an illicit thrill.

'Don't tell to Sister Starling, she don't to like,' Yeshe said, and I said I wouldn't.

The next day, Ammanuel's mum brought him for therapy, dressed in his new outfit. I was so happy to see them and didn't want to waste any time before getting him sitting and strengthening his muscles.

'Do we have anything for Ammanuel to sit in?' I asked Yeshe.

Yeshe scanned the room, wrinkling up her nose. 'Cerebral palsy chair?'

From the side of the room she moved a pile of cardboard folders, a box of plastic pieces and a soccer ball to reveal a small wooden chair. Made of lacquered plywood with high sides and a tray, plus a decorative heart carved on its back, it could have belonged to the littlest bear in the Goldilocks story.

Ammanuel was too little for the chair, and in it, he lolled to one side, so I rolled a towel into a sausage and slid it around behind his hips to prop him up. We pulled clothes from the donations box and each rolled an adult t-shirt into a fat sausage and jammed it in tight between him and the sides of the chair. Then Ammanuel slumped forwards.

'Do we have any bandages?' I asked, and Yeshe dragged a box of old elastic bandages from beneath the physio treatment bed.

I unrolled one bandage across the boy's hips and fastened it like a seatbelt around the chair to hold him in place. Then I used another under his armpits to keep his chest upright. Ammanuel's body was now straight, but his neck muscles were not strong enough to support his head, and it hung forwards. Ammanuel watched Yeshe, and when she smiled at him he beamed back. Now he was sitting up, his mother watched us from the side, looking hopeful.

'Perfect,' I said. We angled the chair by sliding foam tiles beneath the two front legs so Ammanuel's gravity now helped him keep his head up. Yeshe slid another foam tile to support his feet, and I wedged his legs into position, so his feet, knees and hips were at right angles to each other. Next, I slid my hands under his armpits and straightened his spine where he had slumped to one side and tucked the t-shirt sausage-supports in tighter. To finish off, I wriggled his shoulders back so his hips, pelvis and spine gave the best support possible for his head.

Brushing off my knees, I stood back to admire our handiwork. Ammanuel was no longer floppy and unresponsive, too weak to hold his head up. Instead, he sat upright in the chair and although gravity rather than muscles kept him straight, he was still able to see out. Ammanuel made little singing noises while his mum looked thrilled.

In Australia, a specialised supported-seating system cost upwards of one thousand dollars, with custom-made resin inserts, imported precision componentry and hydraulic tilt-in-space mechanisms. But Yeshe and I had made one from locally available material in a Goldilocks chair. Just as we were congratulating ourselves, Ammanuel's head slipped forwards.

'Can you tell his mum to ask him to lift his head?' I asked Yeshe, who translated, and Ammanuel's mum squatted in front of the chair and clicked her fingers above his head. He lifted it a fraction, with a flicker of muscle activity, before it flopped again, but that was a significant progression from lying immobile on his back.

'Bravo!' called Yeshe, applauding while his mum lifted his head back up again. Ammanuel beamed at us with a look that said he was so proud of himself. And I was proud of him too.

After five weeks of working at the clinic I started to settle into the pace and way of working. I saw the full range of patients, from babies with clubfoot to old men with arthritic hips. There was the girl who had become a paraplegic after a car accident, and a twenty-one-year-old who had torn his hamstring playing soccer, and kids with diagnoses I could only guess.

I was enjoying the community feel of the area around the clinic, and of home visits with the rehabilitation workers, picking our way over the dangerous inclines and sharp rocks, watching the mist rising on the foothills every morning and the shadows stretching on the mountains in the afternoons. I had become so comfortable in the *kebele*, the neighbourhood, that when Yeshe suggested we have lunch in a grass-roofed cafe on a Saturday, I took secret pleasure ignoring the sisters' advice that dining out was too dangerous for a *ferenji*.

We started the morning with a coffee ceremony at Yeshe's home. In her room, which she rented in a compound with five other families, she pulled out a low, woven stool for me to sit on. She too sat on a low stool and roasted coffee beans over a burner on top of the gas bottle. We exchanged pleasant small talk, discussing how many family members we had, how long since we finished our studies.

'What are your hobbies?' Yeshe asked, and because it had been so long since anyone asked me that, I said reading, writing stories and watching movies. I wondered if I could count 'political activism' and 'getting drunk' as hobbies, as those were things I enjoyed and did regularly. Yeshe said hers were reading Amharic books, watching movies and going to church. Yeshe went on Saturdays and Sundays as she was Ethiopian Orthodox. I said that as I was Catholic, I only went to church once per weekend, omitting that very often I didn't go at all.

'I met so many Catholic nuns from Australia at the clinic. Is Catholic the official religion of Australia?' Yeshe asked as she lifted the roasted beans towards me and fanned the aromatic smoke in my direction, then added, 'How do you see this smell?'

'It smells beautiful.'

'This is for tradition. You must to smell the coffee cooking.'

I nodded. 'There is no official religion of Australia.'

'*Ara*? Hey?'

'I think most people in Australia have no religion.'

'What would make people think they do not need a religion?' Yeshe pounded the roasted beans with a wooden mortar and pestle. She didn't appear judgemental, just curious.

'I think people in Australia worship things rather than religion.' I felt hypocritical as I looked around Yeshe's room. I had brought more things with me for a one-year stay than appeared in Yeshe's room, which I assumed held all of her belongings. Yeshe's room was immaculate with just a bed, a cane chair, a low bookshelf and a picture of the holy family on the wall. She kept a few saucepans and two plastic plates behind a floral curtain at one side.

'Oh, things like plants and animals? Animist religion, like in the south part of Ethiopia?'

'No, shopping, and possessions really.' I thought about how I had left my bedroom at the convent in a mess, with my ugg boots askew, three novels on the floor with my Lonely Planet guidebook, and the charger for my video camera trailing across my bed.

Yeshe laughed and the conversation trailed off as we sipped coffee in silence.

Later we went to a cafe and ate lamb stew, and Yeshe reminded me not to let on to Sister Starling that I had eaten outside the convent.

Or caught a local bus. 'It costs ten centimes,' Sister Starling had told me over dinner the day before when I queried ticket prices. I calculated that to be about 0.0005 cents. She had added, 'Don't ever travel on a public bus – there are many pickpockets, it's very dangerous.'

An Irish nun had joined in. 'Sure, they'll pick your pockets so well you'll be lucky to get off the bus with your trousers.' Her quip made me snort, which displeased Sister Starling anew.

I felt a double thrill of naughtiness when Yeshe and I caught the bus back to the convent from the cafe. The suspension on the bus was shot and the springs in the seats had loosened, and I bounced and swung sideways with every bump.

'Like dancing.' Yeshe motioned at the rest of the passengers. I swayed along with them, feeling more as if I were on a boat than a bus. I waited for telltale signs of food poisoning, expecting a grumbling tummy or nausea, but they didn't come. It seemed I had proved the nuns wrong: it wasn't dangerous for a *ferenji* to eat out.

On the engine hump of the bus, tinsel and plastic flowers surrounded a 3D cut-out of Jesus and Mary in a small shrine, and the holy duo also dangled on a card from the rear-view mirror. I held on tight to my purse and recited a small prayer, promising God, Jesus and Mary that if they got me home without being pickpocketed or throwing up, I'd be very good from then on.

I went direct from the bus to Saturday evening mass with the sisters. By the opening hymn I started to feel woozy. The light from the candles hurt my eyes and the singing clanged in my ears as it reverberated around the naves. I clung to the pew in front to stay upright when we stood for the second hymn, and when we knelt for prayers, bile rose in my throat. Although I knew it would earn me the wrath of Sister Starling, I tried to sneak from the chapel. She shot sharp looks at me as I ran back to my room and grabbed a bucket from the laundry on the way.

My throat was dry and swollen, my head was swimming and I alternated between hot and cold, one moment fearing I might spontaneously combust, the next fearing chilblains.

Through blurring vision, I consulted the health section of my Lonely Planet guide, realising with alarm I was exhibiting the symptoms of hepatitis A, B and C, typhoid, malaria and dengue fever.

Sister Meaza tapped on my door just before 7 p.m. and popped her head around. 'Julie, would you like dinner?' She glanced from my face to the bucket by my bed.

'You are sick!' She scanned the room, looking panicked. 'And all of your things are all over the room!' as if the two might be related. Possibly she thought I'd thrown my belongings about in a fevered state of hallucination; I didn't let her know this was how my room always looked.

I had no chance to explain, though, as I vomited, retching so hard my eyes strained. My head pounded and I moaned with the pain as I heaved again and again.

'I'll bring Sister Starling,' Sister Meaza said. Though I tried to wave my arm to deter her, she scuttled off, thongs slapping on the tile floor.

Seconds later, Sister Starling demanded from the doorway, 'What did you do today?' She threw her hands to her head when I confessed I'd eaten in a restaurant. She looked at me with a mix of abhorrence and disbelief.

'What did I tell you about eating outside the convent? Gracious, what are we going to do now?'

Although I expected some kind of punishment, I thought I saw her face soften just a fraction, with what might have been empathy. Perhaps she'd made the same mistake in her early days in the country, decades ago. Maybe she knew eating outside the convent brought its own penalty.

Sister Starling called down the corridor, 'Sister Meaza. Please bring Julie some *ambohar*, fizzy water, it will make her feel better.'

Sister Meaza and the other novice sister took it in turns, against my protestations, to empty my spew bucket and bring me carbonated water and dry biscuits for the next twenty-four hours. From time to time, Sister Starling appeared at my door to check on my progress, or at least survival. The novice sisters made me laugh and kept me comforted and safe. In between their visits I flicked through the Lonely Planet health section again. As the vomiting abated I ruled out typhoid and as my fever subsided so did my fears of malaria and dengue. When my appetite returned I crossed off all three forms of hepatitis. That just left hypochondria.

Chapter 4

Right: ትክክል /tekekel/

Once I had recovered, I rejoined Yeshe on home visits. Each weekday morning in November we walked from the clinic to the most distant part of the *kebele*, clambering over boulders and channels, climbing into the hills for forty-five minutes until the air became thinner and Addis Ababa stretched out below us. By the river, girls squatted, scrubbing clothes against rocks and laying them out to dry over bushes, while toddlers waddled in the water. Every day as we walked, kids ran out to squeal a greeting, and grannies with bundles of firewood tied to their backs looked up to puff hello. Young women queuing with jerry cans at the water pump interrupted their chats to shout '*Ferenji*! You-you-you!' with cheery waves towards us.

Yeshe and I nattered on the walk today as we did every day. We passed Teferi's house on the way, next door to the tiny shop that always blared Ethiopian pop music from a tape player. On the hillside we passed the weavers pacing out bright lengths of yarn, waving to us as they looped thread over stakes in the ground ready for their looms.

I stopped for a rest with my hands on my hips. The air was getting thinner; Addis Ababa is at 2,355 metres altitude, about the same height as the summit of Mount Kosciuszko, and today we ascended beyond the city towards its highest point, Mount Entoto. Each breath seemed to draw less oxygen.

'What is the diagnosis for our next client?' I asked.

Yeshe crinkled her nose to think while I panted.

'Mental retardation case. The neighbours told us about her. Not walking.'

The child sat on a hessian sack on the ground outside her house. With a dirty *gabi* shoulder cloth wrapped around her head and shoulders, she looked like a babushka doll.

Yeshe squatted, arranging her long skirt under her knees, and put her face close to the girl, who continued to stare into the distance.

'Fiketu,' Yeshe clicked her fingers in front of the little girl's face.

Fiketu blinked but showed no other response. This child looked plump compared to all my other patients. But looking closer she was not fleshy; she was swollen. The skin over her shins pulled so tight it glistened, and her distended belly stretched the adult t-shirt she wore as a dress. Her eyelids, her eyebrows, and even the spaces between were puffy.

There were no adults nearby, but we did see a toddler chasing a chook.

'*Mamush*, little boy. Bring your parents.' When Yeshe spoke to him he scampered around the hut and returned with a couple who looked in their early twenties.

'How long has she been so swollen?' I asked Yeshe to translate and squatted next to Fiketu, taking her hand in mine.

Fiketu's little brother stood on his toes and rested one hand on my thigh to follow my gaze. Fleas jumped onto my legs from the cracks in the compact dirt around the hut. Yeshe said the family wasn't sure how long she was like this, a few weeks perhaps. They weren't so worried about the swelling, they were troubled that she was five years old and she couldn't yet walk or talk. They wanted the *ferenji* to help her.

When I lifted the child's shirt to assess, I saw even her back was swollen, and her skin was coming off in white scales. My mind raced with things that might cause such swelling. What had I learnt at uni? Could it be congestive heart failure or pulmonary oedema? Unsure, I applied some *ferenji* principles. 'She needs to go to the doctor. I don't know what's wrong with her but she is very sick. They should go today.'

Back at the physiotherapy clinic, Yeshe and I rested with a drink after our hot walk.

'What do you think is Fiketu's diagnosis?' I asked Yeshe.

'I think she haven't enough to eat.' Yeshe took down a text on tropical medicine from the shelf of donated books. 'This one,' Yeshe indicated two sketches side by side.

My eye went immediately to the diagram of a languid child with visible ribs and spindly limbs. This is how I imagined all malnourished kids looked, partly because I had grown up seeing kids like this on TV with a celebrity alongside urging *donate now*.

I read that this was marasmus, malnutrition by insufficient calorie intake overall, where the child has a deficiency of energy. But the other diagram showed a child just like Fiketu, with a bloated face and puffy feet. I skimmed the accompanying text, reading that kwashiorkor is malnutrition by deficiency of protein. While the child gets just enough calories from carbohydrates to survive, the body is unable to function normally without sufficient protein, resulting in widespread swelling. I was on a huge learning curve, and wasn't sure what I could contribute except what I had already done: tell the family to go to the doctor.

That night, I felt guilty for living in relative luxury at the convent while children puffed like balloons because they didn't have any protein. I dished myself only one spoon each from the lamb stew and spaghetti bolognaise set out on the sideboard.

'Julie, eat more,' Sister Starling barked at the dinner table.

'Thank you, Sister, but I'm not hungry.' I willed my stomach not to rumble, feeling too guilty to have more. I couldn't reconcile Fiketu's poverty with my full plate.

Excusing myself from evening card games, I went to bed early. Instead of having a hot shower I changed straight into my pyjamas because I knew Fiketu did not have running water. No-one did in her part of the *kebele*. Every day, her mum would queue at the communal water pump with the other women, and carry home a twenty-litre jerry can on her back.

I had no right to hot showers when this little girl and her family looked as if they had nothing. By denying myself that luxury, I wanted to give myself penance for a lifetime of unfair indulgences.

What I hadn't wanted was to give myself fleas. They must have travelled home with me from Fiketu's house, and when I didn't shower they'd come to bed with me. Sleep evaded me all night, as did the fleas, which sprung aside as I scratched and swatted. Every time I dozed, another flea moved, and I responded with words that didn't belong in a convent. Then I lay back, aware of the rumbling in my belly, drifting off only until the next attack.

The following morning I rose at 5.30 to strip my bed and remake it with fresh sheets from the linen cupboard. I'd scoffed my porridge and left the dining room before the other sisters came downstairs.

At work I wanted to visit Fiketu again, but Yeshe said, 'Not going today, Julie. They are busy working. I'm sure they would have going to the clinic.'

We didn't go the next day or the day after that.

Meanwhile my infestation continued. Every night it was the same. Fleas attacked my shins and my back, leaping out of reach when I slapped at them. I slept only in short snatches, waking with palm poised, ready to kill.

As each dawn broke and the flea mortality rate remained nil, I changed my sheets again and went for breakfast with the sisters, bleary-eyed, upset and irrational.

The sleep deprivation made time slow down and my mental health wavered. Our daily routine never varied and was so restrictive I started to feel depressed. We had prayers before breakfast, prayers after breakfast, work, prayers before dinner, prayers after dinner, washing-up roster, then bed.

Deviations from the convent rules were taken seriously. And the convent had way more rules than I'd anticipated, although not of the kind I'd prepared for. I expected, but didn't find, any rules about sharing a spliff behind the geraniums, or skipping chapel to swig Southern Comfort. I hadn't expected, but found, plentiful rules for maintaining a house of quiet contemplation. My head was so full of my workday challenges I had no space to remember them all.

'This one cannot stay in the bathroom, please, Julie,' the novice Sister Meaza beseeched as she returned my shampoo and conditioner from the shower stall for the third time. 'It is forbidden.' When I asked her if she knew why, Sister Meaza just repeated, 'It is forbidden.'

I gathered I had transgressed other guidelines by glares from Sister Starling or panicked pleas from Sister Meaza. Rules against cups of tea after 5 p.m.; or scraping your dinner scraps into the bin instead of onto the scraps plate (which then got scraped into the bin); or pouring a cup of tea from the kettle instead of filling a thermos first and pouring from there; or decreeing that one should use a spoon rather than a knife in the peanut butter jar. I supposed these things were necessary for maintaining order in a house of many people, and I kept messing up.

Following afternoon prayers, it was time to set the table for dinner, with fresh bowls of the same lamb stew, vegetable stew, and pasta with bolognaise sauce each night. The novice sisters scurried to put out the meals on woven mats on the laminex sideboard, and I scurried next to them with dishes from the kitchen, trying to help. In my state of sleep deprivation I messed up.

'The lamb stew goes there!' Sister Starling bellowed, pointing as I put the vegetable stew on the rectangular hot mat instead of the round one.

Over dinner that night Sister Starling reminisced about a quirky sermon her favourite priest gave during the third week of Lent in 1987. Her face glowed under the fluorescent lights and the spidery capillaries across her cheeks reddened when she hooted at her own anecdote. The other sisters tittered as if under pain of death, so I copied their example.

When the meal was finished the two novice sisters circled the table offering oranges or bananas to each of the other sisters and myself.

'Take fruit, Julie,' Sister Meaza whispered, so I accepted an orange. But since prayers after dinner didn't begin until the last person had finished their fruit, and I didn't want to hold everyone up, I wolfed my orange down so quickly it made Sister Starling raise her eyebrows.

Then the table was cleared, the dinner scraps scraped onto the food-scraping plate, then into the bin, and we washed the dishes, in identical order every night, except tonight, when I stuffed up and washed the large plates before the small plates and got chastised and demoted to drying-up.

Drying-up duty involved setting the table for the following morning. Sister Starling gave a cursory glance over my handiwork. She nodded approval and started to leave, but when she reached the doorway she swivelled as if she'd forgotten something. She stared at the table and turned towards me.

'No, no, no, no!' She narrowed her eyes.

'What is it, Sister?' I panicked.

'You've put the wrong teaspoons out.'

Sister Starling stood over me as I meekly substituted the metal teaspoons for the white spoons I'd set out, with no explanation as to the white teaspoons' fall from grace.

Relations with the ladies of the cloth deteriorated further that weekend, when a nice older colleague invited me to lunch at his family home. Over lunch he and his wife kept insisting, '*Biy*! Eat!' so that I ate too much *injera* to be polite and I had to excuse myself to the bathroom, open my jeans button and rearrange my shirt. I then misinterpreted his question 'Do you like wine?' as a conversational opener, and declared I loved it, and only realised my mistake when their son returned from the corner shop with a bottle and they announced they were teetotal. Sister Starling had told me wine cost one hundred birr a bottle, compared to two birr for soft drink, and I was mortified they had spent that much on me. The Ethiopian wine was thick and sweet as cough syrup, and from the way it went straight to my head, it seemed more like liquor, but I made it through a glass. When my host brushed aside my assurances one glass was enough, and refilled my glass to be polite, I sculled it when they weren't looking. Then his wife refilled my glass when I wasn't looking and I drank that too to be polite. Although it didn't feel very polite to then be drunk, with two sober grown-ups and their teenage son.

So I was tipsy when lunch finished and my host travelled with me in a minibus taxi to drop me outside a cafe where Yeshe and two colleagues waited for me.

'Drink coffee?' Yeshe asked.

'Actually,' I said, full of bravado and cough-syrup wine, 'let's drink a beer.'

It was only 11 p.m. when I banged on the metal gates to the convent, but already the roads were empty of traffic and there were no pedestrians. Waiting for the guard to let me in, I thought I shouldn't be in much trouble. It had not been a wild night as far as parties go – just a few beers followed by a Bollywood film at the Cinema Ethiopia. The most dangerous thing I'd done was to disregard the advice of the sisters about going to the city centre, Piazza, after dark.

The second most dangerous was to wriggle in my seat in the cinema when one of the fleas I was carrying around bit me, which had caused the self-folding seat to slam my knees towards my face.

A sleepy guard opened the gate. He was a stern man with a rifle slung over one shoulder. At his feet padded three beasts that looked to be part Ethiopian wolf with just a dash of domestic canine. I had never seen these dogs in the compound before, and it crossed my mind that the nuns had sent a Welcome Home Squad for Naughty Girls Who Come Home Late.

This was not far from the truth. The next afternoon at recreation time, Sister Starling didn't acknowledge my greeting. Whenever I spoke to her or near her, she stared at the ceiling.

Sister Starling ignored me for a week, and the older sisters followed her example. Life in the convent became miserable. I ate meals in silence, and didn't join recreation time, which I didn't mind, as it involved pretending to watch TV while Sister Starling scowled at me. After meals I went straight to my flea-infested room. But I missed the company of the novice sisters, and I was ashamed that I'd upset the sisters who'd given me a home and a job.

I didn't know what to do, whether to leave, or where to go if I did. I couldn't go back to Australia and explain I'd fallen from grace for disobeying a simple curfew. Hard as it was to stay at the convent as an outcast, I loved my work in the clinic and was seeing real progress with the patients. I tried to focus on work and did my best to do the right thing in the convent. I didn't go out after dark, didn't drink wine or beer; I put the right teaspoons on the table.

Days followed a new routine now. I would go to work, come home, shower, drink tea with the novice sisters (taking care to be cleared away by 5 p.m.), eat dinner in silence, go to my room, leave room to sneak flyspray from kitchen, spray bed for fleas, sneak flyspray back to kitchen, lie awake being bitten by fleas.

The flyspray stunk of kerosene and possessed no insect eradication qualities whatsoever. I wanted to look for flea killer in the small blue shipping container shops lining the road behind the convent. But even if I weren't forbidden to leave the convent alone, I wouldn't have known which shop to go to or how to ask for it in Amharic.

After two weeks, the sleep deprivation got too much for me. At tea one afternoon, I lied and told Sister Meaza I wanted to go for a walk.

'You can't go out by yourself!' she said with a look of alarm. 'It is dangerous!'

'I'll be safe, I am sure. Just please let me go. I just need some exercise.'

'Just to take walk within the compound!' Sister Meaza said, so I put my sneakers on and walked circles inside the perimeter of the compound.

The next afternoon I tried again. 'Please Sister Meaza, I just want to take a walk.' Sister Starling was still not talking to me. All I wanted to do was make a fifteen-minute errand to sort out my flea infestation; it didn't seem unreasonable. I was so angry, so frustrated, and so tired that when Sister Meaza answered me sweetly, my anger and frustration burst through in tears. The harder I tried not to cry the more my eyes welled up and my lips quivered.

'No, no, no, don't cry!' She looked panicked. 'Okay, okay. We will go together.'

I nodded, trying to calm myself. 'Thanks. I know you might be late for afternoon prayers. But ...' I wiped my nose with the back of my hand and wondered how to say it. 'There are fleas in my bed.'

'We must fix this problem!' Sister Meaza marched me out of the convent and into a nearby pharmacy. They didn't have any flea treatment, so we caught a minibus further down the road to another pharmacy to purchase my very own insect spray. It smelt of antiseptic and had a drawing of a flea on the bottle.

By now it was peak hour, and the queues for the minibus were long. Whenever a minibus pulled up, the crowd jostled and shoved each other to get into the van. Sister Meaza and I stood back and let minibus after minibus go, and I kept checking my watch until we had just five minutes left to get back to the convent before afternoon prayers.

When the next minibus approached, instead of hanging back with Sister Meaza, I did what I'd seen the previous passengers do. Clutching Sister Meaza's wrist, I dragged her to the front of the throng and elbowed and shoved us past everyone else onto the minibus. Sister Meaza sat silent until we got back to the convent, worry creasing her forehead.

Sister Starling met us in the entry hall, glaring at me even before I claimed responsibility.

'I'm sorry I was late!' Sister Meaza panted, terror in her eyes.

'It's my fault,' I blurted. 'I have fleas.'

Sister Starling turned her back, and charged off to the chapel. Sister Meaza shuffled after her. I retired to my room in a fury, thankful I was not a nun and prayers were optional. While Sister Meaza no doubt spoke reverential Hail Marys under her breath, I spent the next hour muttering swearwords. I was fed up with convent life but didn't know what else to do.

Dinner that night was even more awkward. The only sound was a few *tsks* from Sister Starling although I did hear her send the maid to help me strip the bed after dinner.

In my room, we pulled back the embroidered coverlets and untucked the floral sheets, as I had every morning for weeks. The maid, who spoke no English, sucked her teeth disapprovingly and said something in Amharic. As usual, I handwashed the sheets and hung them to dry outside the kitchen.

The following afternoon, as we washed and dried our teacups after our daily pre-5 p.m. break, Sister Meaza took me by the elbow and spoke in a conspiratorial whisper. 'Next time, don't use the clothes' – she pronounced it *clothers* – 'from the kitchen for your sleeping.'

With a hand under my elbow, she guided me to the window and pointed at the flapping clothesline. 'These clothers are for eating.'

It had seemed safe to assume that the floral cotton the same size as bedsheets, folded on top of other bedsheets in the bedsheets cupboard, were in fact bedsheets.

'How do I know which are the sheets and which are the tablecloths?' I knew I was whining, but they were all homemade, with no labels to assist the *ferenji* in identification.

'The sheets are in the sheet cupboard and the tablecloths are in the tablecloths cupboard.' She said it as if I were simple.

'But I definitely got these from the sheet cupboard,' I pleaded, although it was possible that in my flea-addled, sleepless state I had confused the two closets.

'Julie,' Sister Meaza looked sad as if she knew what was coming. 'Don't do it again, Sister Starling she don't to like it.'

I tried to avoid her, but Sister Starling confronted me as I laid out the metal-handled teaspoons that night.

'Julie.' Her face was stern. 'Here we don't use the tablecloths on our beds. It is not hygienic.'

I started to explain I wasn't in the habit of it either, but she spun and marched out of the room. And just like I did to Sister Vincent in grade five, I bulged my tongue through my lips and made a face at her departing back, and it felt so good.

To repent for kipping on the kitchen linen, I tried extra hard at Wednesday night chapel. It was a while before mass would start so I slipped my thongs off next to the pile of other sandals, made the sign of the cross, and bowed towards the tabernacle. I padded across the stone floor to a knee-high wooden stool.

There was a tranquillity of the sort that descends when people contemplate in community. The small chapel was full that night with sisters from other houses in Addis Ababa. Two candles flickered at each end of the altar table and the sunset through the lace curtain gave the room an amber glow. Sisters on either side of me prayed with eyes closed and heads down, mouthing prayers.

That's what I'll do too, I thought. I would pray my way out of my misery and confusion. I reached to the small ledge on the underside of my stool for the Bible, planning to read and meditate on a passage to help me reach serenity and patience.

As I fumbled under the seat, I knocked the Bible, scattering it, a hymn book, and fifteen pamphlets around the feet of the elderly sister sitting behind me. I tried to twist and reach under to gather up the mess while maintaining a discreet, serene demeanour. The elderly nun *tsk*ed at me as she gathered the leaflets and replaced the Bible on its ledge even though I had my hand out to take it from her. I got the hint.

The nun sitting to my right passed me a prayer book, which I clutched in my lap until the priest entered, we stood for the first hymn and I dropped five loose-leaf prayers from it onto the floor.

Hell, I thought. Were there not enough prayers in the thousand-page tome? Who felt it necessary to stuff in extras? I could sense the irritated gazes of everyone around me and I launched a stream of unholy words inside my mind although I took care not to mouth them.

By breathing carefully and moving slowly, I made it without further mishap until communion. In the churches of Australia, the priest first holds the holy Eucharist before a communicant and places it either in the person's mouth or cupped hands. But in the convent in Ethiopia on Wednesday night chapel, it was a serve-yourself kind of deal. I was the last to take communion so there was one solitary wafer remaining in the chalice. It popped from beneath my finger when I tried to pick it up and I chased it with my hand around and around the slippery inside of the chalice. The priest rolled his eyes. Was this a sign, a spiritual hint?

The only positive option was to throw myself into work. We visited Fiketu, the girl swollen with malnutrition, again. She was sitting on a hessian sack at the front of her hut when we arrived and Yeshe called inside the hut to her parents.

When the father and mother arrived, I asked Yeshe to translate. 'What did the doctor say when they took her to the clinic?'

'They took blood test, but she haven't ...' Yeshe crinkled her nose to think of the translation. 'How you say ...? Ureen. She haven't ureen so doctor send her home.'

Fiketu's toddler brother ran from the side of the house, waving a stick in each hand. He squatted next to Fiketu, whacking the sticks around her legs. She didn't respond, and she didn't react when her brother ran off again and a hen wandered up to forage at her feet.

The little girl's whole body had swollen so much now even her forehead and cheeks bulged with fluid. Her nose ran, leaving trails down her chin and on her threadbare headscarf.

I felt sick. 'Haven't they been back to the clinic? Can't the doctor do something even without the urine test?'

Yeshe translated my queries, but the father and mother looked blank. The mother didn't reply, and the father gave a quick shake of his head, which I took to mean no, they hadn't been back.

Yeshe's tone was urgent and imploring as she spoke to them in rapid Amharic. I assumed she was urging them to seek treatment, to do something, but the parents looked away. They seemed so disengaged, their faces blank of expression. This was so different to the parents of children with disabilities I had worked with in Australia.

Though I wanted to wipe this little girl's nose, or comfort her, Yeshe said it was time to go. We walked down the mountain to the physio clinic. As we crossed the riverbed where rivulets of water snaked between stepping stones, I asked, 'Yeshe, why don't they take their child to the clinic?'

'Maybe –' Yeshe started but didn't get to finish before three small children called, 'You-you-you! *Ferenji*! *Ferenji*!' They darted from their game to shake my hand before they ran on.

'Maybe ...' I prompted Yeshe to resume.

'Yeshe!' a voice called, and we both turned round to see

another worker from the project. He jogged to join us and he and Yeshe chatted in Amharic until we stopped to let a farmer cross ten brown sheep in front of us.

Without an answer from Yeshe, I churned hypotheses in my mind. Possibly Fiketu's parents didn't understand how sick she was. Why else wouldn't they take her? From here, high up on the side of Mount Entoto, I marvelled at the view of Addis Ababa spreading out below, framed with clusters of familiar blue gum trees. I yearned to ask Yeshe more questions, but I was afraid she would see how little I knew about the world.

'*Anchi*? You?' Yeshe called out, giggling. She and our colleague had walked ahead, the fat-tailed sheep had gone, and I was still standing, staring out at the gum trees. '*Tefash*? Where were you?' She linked her arm in mine when I caught up to them, and I held on tight.

We didn't go to visit Fiketu again. Three weeks later, Yeshe told me that Fiketu and her little brother, who had also taken sick, were dead. The parents had gone to the traditional healer, but it was too late. Yeshe spoke with no expression so I couldn't tell if it was appropriate to feel sorrow for these kids we'd only met twice, and if Yeshe was more experienced at these things than me. So I just said, 'Gosh, that's sad,' without having any idea if that was the right thing to do.

Chapter 5

Mother: እናት /*enat*/

When I had flown out to Addis Ababa my parents collected me from my share house to drive me to Perth Airport.

'Will you email us the phone number for the convent as soon as you arrive?' Mum rearranged a file of physiotherapy handouts and a bag of donated toys in my purple suitcase.

'Yep, when I find it out, I'll email it to you.'

While Mum zipped the suitcase she reminded me of the time I forgot to let them know I'd started a job in England and was no longer backpacking in Egypt, and she and Dad had worried for a full month.

'That was years ago, Mum. Sister Maeve says I'll be safe if I stay with the sisters. Plus, look.' I opened the Lonely Planet to the page I'd marked with a scrap of paper. 'See? It says to phone and register with the Australian consulate when in Addis Ababa. That way if anything happens, they know where the Australian citizens are.'

'What kind of thing might happen?' Mum looked panicky.

'*Nothing*! It's for just in case.'

Mum jammed her knee on my backpack while I zipped it shut.

'Will you register *as soon* as you get there?'

'Yep, as soon as I get there.' I patted her shoulder for reassurance.

While I hoisted my backpack on, Mum lugged the suitcase

towards the door and said, 'You're sure you'll remember?'

I picked up my passport and tickets from the table and checked my watch. '*Mum*! Stop stressing! I won't forget.'

I forgot. Until two months into my stay in Ethiopia when I noticed the bookmark in my guidebook. When I phoned the Australian consulate in Addis Ababa the secretary told me in a thick Ethiopian accent, 'There is barbecued for Australian and Canadian citizens. At this Saturday afternoon. Inside the Canadian Embassy. There is free beer. I think you are interested?'

I was interested. I hadn't met anyone other than colleagues or sisters in the eight weeks since I'd arrived. Although I'd been out with Yeshe to visit a museum and a famous church and had the one poorly judged beer/cinema/curfew violation, I was yet to have proper fun.

With a dry mouth and a thumping heart, I informed Sister Starling I planned to stay in a hotel for the weekend, but she just pursed her lips, exhaled and said, 'Very well.' When I passed her the sheet of paper where I'd written the hotel details she went straight back to her paperwork and I could barely believe I had forty-eight hours of freedom ahead.

After I checked into my room in a budget hotel in Piazza, I waited out the front to be collected by the sister of an Ethiopian lady Sister Maeve had introduced me to in Perth. She took me to the playgroup program she ran for AIDS orphans living in the community. I spent the morning being swarmed and captivated by crowds of children, who had all wanted me to shake hands and inflate balloons. The children played local synthesiser pop, with a register and rhythm so far removed from anything familiar I found it almost unbearable. They demonstrated moves for me to copy with the music so loud it hurt my ears. I was invigorated by the dancing and the heady autonomy away from the strictures of the convent.

At the consulate barbecue I exulted in the liberty to take food in any order I pleased and to use whichever cutlery I fancied. I piled my plate with sausages and steak and took the only spare seat at a full table next to a guy in board shorts who introduced himself as Gary. He looked about my age and when he asked 'Much on for the weekend?' it was such a familiar phrase and accent that I immediately felt at ease. I toyed with saying, *Just hanging out with some orphans*, but instead hedged, 'Just visiting a friend's work.' I didn't want to sound pretentious to this table of strangers. But by my fourth beer and second helping of cheesecake, everyone at the table had heard about my morning with the kids. By my fifth beer and second bowl of pavlova, it seemed a logical conclusion to go out on the town with my new friends.

It was dark when the taxi dropped us in front of a butcher's shop in the Haya Hulett area, not far from the centre of Addis Ababa. A beef carcass hung from an oversized hook, reflecting a yellow sheen from the shop's dangling light bulb. The footpaths bustled with people, and traffic jammed the roads. The air was thick with exhaust fumes and it was hard to chat over the cacophony of car horns as we wandered the street of butchers' shops, each displaying their meaty wares in glassless windows. I was unsure why we were going out for dinner, having just left a barbecue, but I followed the others anyway, until someone called 'This one!' and all the *ferenjis* stopped at butcher shop number 52.

The vendor, a cheery fellow who looked as if he partook liberally of his own products, gave us directions in halting English. He indicated we should go past the chickens and make a right at the beef cheeks. The small shopfront hid an extensive butchery, so we almost took a wrong turn at the mutton, but found our way, between two topsides, into a cramped restaurant.

A waiter seated us in a corner with a table lamp casting an orange glow on the lace curtains and we settled upon his recommendation of *zilzil tebs*. He served the barbecued beef with chunks of garlic and chilli in a burner over hot coals and insisted it tasted best with Dashen beer, returning with a bottle for each of us.

We ate the meat with torn strips of the flatbread *injera*, dipping the parcels in spicy *berbere* powder and *mitmita* chilli paste. Even though I was still full from the barbecue, I couldn't remember the last time I had eaten something so delicious or had so much fun.

After dinner we moved to an *azmari bet*, a traditional dancing house. Over more beers we discussed our lives back home and our work in Addis Ababa. My new *ferenji* friends asked me about living in a convent. They wanted to know, was it hard? Was it boring? Didn't I want to live in a normal house, have a normal life?

I smiled and said it was fine, not sure how to tell them I felt like such a mismatch in the convent, but I loved my work in the clinic and didn't know where else I could go. When I heard about their houses, flatmates and parties I wondered what my life might be like in Addis Ababa if I was an intern at a big aid organisation, or a teacher at an international school like they were.

When synthesiser pop blasted into the room, it was too loud to talk, and five dancers in satin outfits filed onto the stage and performed the same simultaneous neck-and-shoulder dislocation I'd watched the kids do at the group home for orphans that morning.

A bar girl in clinging lycra and heavy makeup slid onto the bench between me and an American guy and started making eyes at him. Then she shouted to me over the music, 'This one from Amhara region, calling *Eskista*. This *Eskista* dance is our culture. How do you see our culture?'

'Oh, I love your culture!' I said.

'Thank you!' She beamed as if she herself had invented *Eskista* and turned back to the American guy.

She called to me again when the beat of the music changed

and three women knelt on the floor with heads bowed. 'Now this one *Oromo*! From Oromia region!' she said.

The dancers untied their ponytails and made slow circles with their heads in time with the music, flicking their hair in front of them. As the music sped up, they swivelled their heads faster and faster until their hair whipped in loops and their heads spun so fast their features almost blurred. We *ferenjis* joined in when the rest of the small audience hooted, clapped and called for the dancers to continue.

It was during the next song, *Guragigna*, where the dancers rippled their bodies backwards and flicked their feet forwards in one fluid movement, somehow looking as if both were off the floor at the same time, that a bar fight broke out. Four men who'd previously been evicted for brawling stormed the bar and threw glasses and bottles across the room.

The bar girl grabbed my arm and we ran, along with all the other patrons, to hide in the storeroom while outside furniture crashed and glass smashed, vibrating the storeroom floor and rattling crates of bottles. Despite visiting lots of bars, I'd never seen a bar fight, much less had to shelter from one. The door was flimsy and, not having much experience with violence like this, I was afraid the brawlers might make it in. I wondered how badly we might get hurt, if I would require hospitalisation, and if so, would I need the involvement of the Australian consulate? It was lucky I had registered with them, although it occurred to me that if I hadn't phoned them, I wouldn't be here.

After half an hour the skirmish subsided and the manager knocked on the door to suggest that although the thugs had gone, we had better stay put for our own safety lest they return. An enterprising waitress sold us warm beers straight from the crate and the party continued until it was time to go home. The other *ferenjis* went to their 'normal homes' and I went back to the hotel I had booked for the weekend, the cheapest hotel listed in the guidebook. When I sat on the sagging bed, I noticed the room's door lock was flimsy, and remembered the owner had earlier told me in faltering English, 'No hot water'. Then I thought of the convent, with guards, high walls and novice sisters who joked with me in the common room after the older sisters had gone to bed. I was glad for my forty-eight hours of freedom, but equally glad to get home on Sunday night.

The following Monday, Yeshe said we needed to visit the home home of Eleni, one of our regular patients. For two months now whenever we heard the nearby bells and excited squeals signalling the end of the school day, we knew Eleni would be in soon. Eleni was nine years old. Partial paralysis resulting from a stroke meant she walked with a limp and had almost no movement in her right arm. She always came alone to the clinic and started her therapy exercises without prompting. After she had finished her exercises to improve her balance, loosen her right shoulder and increase movement in her right hand, she gave us all a big smile and walked home.

I was curious to meet Eleni's parents and wondered how they had instilled such diligence in this young girl. When I was nine it had been my task to feed the chickens. All I had to do was carry a bucket of scraps from the farmhouse to the chookyard but I don't remember being conscientious at all. I jumped on the trampoline or rode my bike in the paddocks until Mum yelled out the window not to make her ask me again, or else. After feeding the chickens I was supposed to practise piano. It's unlikely Mum enjoyed my daily trashing of *Minuet in G* but she never missed a day of insisting I practise. I wondered if Eleni's mum had to nag Eleni to go to the clinic.

At the front door to the house, half a jumper was laid out like a doormat. As we wiped our feet, an old woman's voice called, '*Gebu, gebu*! Come in, come in!'

From the doorway of the hut I saw a wrinkled lady with wiry hair poke her head out from behind a curtain inside. She beckoned us in and disappeared behind the curtain again.

Yeshe and I sat on the sofa, fidgeting with the clean but aged doilies on the arms.

'She looks too old to be Eleni's mum,' I whispered up to Yeshe.

The sofa was lopsided so Yeshe was higher than me.

'Not her mother. She is Eleni's granny,' Yeshe whispered back. 'Eleni is an orphan.'

As the old lady emerged from the curtain, I saw pots and pans stacked on the floor. At the curtain's edge she wiped her feet on the other half of the jumper at the doorway. She wheezed a greeting as she shook our hands then disappeared behind the kitchen curtain.

'*Shai tetechalesh*? Will you drink tea?' she called, but ignored our refusal and boiled the kettle anyway.

Yeshe and I sat without talking as we listened to the old lady pour water from the jerry can. Yeshe picked up a frame from the crocheted doily on the sideboard. She wiped the glass of dust and showed me a black-and-white photo of a girl who looked to be in her twenties.

'This must be her daughter,' Yeshe said. We agreed she was striking.

The old lady shuffled out with a glass of sweet spiced tea in each hand. When Yeshe said her daughter was beautiful she looked sorrowful and spoke in Amharic.

'She's passed on,' Yeshe translated.

'I'm sorry to hear that.' I thought of the pretty face in the photo. 'It must be very hard, especially when she leaves a child behind.'

Eleni's granny shook her head sadly after listening to Yeshe's translation. When Yeshe told me in English that the girl in the photo had no children, I thought how awful for the granny that she should lose two children. 'How long ago did Eleni's father, your son, pass on?' I tried to sound sensitive for Yeshe to translate.

The old woman shrugged and after she'd spoken Yeshe said, 'She don't know, Eleni's father was not her child. She don't know if he is dead.'

I tried various configurations of the family tree in my mind, but whispered to Yeshe, 'I am confused. I thought she was Eleni's granny, but she's not the mother of Eleni's mum or dad. How is she related?'

'Oh no, not related,' Yeshe said, as if it was self-explanatory.

'*Gorabet*. Neighbour,' the old lady explained.

Yeshe relayed that Eleni had been abandoned. No-one knew where Eleni's mother was, and her father had disappeared years before.

'My daughter is dead. I have no family, except Eleni. And now I am old.' Eleni's granny hobbled back to the kitchen to collect a creased plastic bag and shake the crumbs into a bowl. She returned to her armchair, breathing hard.

'*Mimi*? *Daubo gezalesh*? Please buy some bread?' She called Eleni with the affectionate term for little girl.

Eleni appeared indoors and stood by her granny's chair, saying nothing, with her chin tucked shyly to her chest. Her granny folded the blue plastic bag and a birr note into Eleni's hand. Then she straightened the little girl's collar and ran a hand to smooth her braids before flapping her hands to send her on. Eleni grinned to us from the side of her face that wasn't paralysed and skipped out the door, over the jumper-doormat, with her affected arm dangling at her side.

The granny waited until Eleni was out the door before speaking.

'She says when she carries the jerry can from the water pump, she gets a pain here.' Yeshe translated while the old lady held both her hands over her chest. 'She says her breath is small.'

As we listened to the *flip-flop* of Eleni's thongs on the stones outside recede, I considered what physiotherapy might do to help the granny, other than build up Eleni's endurance.

Yeshe stared straight at me. 'She thinks she will die soon. Then what will happen to Eleni?'

Dismayed, I said, 'I'm so sorry. But I don't think this is something physiotherapists can help with. Physiotherapy is more for physical problems; this seems more of a social work issue. Can you please tell her we will ask the social worker at the clinic this afternoon?'

Yeshe continued to look right into my eyes with a strange expression. 'She wants to know if you can help.'

I was confused. 'Sorry, Yeshe? In what way?'

'She wants to know if you have children of your own.'

The granny bent towards me, looking so earnest that clarity emerged. My heart beat fast as I realised she didn't want physiotherapy advice; she wanted me to adopt Eleni.

My mind raced with quick calculations. I tallied clothes, school fees, medicine, dentist bills and health insurance. I didn't have all the things that I surely needed to bring a child home. She wouldn't have a passport and possibly didn't even have a birth certificate. I had no partner, paying job or savings. Since I'd moved out of my share house, I didn't have a home and, as my car had been yellow-stickered before I left, I didn't have a roadworthy car to drive a child around in. I couldn't afford a child. But could this old lady afford a child either? She lived in a one-roomed hut in one of the poorest areas of Addis Ababa.

Flustered, I said, 'I'll talk to the social worker at the clinic. We can make a plan to keep Eleni safe if her granny gets sick.'

But I was distracted while Yeshe talked to the granny. I wondered if I *could* afford a child. Was life only about what we could afford? I let myself daydream about being Eleni's adopted mum. I imagined holding her little hand as I walked her to school at my local primary school. I thought of the assistance she might get there: help with learning English, reading and using her muscles. I mused on whether I would let her walk on her own to visit the Ethiopian family who lived at the end of my street back in Perth, and if we would all chat in Amharic.

My reverie was interrupted when Eleni arrived from the shops, swinging the breadrolls in the blue plastic bag while she tried to skip. Her lopsided hop was playful and light, and again I imagined taking care of her, enjoying life with her as she grew up. She gave us another smile and tried to transfer the bag of breadrolls to her stiff hand, but her fingers got tangled in the thin handles and she held it out for help.

'*Ayzosh*. Never mind.' Yeshe unwound the plastic from around Eleni's fingers, then, taking Eleni's face in her hands, she planted a big kiss on her cheek. It wasn't something we did in Australia but it was normal in the clinic for workers to be affectionate with the children. Eleni grinned even wider and ran towards the kitchen, hugging the bread bag against her chest. She tripped over on the jumper-doormat and spilled the breadrolls onto the floor.

With a cluck, the old lady rose with arthritic difficulty from her armchair, and said, '*Ayzosh, mimi*. Never mind, my little one.'

In the Land Cruiser on the way home from work, I asked Sister Starling what might happen to Eleni if her granny died.

Sister Starling sighed as if my question were an imposition. 'She would end up on the street probably, begging.'

'But she wouldn't last a day on the street!' I heard the panic in my voice.

Sister Starling's voice softened as she conceded, 'If Yeshe can organise it, she may be taken to an orphanage.'

'Could she be adopted out to a family?' I asked.

'Oh good Lord,' Sister Starling's white eyebrows jumped above her glasses. 'Who is going to adopt a disabled child?'

She jerked on the brake for a farmer herding seven sheep past the traffic lights. He wore the characteristic clothes of the peasants from the countryside, with plastic sandals, blue shorts and a green chequered cloth wrapped around his shoulders. Sister Starling sounded the horn and the farmer tapped a stick across the rumps of three sheep, which sent them scuttling in front of the Land Cruiser. He was a typical farmer in Ethiopia, with just a handful of sheep and not much else. My dad was a typical farmer in Western Australia, with thousands of sheep and quite a lot else. Even as a volunteer, I was much richer than this man with seven sheep, or Eleni's neighbour-granny would ever be.

Sister Starling huffed and held her forehead in her palm while we waited for the sheep and the farmer to cross. Her question rang in my ears. Who would adopt a child with a disability? Who would adopt Eleni? How could I *not* adopt her?

There is an Amharic proverb that a person who has too much will start to do useless things, like chewing porridge. When I had set off on this trip I had expected I might feel guilty about having a car, or a computer, a television or a mobile phone. But I never imagined I'd feel privileged to have parents. I had always had so much more than I needed.

Eleni would require very little of me, and yet, it seemed more than I could offer. I didn't plan to move back to Perth or settle down long enough anywhere for her to get through school. Neither could I imagine taking her with me as I moved around in my career. Just two days ago I was stuck in a pub storeroom trying to muster the courage to find somewhere to live outside the convent, as a single person, not as a mum.

I wondered if I could seek people in Australia to adopt her, but like Sister Starling said, it seemed impossible.

Sister Starling revved the engine hard and jerked us into motion again. I rested my forehead against the glass to watch the sheep re-form a mob on the pavement and amble away. The farmer walked on without a backward glance. We hadn't bothered them at all.

Chapter 6

Merry Christmas: መልካም ገና /Melkam Gena/

The mountain air still held the morning chill at 9 a.m. when Ammanuel's mum arrived at the clinic with Ammanuel tied to her back. Her breath fogged as she slipped off her shoes at the door and we greeted each other in Amharic. I lifted the white muslin covering Ammanuel's face to ask, '*Endemeneh*? Are you fine?' From the winning face he pulled, I guessed the answer was yes.

As usual, Ammanuel's mum untied the muslin over-cloth before loosening the material strips holding the boy to her back. Unfettered, Ammanuel balanced on his mother's back as she leant forward, then, in the lightning move that always astounded me, she flipped him forwards, over and into her arms. But this time instead of laying Ammanuel onto the mat for therapy, she held him up.

'Julie! *Eski*! Look!' Ammanuel wore a new outfit. In the two months of regular appointments I'd only ever seen him wearing the same t-shirt. Dark with grime and stiff with his urine, saliva and spilled food, it was so big it covered his feet while the capped sleeves reached his wrists. Initially he'd worn nothing underneath it, not even a nappy, until Yeshe had given his mum some tiny jocks and trousers from the box of donated clothes.

But today he wore a miniature tracksuit of soft blue fleece. The button-down top had a soft white collar and a teddy bear appliqued on each of the pockets, and packet-fresh creases showed in the sleeves and down the middle of the trousers.

‘*Gobez*! Clever!’ I said, because I didn’t know the words for ‘nice’ or ‘handsome’. I addressed his mother, but Ammanuel beamed, taking the compliment for himself.

‘*Endet*? How?’ I asked his mum, and she looked at Yeshe to translate.

‘She is cooking the *injera* and selling for people,’ Yeshe said.

Ammanuel’s mum looked proud as she counted off items on her fingers while Yeshe translated. ‘She has bought for herself from the market: one bowl to mix *injera*, one jug for pouring the *injera*, one disc for putting on the fire, and one small cooking fire.’

Ammanuel’s wheezy laugh sounded joyous. He’d used genuine head control to hold himself up. A baby without a disability would learn this skill at three to four months. At Ammanuel’s first appointment his development was similar to that of a two-month-old: he couldn’t focus his eyes, or move his limbs. But with just six weeks of the right therapy he’d improved so much he could now follow an object and lift his head when he lay on his tummy. I imagined how different things would be for him if he’d been born in Australia. He would have had early-intervention therapy as a baby, and his mum would get social security so they wouldn’t be living this precarious existence.

I laid Ammanuel down on the plinth, facing away from us towards the wall. I rolled two hand towels, one each to go under his right arm and leg. We had practised this movement for a few weeks now, and he was comfortable with it. I shook a plastic maraca just behind his left ear.

‘*Nu*! This way!’ Ammanuel’s mum called him while I stroked his neck muscles to activate them. He turned slightly to look at the toy before giving up and letting his head roll back.

‘*Ciao*! *Ehedalehu*. I’m going now.’ The mother marched on the spot.

With incredible effort, Ammanuel rolled onto his back to see his mum. This movement of just a few inches was the first whole-body movement he had ever performed. His ecstatic mum clapped while Yeshe and I cheered. Ammanuel wheezed a laugh again and bestowed a smile upon each of us as if he had appointed us to watch him roll.

While Ammanuel's mum practised more rolling, I asked Yeshe, 'Is it a good business? To make *injera*, I mean?'

Yeshe looked surprised. 'Of course! She can make much money. Do you see how every Ethiopian likes to eat *injera*? This is our culture. Especially soon as it is *Gena*.'

'*Gena*?'

'Christmas. It's very important for *ferenjis* I think? Your *ferenji* Christmas will be first. Then after two weeks, comes *Habesha Gena*, Ethiopian Christmas.' She handed me the calendar that was pinned by a magnet to the metal wall of our shipping container office.

But the calendar listed Ethiopian dates, taken from the Coptic calendar. The months had different names and durations than the calendars I was used to. I asked Yeshe and Ammanuel's mum what the Ethiopian date was and it took them a while to agree, and then Yeshe converted it to a *ferenji* date, and I realised there were just five shopping days to go until Christmas. And it made no difference whatsoever. It was refreshing to spend Christmas away from the consumer hype, so much so I had not realised the festive season was upon us. I'd seen no advertising at all except at the convent when the sisters turned on the TV on Sunday afternoons and, even then, the single Ethiopian TV channel usually only showed ads for washing powder or fertiliser.

'*Gena*, it is a nice time,' Yeshe said. 'Everyone is eating *doro wat*, chicken stew, and everyone is wearing their cultural clothes.'

Four days later, Yeshe and the rehabilitation workers hosted a coffee ceremony for *ferenji* Christmas, just for me. They scattered long grass and fresh white flowers on the office floor and Yeshe sat behind a charcoal burner roasting coffee beans on a metal disc. When she tossed an orange chunk of myrrh into the coals it sizzled, filling the room with perfume. Smoke from the roasting coffee beans and incense filled the office and stung my eyes in the most delicious way. Yeshe pounded the roasted beans and boiled the grounds in a *jebena*, a traditional coffee pot, while she cooked popcorn on the charcoal burner. We passed the basket of hot popcorn around the room, with another basket of roasted peanuts and cracked wheat.

Earlier that day I had asked Yeshe what I could contribute and she said I could bring biscuits. One of the rehabilitation workers had gone with me to the small hole-in-the-wall shop near the clinic and I had asked in Amharic for three packets of cream biscuits.

Now another colleague served the cream biscuits and glass bottles of soft drink to everyone in the room. It felt so decadent to be bingeing like this on a workday.

'This round of coffee is called *andegna*, the first one. For health.' Yeshe ladled three sugars into each of the cups and passed me a coffee so syrupy and strong it made my heart race. When we passed our empty cups back and she refilled them, she said, 'This is second round, *huletegna*. Second is for happiness.'

I had to decline the third round of coffee against much protestation from Yeshe that third round was for blessing. My belly was full and the caffeine made me jittery.

'Second round, for happiness, is enough for me.' I was being honest. I already felt blessed. I wanted nothing more than to drink hand-ground coffee and eat popcorn and cream biscuits with cheerful company to celebrate Christmas.

'We would like to present you with a memento. We know *ferenjis* give presents at Christmas time, so we all got a present for you,' Yeshe said.

I was dismayed they had spent money on me, but so flattered when I saw the gift. It was a white dress fringed with beads and embroidered with greens, oranges and pinks across the bodice. I slipped it over my t-shirt and rolled my jeans out of sight, then

Yeshe tied the matching shawl as a headscarf.

'Now you have cultural clothes,' she said, and when I twirled, showing off a little, the beaded fringing brushed my ankles. My colleagues shook their heads in a pantomime of amazement and agreed I should parade for the staff in other departments.

A little shy, but pleased, I followed Yeshe across the compound, past ten construction workers levelling the ground. They all put down their tools and gawked. Such attention was not new to me as, being a *ferenji*, I got stared at and shouted at daily. I stiffened, expecting someone to call 'You-you-you!', but instead one of them leaned over his shovel and called in perfect English, 'Thank you for taking part in my traditional culture!'

I wanted to say, 'Thank you for letting me take part in your traditional culture!' I felt useful, loved and welcomed by my community, and now I had cultural clothes. 'You're welcome,' I replied.

I wore my cultural clothes two weeks later for Ethiopian Orthodox Christmas. The only Christmas service in our convent would be in Amharic, Sister Starling told me. In an effort to please her, I asked the other sisters where I might find English mass. When I told Sister Starling I would attend the morning mass at the Indian sisters' convent in Arat Kilo area, she gave a sharp nod of approval that lifted my hopes. If I did nothing else right, at least I would redeem myself a little in the eyes of Sister Starling.

The next morning I waited for a minibus taxi to Arat Kilo area in my brand-new cultural clothes. My dress was fringed with beads of white, green, orange and pink, and it clinked as I walked, and as I bent to tighten the beaded shawl around my waist like a sash, just as Yeshe had shown me. People in white filled the streets. Portly grandmothers in white lugged belligerent toddlers in white, young mothers wore white headscarves and dresses like mine, men and teenage boys were head to toe in traditional white garb. I was so grateful I had cultural clothes; I imagined today I might get fewer stares and shouts.

'*Ferenji*! Beautiful clothes!' a middle-aged man yelled.

'*Ferenji*! Beautiful clothes!' a teenage girl walking arm in arm with a friend called from across the road.

'Beautiful girl!' her friend added, and they both looked over their shoulders to giggle.

After about ten minutes I became so used to the attention I was offended if someone *didn't* compliment me as they passed. A young man dressed in white cotton trousers and a white V-neck vest over a white tunic, with white shoes clipping the pavement, called to me, '*Konjo lebs*! Beautiful clothes!'

Filled with the joy of this Christmas morning ego boost I called to him '*Lehulum*! For everyone!' and I hoped he would understand I meant *you too*, because I didn't know how to say that.

A girl about nine years old flounced towards me, looking down at her own cultural clothes. Each little hand held the ends of the white sash tied around her waist and with each step she flung them wide, watching the beaded fringe shimmer on one side then the other. Engrossed, she almost collided with me, and looked up at me with a start. She took in my cultural clothes, my own sash with fringed beading, with almost the same pattern as hers, and looked awe-struck. She shook my hand vigorously.

'*Konjo lebs*! Beautiful clothes!' I got in first this time. She beamed and ran away, only to return a few minutes later, with her hand outstretched.

'*Mastika tifellegiyallesh*? You want gum?' She dropped two purple pellets into my hand and skipped into the crowd ahead before I'd finished thanking her.

I *liked* Ethiopian Christmas! Compliments, lollies from diminutive strangers, and I was off to an English church service, fulfilling expectations and lifting my reputation in the sisters' home. I rapped on the gate to the Indian sisters' convent at five minutes to nine.

'No church service today. Nine o'clock last night,' the sister wobbled her head apologetically for my mistake. The gate clanked shut, leaving me churchless and unredeemed on the street. I didn't know what to do. If I returned to the convent and Sister Starling saw me, my lack of sanctity would become apparent. I would need to hide in my room, with its sagging single bed and tombstone-cold floor. A minibus taxi passed with a conductor leaning out the window spruiking its destination: '*Menen*! *Menen*! *Menen*!'

I knew where Menen was. I had been going to a group home there every Saturday since the weekend of my bar fight, to help out at the charity that hosted a hundred or so children for playgroup. So I flagged down the minibus and got out at the stop before the group home, in front of the hole-in-the-wall shop.

'*Haya ezziya*, twenty those.' I pointed to a tub of colourfully wrapped caramels, and the shopkeeper counted out the sweets into a plastic bag.

The group home mother greeted me with a familiar hug, and said, '*Gebu*! *Gebu*! Come in! Come in!' while she ushered me into the living area and handed out the caramels. Most Saturdays the courtyard of this home was full of squealing kids, all of them orphaned by AIDS and most of them living with relatives or neighbours. Today there were just five children here, who lived in the group home because they had nowhere else to go. Usually on a Saturday I was engulfed in exuberant pint-sized hugs but this morning the children just stared at me, wide-eyed, saying nothing as they chewed their lollies. A little boy about four picked his nose and the big girl next to him swiped his hand away and glowered at him. They smiled a little though when I started to compare my cultural clothes with theirs. The two older girls showed me the beading on their dresses and pointed out to me how the three younger boys were dressed in miniature white trousers and waistcoats. They stood in a line until I said in Amharic, 'One game?'

'*Awe*! Yes!' said the littlest one, a delicate little boy about three.

'Which game?' I asked and they conferred.

'*Kwass*! Football!' the tiny boy shouted. He stood rigid with his arms at his side until I nodded to him and he ran to his room, scampering back with a tennis ball.

The four-year-old took his finger out of his nose and wiped it enthusiastically on his cultural clothes and all the kids ran to the courtyard. We played tennis-ball soccer in our cultural clothes for almost an hour, with the beaded fringe of my dress clinking against my shins, and sweat trickling down my back. After soccer the girls insisted on playing elastics, which I hadn't played since primary school. I was so bad at it the two girls, aged seven and nine, giggled until they had to lean against each other to stay up.

When I looked at my watch and said, '*Lejoch, ehedalehu*. Kids, I go now,' the kids chorused their disappointment. I tried to say in Amharic that I would come again on Saturday, but there was too much noise and all the bigger kids were crowding me into a hug.

'Stay here!' the littlest one said in Amharic, jumping into the air as if it might make him taller.

If only I could, I thought, but I had told the sisters I would be home in time for Christmas lunch. As the metal gate closed behind me and I walked up the road to flag down a minibus, I could hear five little voices calling out, '*Temeleshe*! Come again! *Melkam Gena*! Merry Christmas!'

Back in the convent, I helped set the table with the good china for Christmas lunch with the shiny teaspoons that I had wrongly set out a few weeks ago. The novice sisters and I set out the bowl of *doro wat*, festive chicken stew, that Yeshe had talked about, as well as lamb stew and vegetable dishes.

When Sister Starling arrived in the dining room, everyone hugged and wished each other 'Happy Feast!' and then we took our seats.

Sister Starling motioned towards the doily in the centre of the table. 'Sister Fantaye from the northern diocese gifted us this doily for Christmas. The embroidery on it is very nice.'

No-one said anything until Sister Starling said, 'Isn't it.'

'Yes, Sister,' whispered the novice sisters, so I did too.

I waited in dread for Sister Starling to ask me about the mass I didn't attend, so I kept my eyes averted, but no-one spoke after that, and the only sound in the room was the good cutlery scraping against the good china, until the *doro wat* was all gone.

The maid took the main meal dishes into the kitchen while the novice sisters and I cleared the table, and she returned with a tub of ice-cream and a packet of wafer biscuits.

After the senior sisters served theirs, Sister Meaza passed me a china bowl.

'Have ice-cream, Julie,' she implored me in a whisper.

I sat at the table with my bowl of ice-cream and one wafer biscuit poking from it, waiting like everyone else until Sister Starling addressed the table.

'It's a special treat. Once a year. It's from the *ferenji* supermarket in Bole area. It's *expensive*,' she said and I felt sure she glared at me. I wasn't sure if I was supposed to feel grateful or guilty, which, being Catholic, did come naturally.

'Thank you, Sister,' I whispered.

Sister Starling gave her opinion on today's Amharic mass and everyone at the table nodded in silent agreement. I focused even harder on eating my ice-cream without letting the spoon touch the bowl, nipping at each spoonful and trying to swallow without noise so that she might forget I was there.

I had expected life in a convent might be hard, but not this kind of hard. In fact, I hadn't given much thought to what living in a convent might really be like. I had assumed that we would all be doing good things, so everything else would be easy.

But now it turned out that I couldn't even find the right church service, let alone the meaning of life. I wasn't sure how much longer I could take of convent living, but I loved working in the clinic and was thrilled to see how Ammanuel and his living situation had improved since he'd started. I wondered if I could live outside the convent but keep working in the clinic, but then how would I go about finding somewhere to live, or even do my grocery shopping? So far all I had bought at the local shops were some cream biscuits, twenty caramel lollies and some flea spray, but even that was with Sister Meaza's help. I guessed that I would become as confident as my *ferenji* friends if I lived outside the convent. Maybe I could find a different job, one that provided me with accommodation and a salary just like them.

Then I worried the sisters would think I was ungrateful for turning down their accommodation and reneging on my offer to work with them; or would they be so delighted I'd gone, they would crack open a second tub of ice-cream for the year?

The room was so quiet that when Sister Meaza crunched on her wafer everyone turned to look at her. Her face flushed and she hunched her shoulders to finish chewing and swallow. It seemed hard to imagine that just two hours ago I had been kicking a tennis ball around a compound with five squealing children.

I wondered what my *ferenji* friends were doing right now. They had invited me to join them for Ethiopian Christmas but I had declined before they gave me the details, telling everyone it was going to be fun to stay in the convent. Because I really wanted it to be fun to stay in the convent, so that I could stay on in Ethiopia and continue my work. It had only been two weeks since *ferenji* Christmas, when I had logged onto my Hotmail and seen pop-up ads demanding my attention:

'Lose weight now! Beat that festive craving!'

'Take our online poll! Is the festive traffic heavy?'

'What are you giving yourself for Christmas this year?'

'It's not too late to get the perfect gift!'

It seemed outrageous that such banalities could coexist with Ammanuel's mum, whose situation was so precarious she was thrilled to have her son roll over, and for Christmas she had given herself some intact clothes. Or that everyone at home was busy buying the perfect gift for relatives who didn't need anything, while here tiny boys needed to live in group homes because they didn't have any relatives.

No, I was a do-gooder and I came to Ethiopia to do good things. So unless something else presented itself, I would have to stay in the convent.

Chapter 7

To help: መርዳት */merdat/*

One morning in mid January I was eating my porridge alone when a sister I didn't recognise came into the dining room. She didn't charge in officiously like Sister Starling, or creep in with fearful glances as the novice sisters did. She sauntered to the table and after serving herself porridge, leant across to shake my hand.

'I am Sister Almaz. Nice to meet you.' Though she spoke at normal volume, her voice jarred in the quiet of breakfast time, when the young sisters always whispered and Sister Starling's greeting was a wordless nod. I noticed Sister Almaz's hair, poking out messily from beneath her veil and as she poured herself tea from the thermos I wondered why she wasn't at prayers with the others. As if in answer, she told me she had some early meetings, as she'd come to the capital for two weeks to sort out administration for her project.

'My project is with the women. In a small town in Welega, close to the border with Sudan. Do you know it? It is very far.'

We chatted while we ate breakfast, and she joined me for tea after work as well. The afternoon sun through the lace curtains dappled light on the table, and the refrigerator in the corner hummed while we drank three cups of tea. I told her about the clinic and its accompanying community-based rehabilitation project I worked with, and she described her project for women's empowerment.

'Sister Starling runs a women's empowerment project in area eighteen, near the Shiro Meda area,' I said. 'Is it like that?'

Sister Almaz gave a surprised laugh. '*Anchi*! You! This is the city. My project is in the countryside. So far away, that when the government changed the name, we still called it the old name. Welega province is not like Addis Ababa at all. Simply we have a school, a clinic and a program with income generation for the women. *Beka*, enough, nothing else. Do you like it here?' She suddenly changed the subject and, suppressing a smile, she motioned upwards with her eyes and circled her head, as if to indicate the hallway of bedrooms upstairs and the communal dining room.

'The sisters are very kind to me,' I said.

'This place is too ... traditional.' She leaned in with a teasing smile. 'Here is for learning sisters. Do you want to be a sister?'

'Umm ... I don't think I would make a very good nun.' She couldn't know what an understatement that was.

'Okay, so stop learning.' Sister Almaz sipped her tea, raising her eyebrows over her teacup and watching my face intently.

Sister Almaz told me about the work she would do while in Addis Ababa. She had meetings with the accountant to sort out finances for her project, visits to government officials to get various authorisations and trips to the Merkato – the enormous central market – to gather supplies that weren't available in her area.

'Will you drink tea tomorrow? Maybe we can talk again?' Sister Almaz said, and I thought how I would like that very much.

Every afternoon for the next two weeks, Sister Almaz and I took tea together. I was awed by her knowledge and her outlook on life, as at thirteen years my senior, she was far wiser than I imagined I would be at her age. All day at work I looked forward to the afternoon when we would talk about the world, its injustices and our place in it, but she would also make me laugh. It was a welcome respite from the daily routine of getting to the end of the workday and dreading the long cold evening in the convent, trying not to break rules I'd forgotten existed.

One afternoon as we drank tea, beside dust motes drifting on sunlight, she asked, 'How long will you stay?' Instead of finishing the sentence she lifted her eyebrows and pointed around the room.

'Another three weeks. I've only got three weeks left on my volunteer visa and I need to decide what to do next.'

'So, come with me! I am looking for a physiotherapist for my project. We have a feeding program for the children with malnutrition. So many disability children.'

I sipped my tea. It would be exciting to get out of the city and visit the border area. But I wasn't certain going to another convent would be wise. Did I want to spend more time with sisters, just to annoy them as I had the Addis Ababa sisters?

'Well ...'

While I hesitated Sister Almaz spread jam onto a thick slice of homemade bread and slapped it onto my plate with a grin as if 'well' had been a proper answer.

In the drive to work the next morning, Sister Starling said, 'I hear from the head sister for Welega that Sister Almaz invited you to work with her.'

'Yes, Sister,' I said, terrified of her disapproval, but relieved I didn't have to bring it up.

'You don't have to go, you know,' she barked. 'The patients like you. I suppose the staff like you. It helps us to have you here. Whichever you decide, you'll need to go Immigration to apply for your next three-month visa. I'll get the driver to drop you there tomorrow.'

I couldn't stop turning the question over in my mind. Should I go, or extend my time in Addis Ababa? I really did love my work in the clinic. When I first arrived I found it frustrating we had no individual times for appointments, but I soon grew to look forward to patients converging for either 'morning' or 'after lunch' sessions. Then, up to five patients might fill the therapy room, while five more waited, giving encouragement to other patients doing their exercises, and toddlers and children, sometimes just the kids from next door, played with the therapy room toys.

That day in the after-lunch session, there was Eleni, Teferi and Ammanuel, plus an old man with a back injury and a young man with a strained hamstring. Yeshi was on a home visit and the community rehabilitation workers were at training. I had no choice except to converse with them in my basic Amharic. After three months in the *kebele* I knew enough to exchange pleasantries, start them on an exercise and progress to the next one. Having the therapy room to myself felt like riding without training wheels. It was nerve-racking but thrilling. Now I felt even more torn about leaving the *kebele* to work with Sister Almaz.

In the evening I wrote down my options in my journal while the sisters were at prayer. I made a list of reasons to stay:

1. I loved my work in the *kebele*. I loved all my patients. I loved visiting all the patients, getting to know their families and the way they insisted we stay for coffee ceremony afterwards. 2. I was beginning to build a circle of *ferenji* friends. Since the barbecue at the embassy, I had a nice life on weekends going out to bars, or pizza and tenpin bowling with my new pals from Canada, Australia and America.

Before I got to write the list of reasons to go, I realised I would be late for dinner. I threw open the door and hurried down the cold passageway to the dining room with my thongs clacking under me on the stone floor.

After dinner there was a knock and Sister Meaza appeared at my door, looking terrified. She looked both ways and whispered, 'Julie, please open your door more quietly.'

'Yes, Sister. Please tell me why?'

'Sister Starling says it is disturbing, the way you open the doors here. And ... please, lifting your feet a little. Sister says your slippers are too loud ...' She pointed at my thongs with an apologetic look.

I clicked the door shut when she left, and clicked it open again when she reappeared half an hour later to say there was a call for me on the communal phone at the end of the hallway.

'*Anchi*? You? Are you coming?' Sister Almaz said.

'But what if I am annoying in your convent? I open doors too loudly.'

Sister Almaz blew through her lips like a horse, as if that was the silliest thing she'd heard. 'So you're coming? I am excited, really!'

We set off for Welega on Friday before dawn, and it was so cold we could see our breath under the streetlights. Sister Almaz had already left so I travelled with the head sister and two other Ethiopian sisters. While we sat in the car, waiting for the driver to pack the boot of the Land Cruiser with supplies from Addis Ababa that weren't available in rural areas, I smiled nervously at the unfamiliar sisters and felt sick in my stomach. I was sure that going to another convent was a bad idea, and wondered how I would make it if the two-day journey was silent and the atmosphere in the car oppressive.

But the sisters were telling jokes even before it started getting light, and as we passed the outskirts of Addis Ababa and the dawn light silhouetted farmers and their oxen, I began to relax. We drove all day on bitumised roads, with the driver only slowing down on the outskirts of towns to coast past roadside markets with vendors sitting on the ground behind produce on wheat sacks. Donkeys and their masters trotted beside the car, so close I could see into the crates slung over their backs, filled with tomatoes and carrots. We stayed the night in the parish house in the halfway town of Nekemte, hosted by young Ethiopian priests, who baked fresh bread for us and waved us off before dawn again the next morning.

As the sun rose and the mist burned away, I saw the open fields had become more forested. Pointed roofs of circular huts, *tukuls*, emerged through the mist, and smoke curled from their peaks. Rectangles of ploughed fields were bordered with banana palms and taller *enset*, false banana trees, with wider dark fronds and tall trunks but no fruit.

Soon the bitumen roads finished and we drove on dirt roads, so flood-damaged in places it felt as if we were driving on creek beds. The Land Cruiser didn't have any seatbelts, so the window-seat passengers in the back steadied themselves by holding onto the strap above the door and the passenger in the middle clutched the front seats. The sisters screeched with laughter as we swayed and bounced, holding tighter when the driver rammed the car down a gear to rev the engine heavily enough to make it up a steep incline. When we stopped for lunch or to pee behind bushes, all the passengers swapped sides so we could hold on with our other arm and rest one aching shoulder.

By the afternoon, the dust from hours of driving on unsealed roads had settled in a layer on my face, in my hair and on my teeth. The foliage at the sides of the road had become so thick in places that the spiked leaves, flat fronds and hanging vines wove around each other and briefly formed a canopy over the road, before the view at the roadside opened out again.

In the late afternoon, when the driver said we were just one hour from our destination, the four-wheel drive struggled up a large hill, and suddenly the land dropped away into a verdant valley so steep I could see the clouds' shadows, while a black-and-white monkey ambled down from a tree. It was as far-removed from Addis Ababa as I could imagine. The head sister told me the last town before the border with Sudan was about one hundred and fifty kilometres away, so we were almost as far from Addis Ababa as you could go without leaving the country. I thought of my co-workers in the clinic, and had a pang of sadness for all my patients that I had grown so fond of, and had said goodbye to just yesterday. But then I thought of my *ferenji* friends, stuck in traffic with buildings all around them, and couldn't think of any place I would rather be than in a four-wheel drive with three sisters, two sore shoulders, a mouthful of dust and this view.

We reached Sister Almaz's convent just on dusk and while the driver idled the engine and the convent guards swung the big gates open, farmers walking livestock home for the evening waved a greeting to the sisters.

Sister Almaz hugged me before I had fully climbed out of the Land Cruiser, and after my shower brought me a cup of chamomile tea, in case I needed something to help me sleep. I didn't at all, and stayed awake just long enough to hear the crickets and frogs outside my window.

I woke to a polyphonic chorus of birds at dawn. Although Sister Almaz had given me a blanket, the night had been warm and I had slept with only a sheet. It felt like freedom after the heavy blankets and fleece I'd needed every night in the Addis mountain chill.

In the dining room, six sisters seated around a small table looked up at me as I entered.

'*Anchi*, you. Hurry up, we are all finished.' Sister Almaz's face remained expressionless.

'But you said seven-thirty!' In a panic I looked at my watch, seeing it was 7.32 a.m. 'I'm so sorry; I must have confused the time. It's okay. I'll go without breakfast if we need to leave now.'

The sisters giggled and Sister Almaz slapped the table. '*Anchi*, you! Joking!' She wrapped her hand warmly around my forearm and pulled out the chair next to her. 'We haven't started yet. Drink tea?' Without waiting for my answer, she poured me a cup and pushed the sugar bowl towards me.

Our first stop that morning was to a therapeutic-feeding program in a nearby village, which Sister Almaz said had a recent spate of child malnutrition. When we arrived, the children were already assembled, sitting around the periphery of a veranda, all dressed identically in a uniform of mustard yellow trousers and button-down shirts.

Sister Almaz introduced me to the head nurse of the program and some mothers, who stirred a vat of lentils and pasta over an open fire and ladled servings into plastic bowls. Some older girls scurried back and forth across the veranda, handing out the bowls. The children didn't look malnourished or emaciated, they just looked like healthy preschoolers.

After their meals, the children handed their empty bowls back to the older girls and slowly the veranda emptied as the children ran into the playground, to kick about a ball of rolled fabric and string.

Only five kids didn't get up to play and sat watching the others from the steps.

The head nurse, a slightly built man, explained in English, 'In this therapeutic feeding program we have five children we are worried for. This boy, two years and three-quarter. He was very severely malnourished before. We feared that he may die, but he is healthier now.'

He pointed out a little boy, who was thinner than the others, with tiny doll-sized features, although his face was full and his cheeks smooth. I sat next to him on the step and he put his chin to his chest shyly.

Sister Almaz had already told me that very few people in this province spoke Amharic so I asked the head nurse to translate for me and ask the little boy's name.

The boy whispered with his chin still tucked to his chest, 'Abissa.'

I squatted in front of Abissa and held his hands in mine. They were so tiny they made mine seem enormous.

'Can you please say "stand up"?' I asked the head nurse.

Abissa's legs wobbled as he stood up, and he stood, feet as far apart as they could go, clutching at my fingers as if he might fall if he let go.

'This is the lasting effect of malnutrition, it is the delayed development,' the head nurse said.

He got the other children on the step to show me their standing too. Although they were older, aged between four and six, they were equally unsteady on their feet.

'What can we do for the delay?' Sister Almaz asked.

I had read about developmental delay following malnutrition in the *Disabled Village Children* book and although I hadn't yet seen any children with this issue, it was fairly easy to find a starting point.

'Let's do an exercise to practise balancing and make their legs stronger. Can you please say "One, two, three, stand up"?' I stood up and lifted my arms in the air to demonstrate.

The head nurse called the instructions and lifted his hands above his head.

Abissa held onto my fingers for support and all the children slowly stood, and then sat straight down.

'Again?' I said.

Sister Almaz carried over a low stool and sat facing the children.

'One, two, three!' she called in the local dialect and threw her arms above her head and whooped. They lifted their arms a little and then sat down again. By the third time we did it, two of the children were smiling and by the seventh time, they were all throwing their hands in the air too.

I said to the head nurse, 'It's an easy exercise, but if they do it regularly, their legs should get stronger and they could join their friends and play in the yard. Who can do the exercises regularly with the children?'

The head nurse said, 'Simply it is me. You know, we do not have any other resource of physiotherapy and we have so many children like this.'

'Yes, Sister Almaz told me there are many children with disabilities in this region.'

The head nurse looked shocked. 'No, there are no children with disabilities in this region. Simply the children with malnutrition.'

In the four-wheel drive on the way home, Sister Almaz explained that very few parents bought their children with disabilities into public here, because of the stigma associated with disability. I told Sister Almaz I had seen how the community-based rehabilitation program in Addis Ababa had reduced the stigma around disability in that community and Sister Almaz wondered if we could use the same approach. We both wondered if I could use the training I had prepared for the community-based rehabilitation workers in Addis Ababa, and modify it slightly for health staff who hadn't had any training in disability issues. It would run through basic understanding of disability issues and some simple physiotherapy solutions for children with disabilities.

'But we need some patients. What if no one turns up?' I asked.

Sister Almaz put her hands together in a prayer position and pointed her eyebrows to the sky with a laugh.

The electricity cut out that evening, so we dined on the veranda by candlelight. It was a hot mid-February night, just like I was used to in Perth. An intermittent breeze carried the scent of frangipanis and lifted blue veils as the conversation flowed and the sisters bantered. When the others finished their dinner and retired for the night, Sister Almaz convinced me to stay for one more cup of tea.

I asked her why the children in the therapeutic-feeding program actually looked healthy, not thin as I had expected.

'Because we feed them.' She looked rueful.

'Do they need a feeding program because the families are too poor?' I dunked a biscuit into my chamomile tea.

Sister Almaz tilted her head to the side. 'Ye-e-s. Also they don't know what to feed their children. They don't know about nutrition. They feed them *bekolo*, corn.'

'And ...?' I prompted. Corn and pasta, I thought. Corn and tomatoes?

'They only feed their children corn. *Bekolo bicha*. Only corn.'

'*Bekolo bicha*? But on the way here I saw women in the markets selling bananas and tomatoes; don't they feed their kids those?'

She shook her head. 'No, they sell those and use the money to buy corn.'

I asked Sister Almaz how entire generations survived if they only ate corn.

'They have lost their traditional knowledge. This is all they know now. Because of handouts. From Bob Geldof and you *ferenjis*.' She pointed her chin at me. 'And from us, the Catholic nuns. But we will change that. I have work for you to do. Can you help me write a proposal for the women's empowerment program? Those mothers in our program you saw today, they need a way to make money and feed their children.'

I nodded, full of zeal. Here was a way to make up for the harm perpetrated by the West. If it meant doing training during the day and writing grant proposals instead of drinking tea in the evenings, I would do it. Sister Almaz, I thought, was a very good do-gooder, and I wanted to help.

We held the therapy training for ten staff members in the clinic, which was a stone building with tiled floors and painted cement verandas. On the Monday morning, I presented some theory and in the afternoon our first patient turned up, a six-year-old boy with severe developmental delay and an intellectual disability, whose mother wanted some ideas to help him walk more steadily. On Tuesday morning a family waited for us with their three-year-old girl, who'd had both legs amputated below the knees, but there were no prosthetic limbs available. In the afternoon, the parish priest turned up because he had heard there was a physiotherapist in town.

He looked about twenty-five years old and told me that because he grew up in a neighbouring village, he already knew all his parishioners. He knew all the people with disabilities in the area, even the ones who never went out in public. He said there was a child with paralysis following a head injury who needed help.

On Wednesday afternoon following the training, he picked me up in his beaten-up Land Cruiser, and we drove for an hour over dirt roads, dry creekbeds, through thick foliage, and up steep embankments until we got to the small village. The parents welcomed us warmly into their *tukul*, round hut, and I assessed the child as she lay on her back on the bench fashioned from adobe. We could hear charismatic prayer, singing and drum beats from the adjacent hut so the parish priest excused himself to go next door and chat with more of his parishioners. I was left to carry out the assessment alone, and when I looked up after a few minutes, five people had filed silently into the hut. Every time I looked up again, more people had come in to watch, and I was relieved when the priest came back to translate for me, as I now counted twenty-five people observing us.

A man in the crowd told the priest his four-year-old nephew also had problems walking and asked if we could visit him next. And in his hut, as I assessed the small boy and saw that his difficulties walking were due to cerebral palsy, another crowd gathered. There, a grandmother asked us to come to her home because her granddaughter was five and couldn't yet walk or talk.

On Thursday morning, three families of children with disabilities were waiting on the clinic veranda for us when we arrived, and on Friday there was a short queue. There was such a demand for physiotherapy that the sisters running the remote outstation clinics asked if I could visit to see their patients as well.

On Monday a sister from a remote outstation collected me in her Land Cruiser and we drove for three hours, stopping only for thirty baboons that lounged across the road and on both sides of it. They looked up with disdain when sister honked the horn and waited fifteen minutes before they sauntered aside. The clinic was set on the edge of a jungle and our patients waited under banana palms. That day I saw fifteen patients – children with disabilities, adults with paralyses and old people with arthritis and painful deformities. I stayed over with the sisters for two days, in their wooden house with no running water or electricity connected. At night the guard lugged a metal bucket of warm water to the bathroom and I bathed by candlelight and then fell into an exhausted sleep listening to monkeys screech in the distance. In the mornings I rose before dawn and attended chapel with the hosting sisters, chanting prayers with them under the light of candle stubs, with the sounds of the jungle waking up around us.

On Monday of the following week, a different order of sisters collected me and we drove for three hours in a different direction, stopping only for two donkey foals taking a dust bath on a road, on a mountain precipice. They didn't move, even when sister held her hand long on the horn. This clinic was set in verdant lowlands and the sisters' house was surrounded by frangipani, mango, apple, pomegranate, papaya and orange trees. There was already a queue when we arrived. That day I saw twenty patients, including a man whose burn scars had rendered his shoulder immobile, children with unexplained paralyses, adults with injuries and disabling pain. I stayed three nights with those sisters, and in the evenings I joined them for prayers on the veranda during tropical storms. We looked over treetops in the valley and sung over the sounds of thunder rumbling in the valley and crickets, frogs and rain.

On my last morning, one of the sisters picked a papaya from the tree. I was delighted to see that as she bent to peel it, a monkey climbed down from the tree and scampered off. That night, returning to Sister Almaz's convent, all the sisters made tea and stayed up late to hear about my trip and I fell asleep to the now familiar cadence of the crickets and frogs outside my window.

I couldn't believe how lucky I was. Although I hadn't given much thought to what living and working with nuns would be like, this turned out to be precisely what I'd hoped for. By day we did good things and everything else fell into place.

The only thing that worried me was the short-term nature of my help. The patients and their families all seemed so eager for help and, while I was glad I could show them exercises, it was distressing to see so many patients with severe functional limitations and such chronic problems with no chance of follow-up. One session of physio and some ideas on different ways to move better wouldn't have much impact at all. I wished there was a community-based rehabilitation program or a nearby physio clinic I could refer them to. All the sisters, in all of the clinics, shared my lament.

Before I left Addis Ababa, I had heard there was a physiotherapy degree in a university in the north of the country, that had started two years earlier. Sister Almaz urged me to call and see if there might be a job with them.

I told Sister Almaz I didn't think I was experienced enough to be a physiotherapy teacher. Although I had worked as a physiotherapist for eight years, I thought I might need postgraduate qualifications to work in a university.

But the Canadian physiotherapist on the end of the line, when I called the University of Gondar physiotherapy department, said not to worry as the curriculum was already set to an international standard. She said there were only a handful of degree-trained Ethiopian physiotherapists, most of whom had been trained outside the country, and they were always looking for new instructors for the course. Send in your CV, she advised and she would talk to the dean.

I had been away from home for nearly six months now, but in Welega it felt so similar to a Western Australia summer that my homesickness felt sweet, almost pleasurable. Every day felt like February in Perth – with dry heat above thirty degrees, although here the heat continued well into April.

The evenings were warm, and I spent every evening working with Sister Almaz, staying up until 1 a.m. the night before we were due to submit the proposal for her women's empowerment program to the bishop of the diocese.

It was my first time preparing a funding proposal, and I left the complicated section asking for the contributing socio-economic factors of the region to the next afternoon.

When I asked Sister Almaz what to write, she said, 'Just write "poor region". *Anchi*, you, hurry up and print, it's almost time! He's here, oh quick, he's here!' We heard tyres on the gravel in the driveway and Sister Almaz ran to the veranda to rattle teacups onto saucers and straighten already straight teaspoons.

The convent cook hurried from the kitchen with a circular loaf of traditional bread, sweet-smelling and still warm from the oven.

'*Anchi*, you. You must be nice to Father Teklu. Make him sign the proposal to give us the money. But be careful. Do not say about his funny physique. He is very old, and short. And, you know, a bit ...' Sister Almaz made the shape of a large belly in front of her own slim waist and hissed, 'He is sensitive.' Then she beamed past me. 'Father Teklu, welcome!' She reached to shake the hand of the tall, thin priest who looked way too young and handsome to be a bishop. When I shot her a look, she pressed her lips together to hold in smile.

Ushering him to the table, Sister Almaz handed him the proposal and budget. It requested funding for Sister Almaz to expand the women's empowerment program, where women could earn an independent income by moulding and firing bricks for sale, by blending and packaging *berbere* spice mix for sale in Addis Ababa, and by sewing school uniforms, for which they required training.

'Will you drink tea, Father?' Sister Almaz poured a cup and pushed it towards him. 'Have some bread, Father.' She plonked a slice of bread in front of Father Teklu. She slid the butter dish close and, while he leafed through the proposal, she inched over a jar of honey so creamy and white it looked like whipped eggs.

Father Teklu looked up. 'Oh! I see you have honey from my home province of Tigray. Only Tigray has honey that is white like this. Is this my gift to you from last time I was there?'

Sister Almaz appeared to think. 'Oh, yes! So it is.'

Father Teklu spread his bread with honey. 'Try some?' He pushed the jar my way.

The honey was the consistency of toffee and I could almost taste flowers in it.

'Do you like this honey, my gift to the sisters?' Father Teklu asked me.

Now was my chance to impress him with my Amharic and impress Sister Almaz by securing the funding. I said, '*Awe! Ewdehalehu*!'

Sister Almaz snorted. Father Teklu's eyebrows shot up and he gulped his tea. He turned first to Sister Almaz, whose face was red, then back to me. He replied uncertainly, '*Amesegenalehu, enem ewedishalehu*. Thanks, I love you too.'

My face went hot. I said, '*Ewedalu, mar*! No, I love it. The honey!' It was only the difference of one syllable, but it was still mortifying.

Father Teklu's laugh was good-natured. He drained the last of his tea, tucked the print-out into his satchel and said, 'I'll discuss the proposal with the diocese committee and inform you next week.'

Sister Almaz shared the story with all the other sisters at dinner that night and everyone laughed. Then one of the sisters recounted her own translation blunders from Amharic to English, and someone else told a joke until everyone was laughing so much the head sister had to take her glasses off to wipe her eyes and I didn't feel bad for my mistake at all.

The next night I sat with Sister Almaz drinking tea on the veranda after the others had gone to bed. I asked her why this region was so poor compared to Addis Ababa, even though it looked so abundant.

She refilled my chamomile tea from the pot before she spoke. 'Because of the political situation since last government. The people are relocated from their original areas and forced to be together. Different people with different language and different culture. They want to be separate but the government doesn't allow it.'

The candle between us flickered and the only other sounds were frogs and crickets. 'Not just here in the south part. In the north too. You know, I am not Ethiopian, and my family is not Ethiopian. I used to be Ethiopian, everyone in my region did. Now they made this line, the border. Now my village is in Eritrea. And the next village is in Ethiopia. Now my family is called Eritrean. Then ... war between Ethiopia and my place.' She motioned with her eyebrows as if 'her place' was just around the corner and not the opposite end of the country.

I tried to imagine how that might feel, but the thought was impossible.

'What were Ethiopia and Eritrea fighting over?' I whispered in case anyone was listening. 'At the border is there gold, or oil?'

'No! Just the land. They were fighting for pride, let me tell you.'

She described her life during the war, telling me about being at university during that time, about things that happened to her family – heartbreaking, terrifying things, with a tone and expressions so whimsical and entertaining it made me laugh aloud. But then we sat in silence for a while as wisps of clouds drifted over the stars. The night was so still I could hear the candle wax dropping onto the table. Before coming to Ethiopia, I had thought all the world's poverty was due to the excesses of the developed world. I thought it was only our greed fuelling current wars, like those in Iraq and Afghanistan. Of all the things that I took for granted at home, like running water, electricity and a full tummy, I had never thought about freedom from terror. Not Terrorism™ that you might find served up in a government security campaign, or displayed on a fridge magnet, but the terror of being caught in a war between two governments.

I was outraged that Sister Almaz, who stayed up past midnight to get funds to make women's lives better, who was so much fun and never made anyone feel bad about themselves, had to endure this. I had never had to endure anything like this. Why was I so lucky and what was I supposed to do with the burden of that privilege?

'*Anchi*! You! Stop worrying!' she guffawed, looking at my face. 'Look at me! I am okay! It is finished, *beka*! Your tea has gone cold! It's time for bed.'

She prised the teacup out of my hand to empty the dregs into the garden and patted my shoulder as if I was the one needing consolation.

I got the email on a hot April afternoon advising that I was to be an employee of the Ethiopian Government. I would be joining the staff of the University of Gondar physiotherapy department, to teach classes and supervise physiotherapy students on the wards of the university hospital. Sister Almaz boiled a celebratory kettle, and we sipped sweet spiced tea on the veranda as we flicked through the Lonely Planet's Gondar section. Sister Almaz was excited I could visit a three-hundred-year-old church. I was excited I could visit a sixteenth-century castle, and we were both excited that I would earn a salary. It would only be one hundred dollars a month but after six months as a volunteer, it seemed a fortune.

On my last evening we walked to the river to get water, as the town electricity and water supply had been off for a week and our stored water supplies were getting low.

We went with the young sisters and some high-school students who boarded in the sisters' compound. We carried our empty jerry cans past bamboo fences with banana palms leaning over the top. It was late in the day, the sun was pleasantly warm and we all laughed and chattered, while passers-by greeted the sisters. As we got closer to the river, the creepers and vines grew in a tangled mass to twice my height, and the air became cool.

The students submerged their jerry cans in the river beside a woman and two small girls squatting to scrub their clothes. When the students tied their cans on to their backs with string so the jerry can became like a backpack, I said to Sister Almaz, 'I'll do it that way too,' and held up my empty fifteen-litre jerry can.

'*Anchi*! You! You won't be able to carry that! You are *ferenji*. Your muscles are soft. You carry the baby size.' She passed me a two-litre jerry can and I felt a little indignant, but a tiny bit relieved.

Returning from the river in single file, with Sister Almaz behind me and a two-litre jerry can of river water under my arm, I felt utterly content, although aware how much more so than if I had been carrying a fifteen-litre jerry can with string cutting into my armpits. While I had loved visiting the clinics here and helping people who would otherwise have no access to physio, I felt excited about joining the physiotherapy department in Gondar. I wondered what the university hospital might look like. I had forgotten to ask on the phone how many beds it was. I imagined it might look like the multistorey Yekatit 12 hospital I had seen from the minibus in Addis Ababa, and felt excited about how many patients we could help, all at the same time. Sister Almaz told me that graduates of health programs were usually assigned around the country and I imagined how great it would be when my future students graduated and a local physio was available for the clinics in this region. Tomorrow, I was off to Gondar to contribute to the wider scheme of things. Finally I was going to make a difference. The sun was just starting to dip behind the trees and oxen's hooves kicked dust into the orange light. I stopped at the top of the hill to take in the view one last time and Sister Almaz almost walked into my back.

'*Ferenji*! Hurry up!' she said, and slung an arm around my shoulder.

I departed on the long journey to Addis Ababa during a colourless pre-dawn. In the bus depot, diesel smoke from revving engines hurt my eyes and formed clouds in the headlight beams. It was hard to hear Sister Almaz over the touts hollering each bus's destination, but she beckoned and I followed her as she heaved my backpack through the crowd to the right bus. She bought a ticket for me and then pushed against the mass again to alight and find me a seat. We hugged and said our goodbyes over the people inside the bus shouting to the people outside the bus. When she was outside, I wiped a clear patch in the dust from my window to wave again and mouth 'Bye!'.

As the bus pulled out, she blew theatrical kisses, oblivious to the crowd, and I wondered if they expected more sedate behaviour from a lady in a habit. I waved as long as I could, twisting in my seat to wave through the back window until the bus turned a corner and I couldn't see her anymore.

Chapter 8

Doesn't work: አይሰራም /*ayserum*/

I touched down in Gondar on a warm April morning in 2005. I was now 658 kilometres and two hours by plane from Addis Ababa, and four days by bus from Sister Almaz.

The airport in Gondar was nestled amongst the green and amber foothills of the Simien mountain range. A driver who had held up a handwritten sign with my name on it loaded my luggage into the back of a four-wheel drive and we drove in silence until he pulled up at an entranceway with a sign reading *University of Gondar Hospital.* Two guards with Kalashnikovs over their shoulders checked our IDs before dropping the chain to let us in. After leaving my backpack and purple suitcase in the hospital's guesthouse just inside the gates, I walked alone, following wooden signs to the physiotherapy office. I counted five tin-roofed buildings marked with signs for various wards. Physiotherapy was in a freestanding timber office about the size of a single car garage, painted a chalky green, adjacent to a large brick building whose sign said *X-ray.* Ten patients sat in the long grass between the buildings, two leant on a rusted car engine, and an elderly woman slumped against an old man's back. They all looked pale, emaciated and unwell and I hoped they were here for X-ray, not physio.

Marieke, the Dutch physio who had organised my contract, was much taller than me, with shoulder-length ginger hair and freckles. Marieke introduced me to my new colleagues – a

Japanese physio, two Canadian physios, two Indian occupational therapists and two Ethiopian physio assistants. She explained each of the *ferenji* physiotherapists was assigned inpatient ward duties and classes to teach. I would be assigned to the paediatric ward and my classes to teach would be determined later. First we needed to get my employee ID card.

The vice-dean's office was a five-minute walk up one hill and down another, past some more offices, until we reached a cluster of buildings. Outside, a throng of youths leaned over the geraniums and daisies in the garden bed, peering at a glass-covered noticeboard.

Marieke followed my eyes and said, 'Exam results,' and it reminded me of my own university days. I remembered scanning similar lists. It didn't seem so long ago, yet here I was, about to be a university teacher myself.

We stopped at a small blue weatherboard building where Marieke said to the secretary, 'We need a staff ID card.'

The secretary continued to click her mouse while she eyed us with disinterest and said, 'Go to dean of students.'

So we went out the building, down the path to an identical building. The secretary there also clicked her mouse and when we asked her for an ID card, didn't look up from her computer screen but said, 'You go next door,' and motioned her head towards a door with a sign reading *Dean of Students*.

Marieke stopped to answer a student's query, and she told me to go ahead.

I hoped my knock sounded respectful as I pushed the door open to see a man signing papers behind a desk plaque that said *Dean of Students*. He wore a brown suit jacket and his hair was dotted with grey.

'Umm, excuse me; I'm here for an ID card?' I said.

The man lifted the corner of a page and signed underneath. He glanced up at me and said, 'You need dean of students,' before returning to his signatures.

I looked from the sign on the door saying *Dean of Students*, to the plaque on the desk saying the same thing, to the man one might be forgiven for assuming was the dean of students. 'Where is the dean?'

'Not here.' The man exhaled and dragged another pile of papers across. He recommenced signing, lifting a corner, signing, letting it drop, lifting the next corner, signing, letting it drop. After a few more signatures, I realised I'd get no further clarity so retreated to the foyer, where Marieke was still chatting with the student.

'No luck?' she said.

'He was not the dean.'

'When will the dean return?' Marieke asked a secretary in a corner that I hadn't seen.

'You wait there,' the secretary said and indicated with her head towards a row of chairs against the wall. A ceiling fan whirred above us but did nothing against the midmorning heat while Marieke and I waited for half an hour until the dean arrived.

For the second time that day I sat at his vast desk. I handed him my confirmation of employment letter from the president of the university, and I requested an ID card.

'*Ayserum*! This won't work!' He looked surprised as he skimmed the letter. 'Where is your memo requesting an ID card? And you don't have two signatures on your ID application form.'

'Where do we get that?' Marieke asked.

'Go to the vice-dean's office.' He pointed to the first building we had come from, more than an hour earlier. I was hot and grumpy, but Marieke remained unfazed.

'Welcome to University of Gondar Hospital,' she said.

I was walking down the hill towards the guesthouse to retrieve paperwork from my luggage when the afternoon intake of patients began. I knew it was afternoon intake, as I had experienced intakes at Sister Almaz's clinics in the countryside of the old Welega province. Patients came in either the morning or afternoon for triage and referral to outpatients or admissions as needed.

When the guards dropped the chain across the entrance to the hospital grounds, the crowd surged. People ran, pushing and shoving up the hill towards the admissions area, an outside area with two booths. Mums carrying babies, old men piggybacking elderly women, young men carrying elderly relatives on bamboo stretchers, senior men in shorts and jelly sandals with white *gabi* cloths and walking sticks across their shoulders, young men in shorts and jelly sandals with their heads wrapped in beehive turbans – all started to run towards where I was walking. I darted to the side of the road as the crowd surged past. The lucky ones made it to the window of the registrar first, while the rest milled around outside, waiting for their turn. This was not like the clinics I had seen with Sister Almaz, and it was confronting to see so many people so frantic for medical care.

I was still shaken when I returned to the office and Marieke said it was time to see my first patients. She walked with me to the door of the adult ward, a detached building fronted by geranium bushes and bordered on all sides by bitumen paths.

Marieke motioned towards a lanky student heading towards us. 'I can't join you but Elias can help you while I'm in a meeting. He's in his second year. He's been on placement for a few weeks, so he knows where everything is.'

Elias had a broad face with big teeth. His skin was soft and fresh, and I guessed him to be twenty years old. He might have been in the group of students I'd seen peering at their exam results: he had an air of enthusiasm about him. He handed me a white lab coat, telling me it was 'to protect the clothes', and with a reassuring smile slipped his own coat over his camel slacks and red t-shirt.

The ward held twenty beds separated by shoulder-high partitions, with a mat on the floor between beds for extra patients. I did a quick calculation – if each of the five wards had twenty beds and twenty foam mats, that made forty patients per ward and therefore two hundred beds in total. But the number of beds was clearly inadequate, judging from the afternoon intake I'd just seen.

The smell in the ward was overpowering: a mix of vomit, the mustiness of unwashed clothes and dirty feet, the pungency of stale *injera*, and of *kibbeh*, the curdled butter that countryside women moisturised their hair with. Just inside the door a man was retching into a bowl.

Bile rose, and I scratched my upper lip to breathe through my fingers to block the smell.

'Righto,' I mumbled to Elias. 'Who do we have on our patient list?'

'Many burns today. One family, all is burned.'

'Okay, where is the nurses station? We should find their medical file.'

Elias motioned to a small office partitioned in the centre of the ward.

'*Yikerta*, excuse me.' I stepped over a woman on a foam mat blocking the way. She moaned without looking at me, but the child next to her, holding aloft a drip bag connected to the IV line in the woman's wrist, shuffled out of the way.

Elias found the file on a wooden table scattered with yellow patient files. Passing it to me he said, 'This patient is first, four children, all in house fire.'

'God, that is terrible. What about their parents?'

Elias clicked his tongue. 'We have seen this family for two weeks now. The mother stayed at home for one week. But now she has dead. Father is burnt, but not admitted. He is here.'

I had not treated a burns patient since I'd been a university student on clinical rotation at Royal Perth Hospital, where there had been an extreme hygiene protocol in the burns unit.

Our first patient was a sixteen-year-old boy lying prone on a foam mattress. Second-degree burns had bubbled the skin along the full length of his spine and arms. His wounds were smeared with white cream but had no dressing. The mattress was split with ragged foam edges and the paint was flaking off the cast-iron bedhead. I knew this didn't look hygienic enough for uncovered burns, and the wounds looked so severe they made me feel nauseous. Well out of my depth, I reverted to physiotherapy supervisor mode and asked stiffly, 'What treatment have you done with him? Can you explain your clinical rationale?'

Elias took a notebook from his lab coat pocket and stumbled on his own handwriting as he read, 'Patient have extensive second-degree burns. With Marieke we did assessment last week. We have assisted the patient to walk, to prevent chest infection, and moving the joints to prevent stiffness from scarring.'

'Okay, great. He should have his pain meds at least twenty minutes before treatment. Can you please tell me what pain medication he is on?' Elias flicked to the medication chart stapled to the inside of the folder. He scanned the page. 'Silver sulfadiazine, topical.'

'Could you look again please? That sounds like cream for wound healing.' I pointed out the white cream on the patient's burns, although I'd never heard of it before. 'Look for some analgesia?'

'No any other medication.' Elias shook his head.

'There must be some mistake. They mustn't have realised we were coming for physio. We can't move him with these wounds without pain relief. I'll write the doctor a note.'

I ripped a page from my notebook and wrote: *Dear Doctor, could you please prescribe some pain cover for this patient for use prior to physiotherapy? Sincerely, Physiotherapy Team.*

I clipped the note under the bulldog clip on the front of the medical file.

'Will it be expensive?' Elias asked, clearing his throat.

'Shouldn't be, why?'

'Because it is must for patient to buy own medicines. And

mother is dead and whole family is also *beshetegna*, patient. There is his brother.' He pointed over the ward to where a boy lay in bed and a man shooed flies from his back with a swatch of a eucalyptus branch.

At the new patient's bedside, the man and Elias nodded acknowledgements to each other. This boy lay on his stomach too. He wore only jocks, and I could see where the flames had lashed him, leaving stripes of seared flesh alternating with unburnt skin. Yellow plasma oozed over fresh scar tissue, pink at the edges where the capillaries had started to regenerate. Burns covered his entire back, right arm and leg and neck. Like his brother, he had no dressing over his wounds, just white cream that had almost dissolved. Two flies landed on the open wound and the father swished them away with the gum leaves.

'Does this brother have any pain cover?' I asked Elias and he flicked through the medical chart.

'Yes, he had paracetamol, two tablet. Thirty minute ago.'

I wondered if it worked. I usually bypassed paracetamol for something stronger just to shift a hangover. This boy needed industrial-strength painkillers. But it did put into perspective why his brother, with far lesser wounds, wasn't prescribed any pain cover, if they only gave paracetamol for such severe burns. There were no stronger pain medication options so we decided to start the physio session.

'What are your assessment findings for this patient?'

Elias read from his notebook again. 'Decreased movement in spine, shoulder, wrist due to burns and scarring. Decreased mobility.'

'Okay, right. And what is your treatment plan?'

He read out, 'One, assisted movement from bed to decrease chance of chest infection. Two, range-of-movement exercises for back, neck, shoulder, elbow, wrist.'

'Good work. Let's get started?'

I tried hard to feign confidence but I had no idea how to

assist someone with such extensive burns. The fire had spared the boy's palms, so he pushed himself upright and we cautiously manoeuvred him to sit over the edge of the bed. He kept silent, just winced with the pain. Elias helped the boy, who told us his name was Berhane, to turn his head left, then right, up, then down. The purple, damaged skin on his neck was already starting to scar and blanched as he stretched for each of the movements.

Elias slid his arm under Berhane's but the scar had already tightened the shoulder so much he could only lift it a few centimetres off the bed. Next Elias asked him to bend his wrist forwards then backwards, but the stretch popped a wide blister on the back of Berhane's wrist. Plasma oozed down the back of his hand and plopped onto the floor, beside a hole through which I could see the ground. Still the boy didn't make any sound, just grimaced.

'Let's get him standing,' I said. I stood on Berhane's left side to offer my upturned left palm. Elias mirrored me and the boy put his hands into ours and slowly pushed himself into standing, his face contorted with pain but only whimpering. Beads of sweat broke out across his brow.

We let him stand for a minute in the new position. I checked his sheet, a square of cotton that was smaller than the vinyl-covered foam mat resting atop his mattress. It was stained with sweat and plasma and crusted with dried *injera* scraps and shards of blackened skin.

Holding the patient's hand, I used my other hand to gather the sheet, pulling the corners together as if it might have been a tablecloth.

'What are you doing?' Elias's brow furrowed.

'I'm going to clean this.'

'Why? What's wrong with it?' He looked puzzled, and I was taken aback. It hadn't occurred to me that the students might have different standards of hygiene.

We reseated Berhane at the edge of the bed, and I went outside to shake the cotton square into the garden bed. The only spot of bare earth I could find was beneath a row of geranium bushes spread with bedsheets drying in the sun. It seemed unhygienic to throw burnt skin flakes there, but there was nowhere else to dispose of them and I reasoned it was better there than contacting the wound.

Back inside, I respread the cotton square over the foam mat and we helped Berhane back onto his stomach. Three flies landed on the wounds immediately and his father recommenced swishing the eucalyptus leaves. I noticed he flinched when he leaned forwards and, on looking closer, his shirt was patched with oozing plasma.

'Is the father burnt also?' I asked Elias in surprise, forgetting he had already told me.

'Yes, father also burnt.'

'But not severely?'

'Oh yes, severely burnt.'

'So he is admitted too?' I was confused.

'No, not admitted.' Elias was equally confused as to my continued questioning.

Even as we spoke, the circular patch of plasma on the man's shirt widened. 'Elias, can you ask him to show us his burns? Maybe we can give him some exercises too?'

Elias spoke to the father, who unbuttoned his shirt and turned his back to us. The skin over the top third of his back was red-raw and covered with yellow bubbled blisters.

'This wound looks quite serious,' I said to Elias, trying to keep my voice level and quell my rising nausea. I wanted to shout, *Why the hell hasn't he been admitted?* But then I looked at the next bed, where an elderly man moaned, mouth agape and eyes rolling back. I looked down the central corridor of the ward where more people moaned and contorted in pain on foam mats, and seeing this man was mobile, and functional, instead I said, 'Let's make an assessment and treatment plan.'

The university administration had advised me I could stay in the hospital's guesthouse until I coordinated a place of my own. The guesthouse was built in the style of the Italian occupation from the 1940s, with two storeys, a curved staircase with a smooth wooden bannister and a paved terrace. I had met the caretaker on my arrival and when I asked her if it was safe, as I was the only guest and my door didn't properly lock, she reassured me that she was here, 'All of the time. Never I am go.' She had clutched my forearm warmly and I felt reassured until she let go to collect her handbag and went outside to catch a minibus into town. She had not returned, and the house was unlit when I returned from the grocer's that first night.

My footsteps echoed on the staircase and down the long corridor to my room. The bulb was so dim, shadows remained on the periphery of the corridor and I jumped at every noise.

The light from the corridor didn't reach the kitchen and only the streetlights through the window kept me from knocking into big obstacles while I searched for the light switch. I ran my hand around the doorframe, across the back wall, the side wall, until I tried reaching my arm as far as I could behind the fridge and finally found the switch.

When I tipped some pasta into a saucepan I realised with dismay I'd forgotten to buy bottled water. There was only half a litre left in my drinking bottle, and Marieke had told me the tap water was not safe for consumption. Feeling bleak, I poured the tiniest amount of water into my pasta and set the saucepan to boil on a standalone electric hotplate while I decided on the least dirty plate in the cupboard to use. In the fridge I counted twenty cockroaches, sedated by the cold, immobile except for waving antennae. More cockroaches scuttled over the cutlery when I opened the drawer. I wondered which would be worse: not washing the utensils or washing under unsafe tap water; drying on the filthy tea towel by the sink or sacrificing my drinking water.

I stared at the knife and fork in my hand for a while, then

spat on them and wiped them on the inside of my t-shirt. I ate a sandwich of tomato and corned beef from a tin and it was only when my water bottle was nearly empty that I remembered how salty corned beef was.

It seemed as if the smells of the ward lingered on me. I knew it was probably psychological but I couldn't get rid of the smell of burnt flesh. Even though we'd worn lab coats over our clothes I wondered if I'd contacted any communicable disease germs from the medical wards today. It took the last of my remaining energy to gather my towel and toiletries, but the bathroom posed a dilemma. Despite a paucity of windows elsewhere in the house, the bathroom's window of unfrosted glass extended the full length of the room and the toilet was right in front of it. A curtain covered only half of the window, which might have been fine had the bathroom not faced a seven-storey boys dormitory, and overlooked the hospital's main bus stop. It was hard to picture a configuration giving more strangers the opportunity to watch me ablute.

Earlier, when I'd tried to buy toothpaste, three men had followed, gawking as I read the labels and made my selection. Pretty much everywhere I went, men loitered, observing, not with menace, just interest, watching the *ferenji* go about her business. The inadequate drapery added a new dimension to the phrase.

I tried turning off the bathroom light, but the switch was in the hallway and, returning in the dark, I stubbed my toe on the bath's claw foot and couldn't see the taps.

With the lights back on, I slid the curtain one way to toilet in privacy, then back the other to shower. The boiler on the wall showed a red light and I was reassured by its bubbling. Surely, after a hot shower and a sleep everything would be fine. The hot-water tap clattered into the bath at first turn, but once I'd re-seated it, the water flowed.

After five minutes, when cold water still ran, I tried the other tap, which also fell off. I fumed as I splashed myself with freezing water. Each individual part of the day could be tolerable, but the combined effect was too much. Couldn't *some* things work? Why couldn't someone make a curtain of the right size, or when extending the effort to install a boiler, check it attached to a tap? The squalor I'd seen today made me want to vomit and cry. If billions of dollars of aid money hadn't made a difference by now, what was I going to achieve? I couldn't even take a shower. It was all too hard, and I was just so thirsty.

I remembered my first day in Ethiopia when Sister Starling showed me around the convent and I'd been disappointed they had hot water. I had wanted to be a hardcore adventurer. Well, here was my chance, but the cold water almost made me shriek. Now I realised I didn't have the strength of character to deal with the squalor on the wards, the lack of hot water, the unsanitary guesthouse kitchen, and the rest of these unnecessary discomforts. I would quit, I decided. I would just go home. Even though it would be embarrassing, I would tell Marieke tomorrow.

I screwed my face up and plunged it under the icy shower. The water was tempting, I was so thirsty. If I took a mouthful of tap water, perhaps I could get typhoid and be airlifted home. People would bring me gerbera arrangements and helium balloons with get-well cards. No-one would ask, 'Did you pike on day one?'

It turns out the will to not get typhoid is stronger than the will for a medevac, so I kept my mouth shut and went to bed thirsty.

Chapter 9

To have discomfort: አይመቸም /*ayimechem*/

On my second day in Gondar, I lay in bed, willing myself to get up and make it through one more day. As much as I wanted to, I couldn't quit, I decided. I had waited my whole life for a job like this.

It was so noisy outside my room. A nearby church had been broadcasting Orthodox scriptures since 4 a.m. The prayers through the loudspeaker were continuous and fast, so it sounded like a race being called where the horses went around and around and around.

From the road below I could make out heavy trucks dropping gears to get up the hill and minibus taxis with conductors yelling, '*Piazza*, *Piazza*, *Piazza*!' The minibus stereos all blasted the same song: 'Ethiooooppppiiiiiaaaa, Abyssinnnniiiiiaaaaa'.

I heard it over and over as the minibuses pulled in and departed, always played so loud the sound was distorted, like music from a transistor radio through a megaphone. The synthesised tune faded off as one minibus pulled out and reappeared as another minibus pulled in, repeating the same line, 'Ethiooooppppiiiiiaaaa, Abyssinnnniiiiiaaaaa'.

Wrapping the pillow over my ears, I tried to look on the bright side. I had a job paying just over one hundred dollars a month, and the guesthouse toilet seat was actually attached to the toilet. Now that was something to be pleased about. The toilet seats in the convents in Addis Ababa and Welega only gave the illusion of connection. I'd had to match velocity and angle in sitting down in order to maintain contiguity between seat and bowl. A hasty sitter could find seat and self skidding off the rim, taking the sitter's unclothed butt to the concrete floor. The group home I visited regularly in Addis had a seat that was wholly detached from the toilet and remained propped against the bathroom wall. It offered the user a reminder of comforts that might have been while the cold corners of the naked rim bit into the under thigh.

Outside my room, a door opened, and I heard the bathroom door open and the tap run. I wondered when another guest had checked into the guesthouse. In the bathroom, the guest gargled, snorted and spat while the tap ran and I heard a man's voice sing loud and out of tune, 'Ethioooopppppiiiiiaaaa, Abyssinnnniiiiiaaaaa'. I lay in bed listening to him gargle, snort and spit a few more times and decided it was time to get up.

Water flowed reassuringly into the kitchen sink when I turned the tap, and the travel-size kettle's light shone red when I flicked the switch. I had the two essentials for a bath, and my morning was working out well. A mere forty minutes later the kettle boiled, and I emptied it into a blue plastic jug, where the gradations inside indicated I had precisely three cups of hot water. In the bathroom, I set the jug down beside the bath, pulled the half curtain to the shower side and realised I'd left my soap in my bedroom. I stepped back out of my bedroom in time to see the other guest, wearing only a short pink towel, stroll back into the bathroom and shut the door. Inside, he recommenced singing 'Ethyioooopppppiiiiiaaaa, Abysinnnniiiiiaaaaa'.

I listened to him hoick, spit, gargle, and sing under a presumably cold shower, while my hard-won hot water cooled. I returned to the kitchen to re-boil the kettle, but the electricity had gone off. The electricity came back on by the time the bathroom was free but there wasn't time to boil the kettle again, only time enough to wash my face and the tears welling in my eyes. I tried to remain positive: at least the toilet seat worked. Then I misjudged velocity and entry angle. The seat snapped from its fixture, sending me skidding sideways and the lid thudding onto my back.

The one consolation was that today, I would be going to the paediatrics ward. Back home in Perth I had accompanied many clients to Princess Margaret Hospital for Children, when I worked as a paediatric physiotherapist. That hospital had colourful corridors and murals of animals and fruit next to the elevators. Although Gondar's paediatric ward wouldn't have an elevator, I imagined the walls might be painted in glossy colours, perhaps with murals of Ethiopian animals. The adult wards were confronting, but I imagined they'd set things up differently for the kids.

The air was thicker in the paediatric ward than in the adult ward. In addition to the smells of unwashed bodies, of *kibbeh*, hair-butter, and fermented *injera*, the ward smelt thickly of curdled milk. Paint came off the wall in chunks and, just as in the adult ward, the floor was pocked with holes that showed the ground beneath.

The ward was an open room with fifteen beds along each side. Foam mats lay on the floor for additional patients between each bed. On my way to the nurses station, I stepped over a father sitting on a mat next to a sleeping girl with a drip in her wrist. He held a bag of saline solution high above the child for gravity to drain the fluid into her veins; I assumed that meant the ward had run out of drip stands.

I was relieved to see the student Elias ready for me in the nurses station.

'Miss Julie, this is our first patient.' He stopped at a bed. 'She is seven years old. And other sister, four years old. Sisters of the brothers we were seeing yesterday. I checked both of charts already. Not have any pain cover prescribed, so can do physiotherapy immediately.'

Like her brothers, the oldest girl was covered in crusting

burns and white cream. Her burns extended from her buttocks to her neck. Her scalp was seared in rows where her braids had burnt away. She lay on her stomach, with nothing on, uncovered by even a sheet. A large fly had settled on her back. Nervous of touching the patient's painful burn, I edged at the fly with the patient file. I felt dismayed, wondering how on earth a child could survive this degree of burn with only silver sulfadiazine cream to prevent infection.

'*Mitu*, little one.' Elias addressed her using an affectionate term. He crouched at her bedside so he was level with her face. '*Semesh man new*? What's your name?'

'Rahel,' she whispered, her eyes widening with fear.

I asked Elias to explain we would do exercises to help her move. Elias's voice was soft, but she still stared at him and when we sat her up she remained silent.

'*Wede ezzi, wede ezziya*? This way, and that way?' I demonstrated turning my head side to side. She copied me, turning her neck so the charred skin stretched and became taut, but she didn't whimper or cry. She didn't even have tears in her eyes. I thought of how easily this big *ferenji* girl got tears and how stoic this little girl was.

'For how long has she been in bed?' I asked Elias.

'For two week.'

'We need to get her to walk, otherwise there is risk of chest infection and loss of mobility.' I squatted in front of her. '*Mitu, lebs yet allesh*? Little one, where are your clothes?'

'*Yellem*. Don't have any,' she whispered back.

'Why doesn't she have any clothes?' I asked Elias.

'Her clothes got burned in the fire. She has no attendant; her village is two days walk from here. Maybe there is no-one to bring her clothes.'

We wrapped her floral bedsheet around her like a cylinder, and when she clutched the ends, it split her wounds a little so they oozed. She padded barefoot over the tiles to look out the door of the ward, at the children playing in the garden. Three toddlers squatted, poking sticks into the dirt. She watched them in silence for a few moments and looked up first at Elias, then at me.

She whispered, '*Dekmognal.* I'm tired.'

We helped her to lie on her tummy, and again she didn't make a sound as she turned in the bed, only bit her lip.

Her sister in the adjacent bed had a round, cherubic face. She was also without clothes, lying on her stomach, but her burns were limited to the back of her neck and the front of her forearms. The unburned skin on her back looked so vital and sweet compared to her sister's wounds. She said nothing when Elias squatted by her bed, just stared at him as wide-eyed as her sister had done.

'*Semesh man new*? What's your name?' Elias asked, but the girl remained silent.

'Mintewab,' her big sister whispered for her.

'Minte!' Elias said. When he asked in Amharic, 'Let's sit up, okay?' the little girl nodded. We assisted her to sit, and we had just finished assessing the stiffness in her neck and wrists when a doctor approached.

'Excuse me, who is the physiotherapist? We have one new patient for you.' The doctor looked about the same age as me. A stethoscope hung around his neck, over a shirt that looked expensive and uncreased. When he reached out to hand me a patient's file, I got a waft of his expensive cologne. His panache seemed incongruous for the ward.

'I am Doctor Tesfaye. Your new patient is here. Partial paraplegia resulting from TB of the spine. Just arrived to the ward now.' He indicated to the empty bed in the back corner where a slight teenage girl piggybacked a younger girl clutching two shopping bags. Clothes spilled out the top of the bags when the teenage girl gently lowered her passenger onto the bed. The older girl refilled the bags, then pulled the blankets back and straightened them over the patient's legs. She stashed the plastic bags beneath the bed and slid X-rays under the pillow.

'Her name is Habtam. You could provide her with physiotherapy please?' The doctor was abrupt, but not unkind.

My head swam. I had never treated a patient with TB before. It was rare to see a patient with TB in Australia; only specialist units would treat these patients from remote Aboriginal populations or overseas, and only for lung issues. I didn't even know it was possible to *get* TB in the spine. I recalled a lecture about TB in Cardiopulmonary Physiotherapy 205, back at Curtin Uni in 1995, but I hadn't taken much in as I'd only slept two hours the night before, having waited until the due date to complete an essay. If only I hadn't been sleep-deprived back then, I might have remembered something useful for now.

Habtam's file said she was ten years old. She lay on her side in her bed, looking morose. Big curls sitting close to her scalp framed her face.

'Can you please ask her where her mother or father is?'

Habtam held her chin to her chest when Elias spoke to her.

'Not here,' Elias translated. 'But she have her sister.'

Both girls looked nervous when Elias spoke to me in English.

'How old is her sister?' I asked.

'Fifteen years old.'

'When are her mother and father coming?'

Elias looked puzzled and said, 'Not coming. Their village is two days walk from here. Simply her sister is her attendant.'

Habtam's face still held the roundness and freshness of childhood, while her sister, sitting on the stool beside the bed, had the leaner face of an adult.

'Can we see her X-rays?' Elias asked the sister, who bent Habtam forwards to fish under her pillow for the scans. The X-rays showed the mid part of her spine had collapsed in on itself so her backbone formed a round curve coming to a point. A large mass was visible in the spine, clearly blocking the spinal cord below.

When we examined Habtam's back, she was so thin her backbone was entirely visible. A sharp hunchback protruded at the point where her spine had collapsed in.

We pulled back the covers to examine her lower limbs. Her thighs and calves had withered, leaving just slight muscle covering the visible bones.

'Can you bend your knees?' Elias asked, but she couldn't. Her legs appeared to be completely paralysed.

'*Kuch bey*, *mimi*? Can you sit up, little one?' I asked.

'*Ayichallem*! She can't!' The sister looked panicked and spoke frantically to Elias.

'Her sister says she can only lying down. She falls over if sitting up.'

'*Amemegn*. I have pain,' Habtam whispered into her chest. She looked so unwell, so miserable. I wanted to comfort her, but it would have been inappropriate. I thought if I just tuned in to my work, to being the best physiotherapist possible, I might be able to help her.

'*Kuch bey*, *mimi*? Sitting up, little one?' I asked again. She nodded but said nothing as Elias and I assisted her to sit over the edge of the bed. Her sister darted behind to gather the edges of the hospital gown that had fallen open around the point in Habtam's spine and naked back.

I demonstrated to Elias how to test her balance. '*Wede ken*, towards the right.' I held my hand to the side, seeing how far Habtam could reach before losing her balance. '*Ahun wede gra*, now towards the left.'

Habtam reached out and screwed up her face with concentration, giving all her effort, but she still couldn't quite reach my hand.

'*Gobez*, *eshi*. You are clever, okay,' I said.

'*Gobez*, *eshi*.' A chorus of little voices behind copied me, only with giggles. I turned around to see five children. Two kids had their chins in their hands, resting their elbows on the bed while another boy leaned against the bedpost. A taller boy, who looked about ten years old, stood with one leg bent up and one arm hanging limp. When he beamed at me I saw that half his face was paralysed. Although I was surprised to see I had a little audience, I hammed it up, pantomiming surprise and saying, '*Tadiyas*! Hi!'

The kids giggled more.

'*Dehna nachihu lejoch*? How are you kids?' I asked.

The kids stopped giggling and sank their heads shyly to their chests, except for the tall boy, who looked around at all the children before replying, '*Dehna*! Fine!' and it seemed he was replying on their behalf.

'*Ante semesh man new*? What's your name?' I asked.

There was fresh giggling from the kids on the bed.

'Gebremeskal,' the boy replied.

'*Tena yistilign*? How do you do?' I extended my hand to him with exaggerated formality and he shook it proudly.

I turned back to Habtam and asked her, '*Dehna nesh*? How are you?' which sent the kids into gales of laughter.

'*Menden new*? What is it?' I asked them.

All five of the kids kept their heads down but I could still hear tittering. A little girl picked at some loose threads on the bedspread.

'*Yene Amaregna*? My Amharic?'

The kids giggled into their palms and finally Gebremeskal said, '*Anchi terunesh*. You are good.'

I knew he meant my Amharic was good, but my flailing self-esteem needed a boost. I didn't feel good. I was completely out of my depth, trying to assess and come up with a treatment plan for a condition I didn't know existed until one hour ago.

After morning tea, I went with two of the *ferenji* physios and two physiotherapy assistants to an orphanage and hospice on the outskirts of town run by an order of sisters.

The sister on the children's wing was a grandmotherly nun, with a downy face and grey hair under her veil. She shook my hand warmly and introduced herself as Sister Deepti from Delhi.

'So many children with the disabilities we are having. Come this way, dear.'

Sister Deepti took me through to the activity room of the kids ward. Although it was spartan, with cement floor, brick walls and tin roof, sunlight streamed in from open windows and my stomach rumbled with the smell of lentil stew cooking somewhere outside.

'Here are the children for physiotherapy.' Sister Deepti indicated six small children sitting on a colourful woven mat on the painted cement floor.

When we joined them on the mat to start the therapy session, a toddler in a striped jumpsuit ran and bellyflopped onto the mat beside me with arms outstretched. An older girl beside him picked him and sat him on her lap.

Our first patient had a round face and soft brown eyes, and when he smiled his tongue poked through the gap where his front teeth should have been.

When I asked, '*Edmeh sint new*? How old are you?', the boy furrowed his brow and turned to Sister Deepti. She cuddled him against her ample bosom and said, 'We don't know his age, but probably he is six, if he is losing his teeth.'

When we did the initial assessment, we found out the boy had some voluntary movement. He could sit alone, and balanced in kneeling on his legs.

'Can he show us how he can move?' I asked the physio assistant to translate and the boy showed us, demonstrating how he could pull himself along on the ground, using his hands to bottom shuffle. Three other children scampered beside him, calling encouragement, while one of the other children ran to the other side of the communal space to cheer him on.

The next patient was a small child with a mild development delay. I had a temporary reprieve from the feelings from yesterday and, this morning, I didn't feel out of my comfort zone.

I had treated children with cerebral palsy and developmental delay back in Perth and in London. I knew how to conduct an assessment and devise a treatment plan. It was so cute to be surrounded by children and it felt similar to being in the group home in Addis Ababa. By the time the minibus taxi dropped us back at the hospital I thought, maybe I could stay. If I can feel like this at the orphanage, once a week, then maybe I would start to feel confident on the ward too.

While the others were at lunch, I scanned the indexes of the fifteen textbooks in the physio office. If I was going to stay, I needed to learn about spinal TB. I could only find one entry about spinal TB amongst the textbooks and I jotted notes in my notebook: *TB spreads from lungs into blood stream. From blood stream enters spine. Forms abscess or cyst that puts pressure on the spinal cord, causing paralysis of the nerves below.*

I looked up when the door opened and a guy about my age walked in. He had broad shoulders, thick curly hair, and a five-o'clock shadow.

He looked surprised. 'You are new?'

'Hi! I'm Julie. I just started yesterday!' I extended my hand and we shook hello.

'Aha. I was sick yesterday, I didn't meet you. I am Tadesse. I am the physio assistant for paediatrics ward. You are a student?' He pointed at my notes and the open textbook on the desk. He smiled a little so I knew it was an amiable dig, but I felt vulnerable. I had offered to work in this place but I had no idea what I was doing.

I tried to act dismissive. 'TB of the spine. We don't have it in Australia, it's new for me. Actually I'm a teacher.' I closed the book and flipped my notebook. 'I just saw a girl, paralysed with TB. Is there anywhere to get wheelchairs?'

Tadesse shook his head. 'No any place for buying wheelchairs in Gondar. Oh! Is this your first time to Gondar? How do you see Gondar?'

I thought of the mountains I'd observed on the way from the

airport and the photos of the castle in the guidebook.

'*Konjo new*! It's beautiful!' I said.

'*Ara! Amaregna techeyallesh*? Hey! Can you speak Amharic?' He pulled up a chair.

'*Tennish tennish echelalehu*, I can, a little bit,' I said.

He spoke in fluent Amharic and although I didn't catch it all, I understood him ask how it was possible I spoke Amharic if I arrived yesterday.

So I told him in English peppered with Amharic that I'd just come from working out near the border with Sudan, in the old province of Welega. And before that, I'd worked in a busy clinic in Addis Ababa. I hoped the more I talked about my experience, he wouldn't guess how far out of my depth I was here.

'When I worked in Addis Ababa I saw wheelchairs when I visited the prosthetic orthotic clinic. We could buy a wheelchair in Addis and can get it sent here for the girl with TB in her spine?' I said.

'But who can pay? These are countryside people. A wheelchair is expensive even for someone with a job.'

I felt silly, of course I should have known that. 'We could get donations? There must be some charity that can help? Or what about the government?'

Tadesse looked shocked. 'Government? No. Not paying for wheelchairs. Not paying for so many things. Where the patients live is all ... the countryside. The ground is full of sand and rocks. There is no *menged*, no pathway, for using wheelchair.'

'So what can we do for the girl?'

Tadesse said, 'Simply physiotherapy, until discharged.'

What use was physiotherapy for Habtam except to keep her joints moving until she went home? I pictured her, legs paralysed, only able to lie on her side because of the sharp point in the middle of her back, not being able to leave her house except by piggyback. It was so overwhelming I wasn't sure of the point in starting.

Marieke lugged a box of books into the physio office and,

seeing us together, said, 'Oh hi! You've met Tadesse. How is day two? How is the guesthouse?'

I thought of spinal TB, cockroaches in the fridge and my dalliance with typhoid. I tried to look peppy. 'Fine! Yep, going great!'

'At least you get a hot shower there, huh?' Marieke pulled a chair up to join us at the desk.

I told them about my evening, the state of the kitchen and the other guest's skimpy towel.

'No trousers?' Tadesse was incredulous and when he laughed a dimple appeared under his stubble.

'No trousers! Cockroaches in the fridge! Ewww!' Marieke said.

'*Yimechal*?' Tadesse asked, and when I looked blank he translated: 'Is it comfort for you?'

I felt the weight of understatement when I admitted, 'It is not comfortable for me.'

'*Ayimechem*! Not comfortable!' Marieke said. 'We've got to get you out of there. Hey, I'm moving into a new place. I'm meeting the housing administrator tomorrow. Do you want to move in with me?'

The next day, I still had not quit, and now it seemed I wasn't going to as Marieke and I sat waiting outside the housing administrator's office. Marieke explained that accommodation was included as part of our contract, in addition to our one hundred dollars a month pay. But the university had expanded so rapidly the staff housing was full and they needed to look for off-campus accommodation for new staff. It seemed like a lifetime ago that I had looked for rental properties in Perth, circling ads in the Saturday paper, filling out application forms and organising bonds. Then I'd been concerned about kitchen bench space and off-street parking. Now, I just wanted hot water and a proper curtain in the bathroom.

'They find it for us? They do it all? What a great service!' I said.

Marieke looked puzzled, narrowing her eyes and tilting her head a little. 'Ye-e-e-s.'

'Enter please,' the housing administrator called us in.

The housing administrator was a small man with grey hair, grey-rimmed spectacles and a grey suit coat.

'Is there any progress on the house you were going to inspect last week?' Marieke asked.

'Aha. The house, the house, yes, you know that house, you know how it is. It's the way it is here, and that house ... the thing is ...'

He continued like this until Marieke asked, 'Have you inspected the house?'

The housing administrator shot a resentful look and pulled his mobile phone from his coat pocket. He swivelled his chair to face away from us, stretching his legs in front of him and as he spoke in rapid Amharic he slid down until his head was resting on the top of the chair. I couldn't understand most of what he said, but I could catch 'house' and 'when can we see it?'.

He ended the call and spoke although he still faced away from us. 'The house is not ready.' We waited for him to continue, but he said nothing. After a few moments, he slowly revolved his chair back.

'Is there another house we could see?' Marieke said.

'There is. But ... well ... the toilet's outside.' He exhaled and stared past her to the wall behind.

Marieke and I glanced at each other.

I asked, 'Can we look at it anyway?'

He continued to stare at the wall, but he said, 'After lunch tomorrow.'

The next day after lunch, I reached the housing administrator's office as a downpour started. The door to the office was wedged open, and I saw the housing administrator was in a meeting. I waited on a wooden chair in the spartan foyer, while outside, heavy rain turned the ground to mud. At least, I thought, we'd get a fair preview of the house: if the roof leaked, we'd see it.

After thirty minutes the rain eased to a light sprinkle and four men in brown suits filed out.

'Come in, sit down,' the housing administrator called to me, without looking up from his calculator. He keyed figures into his calculator, and after a pause, wrote sums with a pen.

'Where is Marieke?' he asked, not looking up.

'She had another meeting. She asked me to look at the house.'

He resumed punching numbers in the calculator. I sat for another five minutes, chewing my lip, retying my shoelaces, staring at the top of his head until he looked at me through his bifocals and sighed.

'Should ... we ... go to see the house?' I said.

He looked out the window. 'Well, it's the rain, you see.'

'Are we walking?' I said, surprised.

He punched more numbers, jotted them down, and put the calculator down with precision. 'No. We'll go by driving.' He sighed again and lifted a memo from his in-tray and inscribed the world's slowest signature.

'I don't mind if we go while it's raining,' I said.

The housing administrator slowly turned the page and took care to crease it at the staple in the corner. He placed it on his desk, straightened it, and then breathed in deeply before a long exhalation.

'Well, it will be difficult. I'll have to arrange a car.'

As he dialled, a finger lingering over the keypad between each number, I considered his low risk for a stress-related coronary disorder. While he made arrangements with the transport department I started to feel excited about moving into a new home with Marieke.

It took a few minutes until he replaced the handset and said, 'Come back tomorrow.'

The afternoon dragged. Now that there was an alternative to the guesthouse, I was impatient to leave. I tried to keep my mind off it while I worked. Tadesse, the physiotherapy assistant, accompanied me to the paediatric ward to see the girls with burns injuries.

We went first to see Rahel, the older of the sisters.

When Tadesse asked her in Amharic, 'Do you want to walk today?', she nodded.

Tadesse produced a small cotton dress from his lab coat pocket.

'*Lebs allew*, I have clothes,' he said.

I looked at Tadesse, astonished.

'The children of my sister,' he said by way of explanation. 'Elias told me these *lejoch*, children, didn't have any dress. My sister have finished with these clothes.'

Once she was standing we slipped the cotton dress over Rahel's head, putting it on backwards so it opened at the rear, leaving her burnt back exposed. In her new dress Rahel walked a little more easily than the day before. She walked to the door of the ward and again looked out at the children poking sticks in the dirt outside until she said she was tired and wanted to go back to bed.

Her little sister Mintewab lay awkwardly in the next bed, contorting her body to avoid the pain from her burnt neck.

'*Kuch bey, eshi*? Sitting up, okay?' I asked Mintewab, and she sat up without speaking just as she had the day before. Tadesse slipped a cotton dress over her too. When we asked her to turn her neck first one way, then the other, I saw her neck had already stiffened from lying on her stomach with her head facing the same way all the time.

'*Mimi*, little girl, lie this way.' I asked Tadesse to translate, and demonstrated she should lie with her head turned the other way.

She looked terrified and whispered, '*Alfelligem*, don't want to.'

'*Lemen*? Why?' Tadesse asked, and she motioned with her

eyes towards her sister. She wanted to be able to see her.

'Alright, let's put the pillow at the end of the bed. That way she can turn her head the other way but still see her sister.' When I moved her pillow, I noticed it was soiled with blood and mucus.

'Why don't the nurses change the pillow?' I asked and when Tadesse looked blank I said, 'Isn't it the nurses' job to change the linen?' Tadesse's mystified look told me it wasn't hospital policy here as it was back in Australia.

'What about her father? Why doesn't he change it?' I asked. We had seen their father yesterday, swishing leaves to keep the flies off their brothers' backs. Tadesse spoke to a mother sitting on the bed of a pallid, lethargic boy.

'Not coming,' he translated back. Tadesse and the woman had spoken at length but Tadesse only translated a little for me. I didn't know why the father wasn't coming to the girls' beds. Maybe there were cultural reasons, or he had to go back to the village to sort out affairs after the fire. Whatever the reason, it meant these two little girls, who Elias told me had lost their mother in the housefire, were now utterly alone in this hospital. No wonder the littlest one didn't want to take her eyes off her big sister.

'So they don't have anyone to pay for their medicine? Is that why they have no pain cover?' I asked Tadesse and he nodded.

Tadesse repositioned the pillow and encouraged the little girl to lie with her head turned the opposite way. Obedient and silent, Mintewab climbed onto the bed and turned her head, the opposite way to how she'd lain for two weeks. She howled in pain, for the stretch it put on the scar tissue and the joints that had stiffened.

She bawled, with big tears coursing down her cheeks, crying more with each sob, which made me think sobbing was painful too. It was heartbreaking to see this little one crying, with no pain medication and no-one to look after her, or even change her pillowcase. I wondered if I should pay for pain meds for her and her sister or if I should pick her up and tell her everything would be fine. But I didn't. She didn't know me; would she want a big *ferenji* stranger hugging her? Instead I stood by her bedside, feeling horrible.

'*Ayzosh*, *mimi*, *eshi*? It'll be okay, little one.' Tadesse squatted next to her and comforted her with an arm across her back as she sobbed. He said to her in Amharic, 'It's uncomfortable now but it will get better.'

That afternoon I went out to gather supplies for my dinner in the guesthouse. I stopped in at the row of stalls near the entrance to the hospital.

'*Dabbo allew*? Have you got bread?' I asked the boy behind the counter.

He shook his head affably and pointed his chin at the stall across the gravel clearing.

I walked over to the stall.

'*Dabbo allesh*? Have you got bread?' I asked the girl behind the counter.

She spoke so fast in Amharic, I must have looked puzzled because she said, '*Ney*, come with me.'

I followed her behind the stall and she leaned back to call, '*DABBO ALLEW*?' I craned my neck to see a man hammering at the top of a power pole.

'*DABBO ALLEW*?' he bellowed across to someone he could see from his vantage point.

'*YELLEM*! DON'T HAVE!' I heard a shouted reply.

'*YELLEM*!' the hammering man called and continued hammering.

The girl from the shop spotted a friend on the street down an embankment and called out, '*DABBO ALLESH*?'

'*ENENJA*! NOT SURE!' the girl on the road below called up. '*NEY*! COME WITH ME!'

I bade thanks and farewell to my first bread tout and

clambered down the steep embankment to catch up to the girl, slipping on the gravel as I manoeuvred around two sheep. She smiled at me and we walked together, not speaking, while birds circled on the currents above the foothills, and the long shadows made the grass mountainsides look like fawn velvet.

'*DABBO ALLEW*?' she called out twice to two small shops high on the embankment, which rose ever more steeply as we walked towards town. But each time the answer was '*Yellem*. Don't have.'

Finally, my stomach growling, I asked, '*Lela migib allesh*? Do you have another food?'

The girl looked at me as if to ask 'Why didn't you say so before?' She led me into an alleyway to a cafe with lentil samosas in a wooden display case.

'*Amesegenalehu*! *Amesegenalehu*! Thank you! Thank you!' I gave the most grateful smile I had, in place of any other conversation.

I walked home, carrying three samosas wrapped in a page of arithmetic homework. Oil seeping from the fried treats had turned the paper translucent in patches where a child's hand had once completed sums. It was getting dark and the first star appeared over the deepening bluc on the horizon. I remembered we always used to wish on the evening star when we were kids, and how we were so confident our wishes would come true. I thought of all the things I'd fervently wished for over the years. And now I wished, *Let this all be okay. It's uncomfortable now but it might get better. Let me be brave enough to stick this out.*

Chapter 10

To be rich: ሀብታም /habtam/

It didn't take long to adapt. After three weeks of living in the guesthouse I got used to washing in three cups of water and to starting my mornings by listening to my neighbour's noisy ablutions. It wasn't comfortable, but it was tolerable. My clinical work was settling into a nice routine while we waited for classes to start. I looked forward to my twice-weekly visits to the orphanage, where I felt confident and every therapy session was accompanied by at least seven giggling little onlookers. Gradually my confidence grew as I saw inpatients on the ward at the hospital, and by now the kids knew it was time for exercises as soon as they saw Tadesse or me.

Today we were greeted at the door of the ward by Gebremeskal, the older boy who'd taken it upon himself to be ward organiser. He shook both of our hands as we entered the ward and limped after us.

Rahel and Minte, the two girls with severe burns, snuggled together on Rahel's bed just inside the door to the ward, each sucking the corner of a foil sachet. Habtam lay on her bed, sucking on a sachet too, so I asked, '*Lejoch, menden new*? What is it?'

'*Ocholoni*! Peanut!' Habtam thrust her sachet into the air so I could read the packet: 'Plumpy'Nut® mega-nutrition paste.'

'*Yetafetal*? Delicious?' I asked.

Habtam shared a look with Minte and Rahel.

'*Yetafetal*!' Habtam repeated through giggles and Minte faceplanted into the bedclothes, sputtering.

The kids snorted anytime I tried to speak Ahmaric, but it was too cute to feel offended by it, and their giggling was contagious.

'*Gin yetafetal*? But it's delicious?' I asked, trying to keep a straight face myself.

'*AWE*! YES!' Habtam shouted with a grin so broad her apple cheeks folded up to her eyes.

I turned back to the sisters. They looked so little, lying on the high cast-iron beds with towering mattresses.

When I asked '*Esporte*? Exercises?' it made Minte, the smaller one, giggle and hide her head in her big sister's armpit, repeating '*Esporte*!' It was nice to see her happy and cuddling with her sister after she'd looked so miserable for so long.

'*Behuala*? Afterwards?' Rahel pointed to the sachet, meaning: could they do their exercises after they finished eating their Plumpy'Nut? Their physio could wait. Three weeks on from the first time I'd seen them, their wounds were healing. The burns had crusted over into dry scabs and were no longer weeping.

'*Ke mesa behuala*? After lunch?' This was a new phrase that I tried out on them, but they were both in fits of giggles and couldn't answer as I walked over to Habtam's bed.

Habtam seemed ready to progress to doing her exercises in the therapy room. Over the last three weeks she had practised in bed and there had been a gradual return of movement. With the anti-TB medication, the cyst in her spine had shrunk, reducing the pressure on her spinal cord, and with improved nutrition she had more strength.

She had twice-daily physiotherapy, and her older sister helped her do exercises an extra three times a day. Yesterday, when she lay on her back, she could bring her feet up towards her bottom. Today, when we sat her up, Tadesse and I helped her inch her bottom forwards until she perched right on the edge of the bed. She steadied herself enough not to fall to the side. Without waiting for Tadesse to translate I said, '*Wede esporte bet*!' I wanted to say 'Shall we go to the therapy room?' but actually declared: 'Towards the exercise house!'

Habtam and the two little sisters guffawed.

'Where is your sister?' Tadesse asked Habtam, and she pointed her chin outside the door, to where a collection of parents squatted on their haunches under the tree outside the cooking shed.

'*Ene echelalehu*? I can?' offered Gebremeskal, who had been leaning against the doorframe, watching proceedings. I thought what a sweet boy he was, offering to run for Habtam's older sister, but he didn't run. Instead, Gebremeskal limped to the open window and stuck out his head. Cupping his mouth with his one functioning hand, he bellowed for her to the ladies in the cooking shed and the reply came, '*YELLECHEM*! SHE'S NOT HERE!'

'*YET ALLECH*? WHERE IS SHE?' Gebremeskal shouted.

The same woman's voice called again, and this time a man shouted back.

Gebremeskal turned to us and nodded professionally. '*And gize*. One moment please.' He limped out the door to return a few moments later with Habtam's sister.

She squatted by the side of Habtam's bed so that Tadesse and I could help Habtam into a piggyback. The girls were nearly the same size, and the older sister bent forwards with the weight of her passenger. She hoisted up Habtam's legs and held them tight at her sides, while Habtam clung on around her neck.

'*Enhid*? Let's go?' said Gebremeskal, as if he had a schedule to keep.

Outside, the ten o'clock sun was scorching. Habtam's sister was puffing already at the bottom of the three big steps out of the ward. We kept going, up the forty cement steps cut into the hillside to get to the upper embankment of the hospital. She stopped at the top, red-faced, with sweat trickling down her temples, to catch her breath. Beside them, I felt the idiocy of my walking empty-handed. I felt terrible the teenage girl should carry her sister on her back and wished that patients needn't be carried to the therapy room at all. It would be so nice if we had wheelchairs to transport them and smooth paths for the wheelchairs to roll over, I thought. Then I wished for people to sweep away debris on the path, and a budget to pay the people who did the sweeping. I wondered if Tadesse would offer, but I never saw any hospital staff carry patients.

Gebremeskal walked at my side, lurching up the steps, putting his strong leg first, and dragging his weak leg behind, holding his paralysed arm up in a constant shrug. Although he was taller than the other kids, he was still short enough that he had to lift his whole head to see Tadesse's face as he chattered.

'He wants to know, what is the meaning of the name "Julie"?' Tadesse translated.

'Well, *ferenji* names don't really have a special meaning like Ethiopian names. Maybe it means "Great One", like Julius Caesar.' (I read that in *Women's Weekly* once.) 'How about "Gebremeskal", what does it mean?'

Gebremeskal prattled a long sentence to Tadesse, with eyes squinting against the sunlight, and Tadesse translated the abridged version: 'Gebremeskal means "is one of the angels".'

'He *is* like an angel,' I said and when Tadesse translated, Gebremeskal beamed at me.

'*Habtam mallet*? What does "Habtam" mean?' I asked Habtam.

'*Mallet habtam*! It means habtam!' Gebremeskal interjected.

Tadesse said, 'It means "you are rich". It's a word and a name.'

When we reached the therapy room, Gebremeskal said, '*Bezzi*, this way,' and patted the plinth. Habtam's sister squatted by the edge of the plinth and let Habtam slide off to sit at the edge. She fussed about, smoothing out her sister's hospital gown and tucking it in under and around her legs before she wiped the sweat from her forehead with the sash that was tied around her waist.

Tadesse lifted Habtam to sit on a large therapy ball. I sat

behind her on the plinth, with my legs holding the ball steady on either side. With my hands on her thighs I palpated for muscle contractions. There was definite improvement from just a few weeks back. Her leg muscles were so weak when she first started physio that it was difficult to feel them when she contracted her muscles. Now, when she sat on the ball and I rolled her gently forwards and backwards, her thigh muscles bunched and relaxed beneath my hands.

'Can you try standing?' I asked, and Tadesse translated. I expected the act of initiating standing might prompt her thigh muscles to work. But instead, she put her hands onto her sister's shoulders, leaned forwards and stood up. Astounded, I did what any professional should do – I hollered for everyone to come and look. The other *ferenji* physios and the adult patients crowded around her, saying '*Gobez*! Clever!' She gave a hesitant smile, but there was hope in it. She sat and stood again, with her hands on her sister's shoulders.

'*Dekemesh*? Are you tired?' I asked her.

'*Aldekamegnem*. Not tired,' she said, so I got her to try mini-squats, small up-and-down movements to work the thighs.

By the fifth mini-squat she was grimacing.

'*Ahun dekemesh*? Now are you tired?' I asked, but she shook her head with determination.

Only when her legs gave out did she admit, '*Dekmognal*. I'm tired.' She plonked down onto the ball, looking weaker but triumphant. Triumph was what I felt too. Three weeks ago she had almost no movement, but now it was returning.

Marieke and I bumped into the housing administrator on his way out from a meeting late that afternoon. He responded to my outstretched hand with a limp handshake and without prompting said, 'The committee has inspected the property which Marieke found. The rental committee meeting has approved the property for rental.'

I spoke first. 'Well! Great news! We got the house! When can we move in?'

'However, the owner requested rent that exceeds university guidelines.' His eyes glazed over, looking behind my shoulder.

After a pause I asked, 'Does ... that mean ... we are not moving in?'

He studied the ground for a few moments before saying, 'Yes, it's not possible.'

Marieke said, 'The owner told me the price is negotiable. He said if he hadn't heard from the rental committee by the end of today he would rent it to someone else. Could you call and negotiate the price with the owner?'

The housing administrator raised his eyebrows as if his hairline was heavy, and blew out his breath.

'Or can *I* call and negotiate with him?' Marieke said.

'As you like.' He shrugged and walked on.

There were just thirty minutes until the end of the day. It had taken three weeks to find the property and get this far in negotiations. There was a shortage of rental properties in Gondar; if we missed this one, who knew how long it would be until we found another?

The phone in our physiotherapy office was busy for fifteen minutes as the secretary wrote detailed notes with the phone wedged between her ear and shoulder while I fretted. When she eventually hung up, Marieke dialled, but the phone, which gave only sporadic service, was not working. The phone in the radiology department next door was dead too. We power-walked to the head dean's office, up a small incline, across a bit, then down a hill, with elbows swinging and hips swaying side-to-side like Olympic competitors.

'We need to use your phone please!' Marieke puffed. The secretary sat with hands in her lap, looking at her screen saver.

'*Ayserum*. It's not working.' The head dean's secretary spoke in an amiable tone and continued to smile at us, as if prompting us to continue.

This time we ran across the campus and up the hill to the housing department. The secretary there let us use the phone, but when Marieke dialled 0 for the switchboard the operator advised, 'It is not allowed to make external calls,' and hung up.

By then we were frantic. We ran down the hill and back across the way to the dean of health sciences.

'Our phone doesn't work,' Marieke panted to the secretary of health sciences. 'Can we use this one?'

The secretary gave us a beatific smile. '*Manem chigger yellem*, no problem.' She glanced at her computer to click on her game of solitaire and turned back to us without changing expression. 'Please give me your permission slip.'

'Sorry?' Marieke asked.

'Permission slip. For using another department telephone. Signed by head of department.' Still beatific, she looked from Marieke to me.

'We don't have one,' Marieke said.

'Sorry. Without permission slip cannot using the phone.' The secretary tilted her head in sympathy.

Marieke and I looked at each other, at a loss. 'Oh! Doctor Tesfaye!' Marieke pounced as the handsome doctor from paediatrics entered the foyer. 'Do you have a mobile we could use?'

'Sure!' Doctor Tesfaye first slid a form into the secretary's in-tray and then passed over his mobile. While Marieke negotiated with the house owner in fluent Amharic, I considered flinging my arms around this near-stranger in gratitude. Handing the doctor's phone back, Marieke was jubilant.

'He agrees! He agreed to the university guideline price. He says we can move in tomorrow!'

I joined in Marieke's victory jig. The next day would be Friday. After six months of living in convents and guesthouses and other people's spaces, I would live in a place of my very own.

Moving into our new house was quite simple, in theory. All we needed to do was phone the owner, organise to collect the keys, and arrange a hospital vehicle to transport our things.

'The network is busy. Please try again,' the Ethio Telecom message droned when I tried to dial the house owner's mobile the next morning. The physio phone had resumed service so I dialled fifteen times over four hours from the office, and on the sixteenth try, the network was not busy. The owner said, 'Why haven't you called earlier? I've been waiting. My representative is at the house with the keys.'

Arranging a hospital vehicle to collect Marieke's furniture from her old house, along with my suitcase and backpack from the guesthouse was, in theory, just a matter of filling out a request slip and getting it signed off. Tadesse took the completed form for authorisation to the most appropriate person's office, but that person was out. So he went to the next most correct person's office. That official was also absent, so Tadesse gave the form to the office messenger, who slid it into the wrong in-tray, where the form sat, unsigned, for four hours until Marieke realised the mistake. Tadesse ran to once again seek out a somewhat appropriate person, and by four o'clock, just four hours after we'd begun, we had a signed permission slip.

There was no time for jubilation though, and we dashed to the transport department. Tadesse called to our assigned driver, who waited with all the drivers under a shady tree. Although it was close to home time, our driver rose with lackadaisical ease and then strolled across the car park with the urgency of a sleepy cat.

Once behind the wheel, he was like a Formula One driver escaping a shootout. He missed two buses, careened around a horse and cart with four stacked sofas, and swerved past a man squatting in the middle of the road painting a yellow line. When he cut in front of a cyclist I heard the bike tyres screech, and saw the bike rider go down but still we drove on.

Swivelling in my seat, I saw in the receding distance the rider dusting himself off, lifting up his bike.

By the time we got to Marieke's old house, my chest was tight and my legs shaky. The adrenaline subsided while we stacked the back of the ute with her furniture and belongings, but surged again in the ten-minute journey from there to our new house. I was still a little shaky when I went inside and used the bathroom. But I forgot all that when I saw the bath – with water boiler, spout and a length of garden hose to make a shower, all connected, so that when I turned the tap, hot water flowed. With warm hands and joyful heart, I lowered myself onto the toilet seat with extreme care, then, growing bolder, I twisted a little, and was euphoric when the seat stayed unseparated and intact.

It was not a fancy house by Australian standards. It had stone-tiled floors and wooden walls. The kitchen had a gas cooker, a large fridge, a table for a bench, and four wooden shelves. My bedroom had a single bed, a table with a wooden chair, a chest of drawers and a wardrobe. It was not stylish, but to me, it was perfect. Giddy at having a place of my own, I unpacked my clothes into my new drawers. In the bathroom I set out my shampoo and conditioner on the rim of our bath, knowing they could stay there and no nun would tell me off.

At dusk I sat on the back step of the kitchen door with a tray of dry rice on my lap. I had bought the rice at the market and, as I'd seen Ethiopian women do, I had poured it into a tray to clean it. The rice was flecked with chips of dirt and stone, and I picked these out and pushed the cleaned rice to the other side of the tray.

I leaned against the doorframe, looking beyond the garden. Trees stretched all the way to the silhouette of a mountain, and the valley was filled with a late-afternoon haze. Golden light from the sunset fringed the treetops, fading as the clouds turned from orange to tufty pink. It looked like one of those Inspirational™

scenes on prayer cards the sisters used to give us at school.

Back then, I had been filled with idealism, filled with conviction the world could be a better place if only everyone tried harder. But that was before I'd realised the complexity of problems that made the world as it was and what minor bit-parts each of us play.

But today, before sorting rice for a first meal in our new home, my bit-part had been to help a girl stand again. Her name, Habtam, meant 'you are rich'.

I had this glorious house, with a view of a valley at sunset, with hot water and a toilet with a reliable seat. I felt rich indeed.

Chapter 11

To feel nervous or afraid: ሀብታም /eferalehu/

A week later the novelty of having a hot-water system attached to the tap had still not worn off. On the Monday morning in my new bathroom I showered under the length of garden hose from the bath spout. In the new kitchen I cooked porridge for Marieke and myself on the gas cooktop, then we walked to the main road to catch the service bus that brought staff to the hospital. It normally came sometime between 7.30 and 7.45 a.m. but today it was yet to arrive by 8 a.m.

A man from the radiology department told us the service bus was cancelled and the roads closed because of a political protest.

Marieke and I flagged down a minibus that took us through backstreets and stopped far from the hospital entrance. As we walked the rest of the way we saw the main road in front of the university hospital was indeed closed. The national anthem blared from megaphone speakers tied to the roof of a utility. Crowds of students milled about, waving Ethiopian flags as well as flags of the ruling party's logo. Policemen with rifles slung over their shoulders lined the periphery of the mob.

The crowd cleared for a youth riding a bony horse. The horse's bridle was decorated with blue and red pompoms, and its saddle cloth bore intricate, faded embroidery. The young man galloped past the crowd, reined, and galloped back again to cheers. After him ten elderly men slowly rode out on thin horses, all with white *gabi* cloths around their shoulders, in turbans of scarlet, cyan or magenta, each brandishing a rifle or long stick.

More than one hundred men advanced behind the horsemen. Unlike the students, who wore jeans and t-shirts, these men all wore the same style of countryside clothes – blue safari shorts and button-up shirts of the same material, all patched and re-patched. Each wore a white turban, with a white *gabi* cloth around their shoulders, and they all held a stick, an umbrella or a rifle against their right shoulder. Their hundreds of plastic sandals clacked against the bitumen.

The cavalcade waved their implements high, so that even the umbrellas and sticks looked like weapons, and the crowd cheered. This was nothing like the political protests I participated in at home. I wondered if it was the beginning of civil unrest. I was nervous and relieved to see Tadesse pushing through the mob towards us.

'What does all this mean, Tadesse? Should we be worried?'

'Don't be worried. It's the government – just they give the countryside people food and put them on the bus, to making everyone think they have lots of supporters. Those people don't care who the government is. And they are making us to be late for work.'

He led us through to the gates, and the guard dropped the chain to let us through. I didn't want to be late today, not on my first day as a physiotherapy lecturer.

In the classroom I wiped down the blackboard from the previous day's classes, took out my folder and spread out my lecture notes, additional notes and the transparencies for today's class. With the first transparency ready, I switched on the overhead projector to check it was working. Illuminated on the wall behind me was:

Cardiopulmonary Physiotherapy 201
2nd Year
Topic: Skeletal Anatomy of the Thorax

Underneath, I had typed my name. I liked how that looked. Feeling more confident, I dragged the skeleton on its stand from the corner of the classroom to beside the blackboard, to have it within reach for pointing out the relevant anatomy. I dragged my chair next to it and waited. I was early so there was time to wait. My heart beat fast and I felt queasy. Today I would be leading a class on my own; I hoped I would be able to lecture well enough to answer all the students' questions. I looked at the clock to see it was 9.10 a.m., then 9.15, then 9.25. Class was supposed to start at 9.30 a.m. but by 9.35 still no-one had showed up. I flicked through my diary to the page where I had written the details: it said today, 9.30 a.m., Cardiopulmonary Physiotherapy 201. I continued to wait, wondering what had gone wrong. At 9.40 a.m. the metal door scraped over the tiles and Elias the student poked his head into the room.

'Miss Julie? No-one is coming for your class today. I want to tell you.'

'Oh! Why not?'

He looked apologetic. 'Everyone is at the political meeting.'

'Oh, for the rally at the gates?'

'Maybe.'

'And every single student is there?'

'Many?' he shrugged.

I found it hard to believe the entire second-year class were so politicised but nonetheless switched off the projector and slipped the transparency into my folder. I was disappointed to have missed my first class, and part of me wondered if the students had heard I was new and thought my lecture not worthwhile.

'So, Miss Julie, see you on Saturday, for the make-up class,' Elias said.

I must have looked surprised because he said, by way of explanation, 'All class from today will be on Saturday.'

I packed up, feeling dejected at both my first attempt to be a university lecturer, and the idea of working on a Saturday. As I yanked the sticking metal door behind me to lock up, I heard chanting drifting down from the hospital entrance and heard a little voice calling '*Ferenji*!'.

I looked across to where Rahel and Minte, the two sisters with burns, waved from the high concrete step of the paeds ward.

'*Foonya allesh*? Have you got a balloon?' Minte called, her face creasing into an expectant grin. Tadesse had given them each a balloon in their first week in hospital and since then they occasionally asked for one.

I exaggerated large pats to my front pockets, then my back pockets, then my shirt pocket.

'*Yellem*. Don't have,' I called.

Minte waited for me to walk past and, when I reached her, she poked my shoulder bag with one miniature index finger.

'*Ezzi wust*? In here?'

I rummaged in my bag and shook my head with big movements. '*Yellem*.'

Minte pointed again to my front pockets, holding her lips tight as if a giggle might escape. I pulled out the linings of my trouser pockets, left then right, to show they were empty.

She pointed to my back pockets, '*Ezzi wust*?'

'*Yellem*!' I pantomimed surprise. I bent forwards to her level. '*Ebde nesh*? Are you crazy?'

Minte and Rahel squealed and ran up the steps inside, calling in Amharic, 'She said, "*Are you crazy*?!"' I waited on the step as the two sisters skipped out of the ward again.

'*Esporte bet allew*? Are there balloons in the therapy room?' Rahel asked.

'*Menalbat* ... Maybe ...' I drew the word out. There was a jar of donated balloons in the therapy room that we saved for special occasions, but I thought it couldn't hurt to give the girls one each. I motioned up the hill with my chin and Minte took my hand and jumped off the step, her bare feet landing on the gravel.

'*Chama*! Shoes!' seven-year-old Rahel chided, and they both scrambled to return to the ward. I followed them in.

'*Foonya allew*! *Enhid*! There's balloons! Come on!' they proclaimed to the children in the other beds as they slipped on their plastic shoes. Minte was so excited one shoe spun out of control and she hopped across the room to catch it with her toes.

It was just over a month since these girls were admitted. I had never seen anyone visit them and Tadesse had told me their father and big brothers had returned to their village. I wondered if they didn't have any extended family to visit them, if they were abandoned, or if this sort of thing happened all the time. I had taken it personally no-one turned up for my class today. How would I feel if I were five years old and no-one visited me in hospital for a whole month? A balloon was a poor substitute for a visitor but it was something exciting at least.

'*Enhid*? Let's go?' Rahel and Minte flanked me and each slipped a hand into mine. I figured since we were going to the therapy room, we may as well make it worth our while.

'Habtam and Gebremeskal,' I called our other physio clients. '*Enhid*? Let's go?'

Gebremeskal checked that Habtam was safely on her sister's back before he nodded to confirm, '*Enhid*.'

We all walked up the hill together – Habtam being piggy-backed by her teenage sister, Rahel and Minte now holding hands, and Gebremeskal limping beside them, his right arm swinging loosely while he gesticulated with his left, giving a running commentary: 'Mind the rocks! Here's a step! It's a long way but you'll be okay!'

The kids seemed to have forgotten about the balloons by the time we got to the therapy room and the two little sisters ran to greet Tadesse and play with toys in the corner while we set up for Habtam. Gebremeskal started his exercises without prompting; he had been doing them for weeks now. He sat at a wooden board with holes drilled in it, removing and replacing golf tees from the board to rebuild the coordination in his hand that had partial paralysis.

Tadesse put a chair for Habtam inside the parallel bars, the two metal bars standing side by side for walking practice, and her sister lowered Habtam to sit in it. The older girl bent forwards to wipe the sweat from her face with the sash tied around her waist.

'*Kena bey techeyallesh*? *Tenkaranesh*? Can you be upstraight a bit? You are strong?' I asked Habtam, and she found that so hilarious she could only nod to agree through her giggles.

Habtam held onto the parallel bars and I helped her to stand up, with one hand around her back and one in her armpit. I bent her stiff knee upwards while Tadesse slipped a ball underneath her foot. I sat on a low stool and guided her foot, rolling the ball backwards and forwards to activate her thigh muscles.

'*Yehe tenkara yimetal.* This strong will come,' I pointed to the back of her thigh. Habtam laughed, but only a little, as she concentrated on rolling the ball back and forward, until she was ready to do her next exercise. Walking between the bars, she held on tightly, with each step hitching one leg up to swing it through, then dropping down and hitching the other leg up to repeat. I walked behind her with my hands ready at her waist to catch her if she fell.

When she had been forwards and back twice I asked her in Amharic, 'Can you stand without holding on?'

I supported her hips as she lifted first her right hand, then her left, from the parallel bar. Slowly, I lifted my hands away until she was balancing on her own.

'*Gobez nesh*! You are clever!' A few weeks ago she had barely been able to move her legs and unable to stand. Without medical treatment the tuberculous cyst in her spine would still be pressing on the spinal cord, but without physiotherapy she would not have relearnt the skills to walk again. Although she had been walking by holding onto the bars for a few weeks now, balancing on her own represented a tremendous achievement.

'*Bizu gobez nesh*! Many clever!' I said, thinking I was saying 'very clever,' and she gave huge nods, with her apple cheeks scrunching up beneath her eyes as she smiled.

There was a roaring again as the sounds of the political demonstration surged up the hill from the hospital entrance. When I wondered aloud if we should be nervous, if things might get out of hand, Tadesse said he would check. I felt reassured, although that left me with no-one to translate. Before he left, Tadesse showed Rahel and Minte how to turn the shoulder wheel, a physio equipment like a ship's steering wheel attached to the wall. He put a step beneath it for them to stand on and helped them to turn the wheel high, to reach up and improve the movement in their stiff and scarred shoulders.

I stood with Habtam in the parallel bars and, watched as Minte spun the shoulder wheel first, stretching out her shoulder. Rahel supervised, then they swapped. I busied myself with Habtam until I noticed the two girls had abandoned their wheel-turning and were standing on tiptoes at the window separating the therapy room from the storeroom. They whispered to each other, glanced at me, then gazed back through the window.

'*Menden new*? What is it?' I asked.

They giggled into their palms but didn't say anything. Gebremeskal limped across and peered over their shoulders.

'*Foonya*. Balloon.' He gave an authoritative nod towards the glass while Minte and Rahel made blowing sounds.

I left Habtam standing in the bars and, on unlocking the storeroom door, saw the jar of balloons in full view on the bench behind the glass. Rahel and Minte waited with eyes wide, holding their breath. When I emerged with a handful of balloons, the two girls stood so close they were almost leaning against me. They had their hands out, chests fully inflated with anticipation.

'*Hulet sewoch*! *Gobez allew*! *Allew*! Two people! Clever you have!' I declared in my terrible Amharic and I dropped a balloon into each of their hands. The girls both passed their prizes back to me, indicating with puffs that I should do the inflating, while Gebremeskal was happy to blow his own balloon. When I had blown up one blue and one yellow balloon I looked across to see Habtam wobbling by herself, out of the parallel bars, across the open floor, heading towards another set of rails.

I called out 'Wait!' in English, and ran to her, but she careened over the open space with arms flung out like a novice ice skater. She grabbed the rails before I reached her, and gasped for breath and then burst out laughing, jubilant at her own achievement. Her sister laughed too, but with a nervous expression.

'*Eferalehu*! Afraid!' I held Habtam under the armpits, even though she was already holding on.

She looked perplexed. '*Lemen*? Why?'

Still holding her, I stayed silent for a minute. I didn't know how to explain in Amharic, and I wished Tadesse would return from the demonstration. It was dangerous for Habtam to walk alone; she might fall and injure herself even more, maybe even fracture one of her fragile bones. The crowd in the distance roared again. My stomach was queasy for the second time that day but Habtam looked right into my eyes and said, '*Atefera*, *eshi*? Don't be afraid, okay?'

There was an almighty bang. I jumped and spun around, my heart beating wildly, thinking of the rifles that morning. But it was just Rahel looking sheepish, holding the remnants of a blue balloon. Minte had eyes screwed shut and hands clasped over her ears.

'*Wuyi*! *Lejoch*! *Eferalehu*! Oh my goodness! Kids! Afraid!' I said.

Habtam laughed so much her sister had to bring a chair.

Although I wished I wasn't working on a Saturday, I was excited to be taking my first class. And this time, as I cleaned off the blackboard, set up the overhead projector and dragged the skeleton into place, the room filled with students.

I delivered the class like the ones I had attended in Australia.

After a quick introduction of myself and the course, I slid the first transparency onto the overhead projector. No-one asked any questions, but everyone in the room was bent over, writing furiously, peering up at the screen and back down again. When I replaced the first transparency with a second, there were many sighs and people clicking their tongues with disapproval.

'Shall I put it back again?' I asked, and everyone nodded. No-one listened to anything I said – they were too busy jotting the notes down as quickly as possible. Although most of the students spoke only a small amount of English, all education from secondary school onwards in Ethiopia was delivered in English. This was partially a reflection of the country's longstanding ties with England and of the difficulty of getting textbooks in Amharic. Marieke had warned me class would be like this. Learning in English was hard for these students – they were trying to learn a new subject in an unfamiliar language, so most learning in the course was by rote.

After considerable note-taking, I attempted a more interactive mode of learning. At the front of the class I said, 'Okay everybody, I'd like you all to form groups of four, as you are going to have group discussion.'

The entire class looked at me with blank expressions. I pointed to four students in the front row and motioned them together with my hands. 'You're a group.'

'And *you* are a group,' I said to the next set of four students. I went around the entire room, counting out groups of four, making eye contact with all thirty-five students. Returning to the front I said, 'Now, we will do activities in our groups. Everybody please sit in your assigned groups.'

The class remained still, staring at me. Seeing my instructions were insufficient, I went back to each group and gave them directions: 'You go to this corner, and you go with her. Now, you go to that corner, and you four work at the back of the room.' It was slow going, but finally, I managed to get each group in its own section of the room, facing each other, and I distributed handouts with written instructions for each station. After ten minutes, I attempted a rotation.

'Leave your activity behind and move to the next group's activity,' I said. Once again, no-one moved. Everybody stayed sitting where they were.

I was proud of my explanation: 'Group one, now you stand up and move to group two. Group two, stand up and move to group three, and so on.' The students left their chairs and milled about confused, with no movement towards the next station.

With still more choreographic effort, I finally got them to move along to the next station, and working on their class content. After ten more minutes I announced we would rotate again. I asked, 'Do you all understand about moving stations this time? Move to the station to your right.'

The entire class nodded and returned to their original seats. I was amused and astounded – I knew they were listening to me as best they could and they wanted to please me and to learn the material. And somehow, they all misunderstood my directions in the same way.

I regrouped the students and persisted with the group activities until they were all complete. When the class was over and the classroom almost empty, Elias, the student I supervised on the ward, thanked me for the class.

'You're welcome, Elias,' I said, surprised. 'Thank *you*. How did you enjoy the class?'

'This moving around the classroom is something new for us. Most of the time is simply sitting and writing the notes. But this class was nice. *Ferenji* style.' He smiled again as if I needed reassurance, which I did.

It was a relief my first class hadn't been a total disaster. Although it hadn't gone quite as I had planned, it hadn't entirely bombed. The students seemed to have learnt something, and I had learnt an important teaching lesson – to check in to see if they really did understand, rather than just taking their nods at face value. Moving from one station to the next was something I took for granted but it probably seemed illogical to those who'd never done it.

I locked up the classroom, and as I stood on the top step, pulling the door tight behind me, I heard familiar little voices calling '*Ferenji*!'. Minte and Rahel poked their heads out from the paediatric ward next door.

'*Foonya allesh*? Have you got a balloon?' Minte called. The two girls edged out of the doorway.

'*Yellem*! Don't have!' I pulled out the linings of my pockets.

Minte and Rahel giggled into their hands. '*Bey*! Say it!' Rahel screwed up her face in expectation.

'*Ebde nesh*? Are you crazy?' I called, which sent them snorting and scurrying inside the ward. As I walked back past their ward, Minte and Rahel's heads peered over the windowsill.

'*Ebde nesh*! Are you crazy?' they singsonged in unison and this time it made me snort. Usually by this time Gebremeskal would have appeared at the window but he wasn't here today.

'*Lejoch*! *Gebremeskal yet new*? Kids! Where is Gebremeskal?'

'*Wede bet*! Gone home!' Rahel called down to me from the windowsill.

I don't know why Gebremeskal went home. Like Rahel and Minte, he seemed to be alone. I never saw him with any family member or attendant. He busied himself overseeing ward proceedings, he did his physio exercises diligently, and then suddenly he wasn't in hospital anymore. We didn't have time to create a discharge plan for him or make an appointment to follow up. He lived in the countryside, without a telephone, or an address to post a letter to. He was just gone. He was the first of my patients to disappear without any notice and I felt his absence keenly. I didn't know it was something I would need to get used to.

Monday was payday. For three days there had been a long queue outside the cashier's office window, where employees queued to collect their monthly salary. I followed the rest of the *ferenjis* to stand in the queue. Even though it was only 10 a.m. the sun was already scorching my skin and making me feel sleepy. The queue snaked from the small asphalt area surrounding the cashier's window, past the garden bed with the geraniums and daisy bushes, and down the hill. After thirty minutes I neared the front of the queue.

I was looking forward to my salary. It would be five hundred birr, with an exchange value of one hundred Australian dollars. It felt really hardcore, earning so little. Here I was, earning a local wage, being a do-gooder. I hadn't had any income since I left Australia, seven months previously. Although I had received food and board in return for volunteer work, I was excited at the idea of being paid a salary.

My turn was next. The *ferenji* in front of me folded her wad of green one hundred birr notes and tucked it into her purse while the cashier called me over. She greeted me with a belligerent glare.

'ID card.' She flipped her palm.

I handed over my foreigner's ID card, a green card with my photo on it. She ran the edge of the card down her print-outs, using it to compare my name to the names on her list.

Then she said, 'Name not here. No salary.' She slid my card back to me and looked over my shoulder. 'Next.'

For a moment I was baffled. Before the next person edged in, I asked, 'What should I do?'

The look on the cashier's face said she didn't care as long as it didn't involve her.

'Go to finance office.' She was already licking her finger to count off one hundred birr notes for the next employee's salary and she beckoned him with a nod.

At least the queue at the finance office was shorter, and the customer service window was inside, so I wasn't getting sunburnt. The door had a window in it, like a stable door, with the top half open. Leaning over it, I sneaked a look into the finance office. Six desks were piled with reams of paper and a clerk sat at each desk.

A clerk saw me and I attempted to catch his eye. I tried four times, and on the fifth he sighed, put down his papers and approached the window. I explained my situation and he called to someone at the back desk. That person called to someone centre left, who then called to someone front left, who returned the question to centre right. Thereupon the clerk asked me, '*Ferenji*?'

'*Awe*. Yes. I'm the *ferenji*,' I said hopefully.

He said, 'Come back tomorrow please.'

Disappointed, I walked to the ward. When I did a quick calculation in my head, I realised I was down to my last one hundred birr note. That was worth about twenty Australian dollars, enough to keep me in groceries for a week but not much longer. I was afraid I would run out of money. There was no way to withdraw from foreign accounts in Gondar. Before I'd left Addis Ababa, I had withdrawn a large sum of money from my credit card from one of the three places in Addis that serviced foreign accounts. I would have to pay the credit card back, of course, and I wasn't keen to make a four-day round journey to Addis to borrow more money.

So it was with great trepidation I returned to the finance office the next day. This time when I leant into the opening atop the half-door, not one of the clerks looked up from paper shuffling. After waiting a few minutes, I cleared my throat. After a few more, I coughed. A lady in a polyester frock noticed me, and she prodded the clerk from yesterday. On seeing me he fished in the top drawer of his desk, closed it and opened the next drawer down, fished around in there, pulled out a ream of paper, flicked through it and put it back again. He combed through piles of paper on his desk and in-tray, and I watched, full of hope, as he took a few pieces of paper to the desk of an older man. The two of them murmured together, looked up at me, reviewed the papers, looked up at me again, and seemed to agree.

'Get inside please,' the clerk called.

The room smelt musty, like old books. Every available space in the room was overflowing with forms, balance sheets, blue sheets, ledgers and documents. The shelves lining the room were filled with stacks of paper and yellow cardboard folders beside bundles of lever arch files, some full, some lying open. The clerk resumed his seat and waved me over with a piece of paper. As I stepped around the filing boxes beneath his desk, he reached out to shake my hand and ask how I was. When I answered that I was fine, he said, with solemn import, 'Come back tomorrow.'

Chapter 12

Patience: ትዕግስት/*tegest*/

Most days Marieke and I checked our emails over breakfast, taking it in turns to plug our laptops into the dial-up internet. One morning in early May I received an email from the Australian consulate and read it out to Marieke while she made coffee.

'It says the elections will be held next week and the risk of violent escalation remains high. We need to stock up on adequate quantities of food and drinking water, alternative cooking fuels and candles. Also, they've advised us to avoid political demonstrations and public gatherings of any kind.'

When Marieke's coffee was ready she plugged her laptop in and found a similar email from the Dutch embassy.

After work that evening we set about preparing. We sanitised our drinking water like we usually did, by boiling tap water on the stove before pouring it into a water filter. Normally two huge saucepans might last us a day or so before we'd boil more. But in the days leading up to the election, we emptied the water filter into jerry cans and boiled, poured and filtered again until we'd filled four jerry cans.

The Saturday before the election I shopped in Piazza, with a wad of notes from my salary when it was finally released. The Dashen grocery store, at four metres square, was the biggest food shop in town. Dry goods lined the walls right up to the ceiling, and everything was behind the counter. The grocer made a pile on the counter for me as he fetched and stacked items from our list:

2 kg macaroni
2 kg white rice
1 jar freshly milled peanut butter
1 packet dates
2 packets Laughing Cow cheese wheels
1 tin Nido powdered milk
1 litre vegetable oil

On an impulse I requested three packets of Hip Hop cream biscuits. I was sure Marieke would approve.

Weighed down with enough simple carbs to see out the elections on a sugar high, I flagged down a minibus. At my stop, just outside the Hip Hop barber shop, I struggled out with a plastic bag in each hand and a loaded backpack.

'Julie!' Tadesse waved from inside the barber shop. Eponymous beats blared at full volume. He waved goodbye to the seven young men gathered around the two barber chairs. They all waved hello and two of them called '*Ferenji*!'.

On the steps to the shop, Tadesse shouted over the gangsta rap and pointed at my laden bags. 'WHAT IS THIS?'

'GROCERIES!'

Tadesse took one bag without asking and walked beside me towards home. I looked again at the quantity of my groceries. I felt mortified. Most people only made meal-sized purchases from hole-in-the-wall shops. My shopping extravaganza had cost the equivalent of Tadesse's weekly salary. To explain myself, I indicated the bags and said, '*Mekniyatum, menalbat chigger allew*. Because there might be a problem.'

Tadesse looked around to see no-one was in earshot before he spoke. '*Liknesh*. You are correct. Maybe there will be a problem. This is our first democratic election. Last time, if you said something you must worry, maybe the government comes to take you away. I think you know the last government?'

'Uh huh.' I thought of my friend Genet, whom I had met

through friends in Addis, an older lady with a painful back from torture she hinted at but never explained. The history books I had read said the previous government was responsible for the deaths of millions of their civilians.

We walked past a tape shop with a boom box on the counter playing a familiar tune: 'Ethiooooppppiiiiiaaaa, Abyssinnnniiiiiaaaaa.'

'Why do I keep hearing this song?' I asked.

Tadesse said, 'He is singing about the government.'

'Singing good things or bad things?'

'About democracy, human rights. He doesn't like this government.'

'Aha, so that's why it's always on the radio.'

Tadesse looked shocked. 'No! No! It's not on the radio! By cassette only! You think the government would play a song like that on the radio?'

Sometimes I still felt so naive. I had forgotten that the country's only TV and radio stations, one each, were government controlled.

Tadesse said, 'Could be the government won't win, but maybe they will cheating and take power. Then maybe the opposition will fight. But who can fight the government?'

It was late in the day so shadows were long, and a haze settled over the mountains in the distance. A bunch of kids played hopscotch on the gravel road. Two women conversed from opposite sides of the street, both leaning out of their gates, their amiable chatter loud enough for the sound to carry through the neighbourhood. There seemed no place for armies or conflict on this sunny afternoon.

There were two kittens in the hallway when Tadesse and I reached home. The kittens were so young their limbs trembled to hold themselves up.

Marieke looked thrilled. 'I got them from a *ferenji* who lives on the hill. I ran into her in Piazza and she said she had kittens to give away.'

Tadesse and I were equally enchanted by the duo, and I made tea for Tadesse and a saucer of milk powder and water for the kittens.

The night of the election, Marieke and I were reading in the lounge room with jazz on the CD player. I put my book down to give all my attention to the two balls of needy fluff clawing up my legs. Outside, our guard, Mesfin, switched his radio on and the theme music for the Amharic news drifted through the open window. I thought of election nights in Australia with half-hourly televised updates on polls. I wondered how it might be here when the election result was announced, and how the predicted madness would descend. Marieke and I went onto the veranda to listen to the news with Mesfin. The streetlight cast a yellow glow and it was a warm, still evening. Usually at this time of night I would hear people calling to each other in the streets, or the music still blaring from the Hip Hop barber shop. But tonight there was only the stereo crackle of the same news broadcast, from neighbouring guards' transistors.

It was both disquieting and comforting to have a guard. Disquieting because it felt bourgeois, but comforting because he guarded us. Every compound had guards, although most shared the one guard for three or more small residences. However, as ours was the only house in this compound, Mesfin guarded just us. He lived in a small tin hut behind our house. We would pay him monthly from our salary, with his earnings being just a fraction of ours.

I guessed Mesfin was in his early twenties. He was slightly built, with cropped hair, a small round face and roughened skin.

Despite the warm evening Mesfin had wrapped a yellow-and-black tartan blanket around his shoulders. He turned up the volume on his transistor radio and put a finger to his lips, signalling us to be quiet.

Marieke and I each held a kitten while we listened, although the announcer spoke so fast, I could catch only familiar syllables and the distinctive cadence. I craned my neck towards the radio as if that might help me to understand the Amharic. Had the government won, and would the opposition rise up? Or had the opposition won and now the government would retaliate? Would there be unrest?

A folk tune followed the news. Mesfin shook his head, clicking his tongue against his teeth, but saying nothing.

Marieke spoke with Mesfin, and I wished she would hurry and translate.

'So, who won?'

'They haven't finished counting yet.'

Days passed and no election results were announced. Depending on who I spoke to, and which day I asked, I was told the election results would be announced in three days, or ten days, or five days and soon I stopped asking.

I tried to forget about politics and got on with work. I relished seeing the kids on the ward improve and seeing the kids with disabilities at the orphanage start to have more functional independence. By now I also taught three classes – Cardiopulmonary Physiotherapy for the second- and third-year students, and Clinical Communication Skills for the first years. I loved being a lecturer. Since the start of semester, the weeks had blended into each other – a pleasing blur of staying up late to prepare for classes, delivering classes, marking assignments and setting new ones.

I loved being on the other side of the classroom, watching the students do the same things I had at university. When a student raised their hand and asked, 'Will this be in the exam?' – then glazed over if I said it wouldn't be – I recognised myself as an undergraduate.

I memorised names and faces until, with time, I recognised all my students, in class and when we passed in the market, in coffee shops, or at my new after-work hangout – the fitness centre.

Since arriving in Ethiopia eight months earlier, I had barely raised my heart rate, and there had been nowhere to exercise while I stayed with the nuns. So I was overjoyed when, the week after the election, Tadesse took me to the newly opened university gym. It was inside a tin shed with carpet laid over a compacted dirt floor, with a velvet curtain strung over a beam sectioning off a corner as a change room. Amharic hits belted out from a tape player in the corner.

Most of the equipment looked well used, as if it had been assembled from donations, and bore labels with company addresses in Minnesota and Illinois. There were two treadmills, some free weights, an exercise bike, a rowing machine, and a few unidentifiable gimmicks that looked straight from impulse teleshopping.

Thrilled to finally get some wear from the gym clothes I'd packed all those months ago, I jogged for a while on the treadmill. My muscles burned, my heart pounded, and the feel-good hormones flowed, despite the tape of 'Ethyiopiaaaaaa Abysiinniiiaaa' playing the same song on A side as well as B. I waved a sweaty hello to other teachers, some doctors from the hospital, and some of my students too.

Three of the older secretaries from the university admin department enthusiastically beckoned me to join them in the back corner. They were all having a go on a machine with fluorescent wording that proclaimed 'FATBLASTER!'. This was the type of machine advertised on Australian breakfast TV. The user slips a vibrating belt around the body part in question and the machine jiggles the bejesus out of the cellulite, resulting in terrific weight loss. (Disclaimer: only in conjunction with calorie-controlled diet and strenuous exercise.) I wondered what thought process had led to someone donating a FatBlaster to Ethiopia.

The three middle-aged secretaries defied the Ethiopian cliché though, and had ample buttocks and tummies, as to be expected with their good salaries and sedentary jobs. They each took a turn on the FatBlaster, twisting with practised efficiency for the blaster to jiggle their tummies, their butts and thighs. They were insistent I trial the machine, and I was flattered to be included in their fun.

After discussion and subsequent inspection of my area of greatest need (a step I preferred to skip), they looped the belt around my thighs and buttocks and turned the machine on. The jiggling blurred my vision and I couldn't control my giggles.

The gym instructor dashed to the front of the gym to change the tape to a traditional *Eskista* song, at full volume, and the ladies broke into dance, laughing along with me. They danced *Eskista*, shrugging their shoulders and *tzzz*-ing through their teeth while my own teeth chattered and my saddlebags zinged. Another of the secretaries took my place when my fat was suitably blasted and, dancing in rhythm with the ladies, singing the *tzzz*-ing through my teeth too, I felt joyous.

When I left the fitness centre, the dusk air was warm and heavy, and the first star was out. The endorphins were flowing, my heart was light, and I felt optimistic about Gondar, about my saddlebags and about life.

There was a new patient on the ward, a child named Tigist. Soon after she arrived, Doctor Tesfaye called Tadesse and me over to the nurses station to discuss the case. As usual, I stood close to Doctor Tesfaye to breathe in his expensive cologne, which was a more familiar scent than the ward's thick smells of hair butter, fermenting *injera* scraps, smoky clothes and a smell I could now recognise as infected wounds.

Doctor Tesfaye passed the yellow patient chart over. 'TB of the spine. Patient is in serious condition. She has pressure sores on her buttocks. Very big.' He led us to Tigist's bed, in a nook behind the nurses station. The ward was even more overcrowded than usual. In every bed, and on each mat on the floor between beds, lay tiny bodies, contorting in hacking coughs, or moaning and crying.

Tigist looked about twelve years old, with the skin sunken around her emaciated cheeks. Her hair wasn't in tight curls, but was wavy, and long by comparison with the other girls on the ward. It looked long enough to reach her chin, but it was wet and lay plastered on her forehead and on the sides of her face. Her grandma sat by her bedside, looking up at Doctor Tesfaye with eyes huge and a bewildered expression. She was as thin as Tigist. It was clear they didn't get enough to eat.

The medical chart family history read: *Patient exhibits partial paralysis of lower limbs. Lives with family of eight in one-roomed hut. Parents are farmers.*

'Do you know the town she is from?' I asked Tadesse, showing him the yellow folder.

'Oh, very far, very poor place,' Tadesse shook his head. 'It is in Amhara – almost in Wollo region. Before many years it used to be a famine place.' He clicked his tongue against his teeth to indicate just how bad this place must be. 'This place, never it gets rain.'

When Tadesse spoke to her, Tigist stared through him. When her grandma spoke, she looked at the old woman but didn't register any emotion. Her breath came in rasps. She was too tall for the bed she had been allocated. The bed was midway between a cot and an adult bed, with tall iron bars at each end, and her feet poked through the rails, dangling in the air.

'Let's examine her. Shall we see the pressure sores?' Tadesse and I drew her sheet down, and the ammonia smell of stale urine hit the back of my nose. I tried to breathe through my mouth as we examined her but the smell was overpowering.

The sheet beneath Tigist was soaked, and the urine had soaked into the dressings. The wide gauze pads attached with Micropore tape stretched over most of each buttock, no doubt covering enormous pressure sores. Her hipbones jutted out, and she had barely any muscle. The bottom sheet had bunched up underneath so her legs lay against the brown vinyl mattress, and a puddle of moisture pooled beneath her.

There would be no way for her to get to the toilet. Her legs were completely paralysed, and her grandma was too frail to carry her. I wondered how long she had been like this, immobile and incontinent, with the urine eating into skin already breaking down from the pressure.

'Let's see her back, shall we?' Tadesse and I rolled Tigist over from her side, comforting her with gestures and words, trying to be as gentle as we could. The TB had made the spine collapse in on itself, so it jutted out in a triangle to a point. Someone, probably her grandma, had bunched the sheet around the protrusion, filling in the gap between the sharpness of her spine and the mattress, and had padded it with clothes. I wondered how this child ever got comfortable with such a deformity, and how much the urine stung.

Tadesse shook his head and clicked his tongue. 'This is no good. The smell is very bad, and it will result in damage to skin integrity. I will find a clean sheet.'

I held the girl's hand and looked out for a nurse. Where were they? Anger rose up as I wished I could find a nurse just to tell them off for letting a child lie in such filth.

When Tadesse returned, we rolled Tigist onto her side to replace the sodden sheet with a dry one, and covered her with a fresh top sheet.

'Why don't the nurses change the bedlinen?' I asked, forgetting that we had already had this conversation a few weeks ago.

Tadesse looked puzzled. 'It's not their job.'

'Whose job is it then?'

'*Beshetegna*, patient family job. Patient is given one sheet – it is must for patient family to wash and keep it clean.'

The idea of nurses leaving a family to change their own paralysed child's bed linen seemed callous and so far from my own experience of hospital that I must have looked horrified.

'Nurses' salary is very little.' Tadesse turned his palms out in a gesture of helplessness.

We showed Tigist's grandma how to do exercises to help Tigist maintain movement in her knees and hips. Even as Tadesse explained to the grandma to wash this sheet, to ask for another sheet to use while this one dried, the urine seeped from the dressings into a damp patch on the new sheet. Tigist didn't show any emotion, she seemed oblivious to us. I couldn't tell if she was more comfortable after we had finished, but surely, a dry sheet and a change of position must have helped.

We had just ordered our tea when the eleven o'clock news came on. In the open-air tearoom we sat in dappled shade while birds called to each other and hopped over the radio tied in a crook of branches in the tallest blue gum. When the theme music played, the room's patrons held their drinks midway to their mouths, craning towards the radio. The usual chatter in the tearoom didn't resume after the news ended and I wondered if the election results had finally been announced. After a few minutes, subdued conversation began again.

Tadesse and the older doctor he sat beside spoke to each other in low murmured Amharic.

'What is it? Is it the election result?' I asked.

Tadesse snorted. 'Still not. Government have banned demonstration. This is very serious.'

'For maintaining democracy, it is not allowed to demonstrate,' the doctor said, and they both laughed, although they looked rueful.

The doctor said to me, 'Did you know the students are demonstrating in Addis Ababa? They are hunger-striking because they think the government cheated them and that is why they don't announce the election results.'

'What will happen? How do you think the government will react?' I asked.

'I don't know.' The doctor's brow furrowed and he looked at the ground, seemingly lost in thought. A finch with iridescent green and blue feathers flittered from the tree above and darted about at our feet, nipping at scattered breadcrumbs.

Tadesse broke the silence. 'I have a meeting.' He extended his hand to the older man.

'*Eshi*! Okay!' The doctor looked up, startled. He shook my hand too and Tadesse and I walked back under the scorching sun to the physio office.

One Monday in early June, three weeks after the election, a phone call came from Addis Ababa for our department secretary. She replaced the handset with a trembling hand, saying, 'My brother, he is in Addis Ababa University. Police and army are surrounding them. Many students are there.' She clicked her tongue against the back of her teeth. '*Chigger allew*, *chigger allew*, there is trouble, there is trouble.'

There were rumours everywhere.

'... hundreds of students have been shot,' said the new graduate radiographers in the X-ray department next door.

'... twenty students have been shot,' said the environmental health lecturer.

'... war is about to start,' said the girls serving tea in the tearooms.

'... this is only a minor hiccup. No-one will get hurt. Relax,' said a portly doctor from the surgical ward, when he stopped by to drop in a referral form.

At the end of the day a few of us from the physiotherapy department went to the tearoom to listen to the news. Tadesse translated there had been a crackdown on the demonstrating students outside Addis Ababa university, and the government had arrested five hundred students across the capital for defying the protest ban. That afternoon I walked home from work on the path I always took. As usual the shadows were long and the eagles circled on the currents above the mountains ringing the town.

But some things were not as usual. Usually when I passed the police compound, I saw the same brown cow grazing on food scraps and got a languid wave from the fuzzy-cheeked cadets reclining atop the brick wall. But today three guards sat upright on the steps and, as I rounded the corner, one of the cadets looked down the barrel of a rifle resting on the brick wall.

I jerked to a stop, realising I'd walked into his sights. He looked up and, recognising me from my daily walk, gave me a shy smile over his Kalashnikov.

'*Endet welsh*? How's your day?' he asked, as usual.

'*Teru new.* Good,' I said, though I was unsure of the correct response in this situation. I continued on to my house, knowing there was an AK-47 directed at my back, praying Hail Marys the whole way.

On Tuesday, more students in Addis Ababa protested for the release of their compatriots, and the rumours said the students were brutally repressed, beaten by the police with the butts of their rifles.

On Wednesday the minibuses and taxi drivers of Addis Ababa went on strike as demonstrations spread across the city. We heard rumours that police opened fire on the crowds, that the official reports said twenty-two civilians were killed but that the numbers were much higher.

Marieke and I had trouble keeping up to date. Without a TV, radio or English newspapers, we had no access to local news. We had a dial-up internet account that gave sporadic access, just like the telephone line it ran through, and the electricity supply our laptops ran on. On Wednesday night we logged on from our laptops at home to check the BBC World News site, but it contained just one or two generic articles on the crisis. I read about how the government claimed the crowd was culpable for disobeying the protest ban, but the opposition party should take the blame for inciting protest. The next article said the leaders of the opposition party were now under house arrest and that, indeed, the official reports said twenty-two civilians were shot by police but unofficial reports gave a much higher deathtoll estimate. But there were no more reports on Ethiopia so I checked my emails. Next to my Hotmail login was a banner for a new TV show in Australia about home demolition and rebuilding, and against my better judgement, I clicked it. The ad showed a woman with fake hair, fake tan, fake breasts brandishing a likely fake pickaxe, smashing the wall of a 1980s brick kitchen. The ad said, *Australia's newest reality TV show!* The idea of reality jarred, and I thought of how inconsequential this reality, of people being shot for requesting a fair election, was to those whose reality was demolishing a perfectly good home to build another.

I felt powerless and angry and wished something, anything, could be done to change this injustice. I logged off and lay on the couch to read, letting the kittens nuzzle and purr into my neck until I'd calmed down enough to sleep.

Two days later, the trouble arrived in Gondar. Marieke had gone into work early so I was home alone, with our guard out the front. As I showered and ate breakfast, I heard the distant roaring of a crowd. It was only 8 a.m. but it was already hot when I opened the front door to leave for work. Mesfin was peering over the gate into the street, using both hands to balance. On seeing me, he hobbled over, and the tall staff he used as a walking stick clunked on the cement.

'Julieyea! *Wede sira alhedeshem*! *Chigger allew*! Don't go to work! There's a problem!' He rested the staff against his chest to wave his arms and tried to usher me back into the house. I didn't understand all his Amharic, but his arm-waving and the pointing told me as much as I needed to know.

I was just inside the door when there were three gunshots and distant screams. The white kitten jumped up, arching her back with fur bristling. If I had fur, it would have done the same. I opened the door just a crack and Mesfin pointed at my face and burst into laughter.

'Ah Julieyea! *Ayzosh*! Relax!' he mimed shooting upwards into the air, as if that should reassure me. '*Eshi*? Okay?'

I was not okay. I edged my way outside and sat stiffly beside him on his bamboo guard's bench. The white kitten tottered to the open front door until the next burst of gunfire made her skitter back inside.

'*Endezzih*? Like this?' I asked Mesfin, and mimed shooting at him. '*Woym endezzih*? Or like this?' I mimed shooting upwards.

'*Ayzosh*, relax, Julieyea.' When Mesfin laughed again he pointed his fingers upwards, speaking so fast the only word I understood was 'never'. He pointed his imaginary gun at me, then shook his head as if to say 'This would never happen'.

After a little while, Mesfin urged me, with mime and Amharic, to look into the street. He acted out opening the gate and putting an eye to it, so I did. I inched the gate open and peeked through to see a bunch of youths sprinting around the corner. Just then there was a crack of a nearby gunshot. I slammed the gate and charaded: *I'm terrified, my legs are like jelly*. He didn't exactly understand, but he thought my mime was hilarious and he set me giggling too. It was such a surreal situation, and Mesfin turning it into comedy made it less scary.

After a few minutes I opened the gate a slit again. The only spots of colour along the grey walls and road were other people leaning out of the gates to their compounds, surveying the street. Seconds later an army jeep crunched around the corner, with two soldiers standing on the back, bearing Kalashnikovs. I flattened myself against the back of the gate as if the guards could see through the slit, which made Mesfin double over. This set me off laughing too, and we were both laughing so much that when he spoke, waving his arms, I couldn't catch it all, but I thought he said, 'Ah Julieyea, you are so afraid.'

The jeep rumbled down our street and turned down towards the local high school, and I heard children screaming. The screams abated and within minutes the jeep rolled back past. I saw the troops standing on the back, elevated above the level of our compound fence. I stayed next to Mesfin on the bamboo bench outside our front door until the adrenaline dispersed and my legs didn't shake when I stood up.

Some hours later, the sounds of rap floated over from the Hip Hop barber shop and the *Eskista* blared from the tape shop so I knew things had settled. I ventured into the street and down the hill towards the hospital. Most things seemed normal – the familiar cows grazed outside the entrance to the football stadium, a man led a herd of sheep past the Hip Hop barber shop.

The only difference was the soldiers everywhere. I counted more than one hundred soldiers on the twenty-minute walk. With the sounds of the gunshots from earlier in the day still in my head, the sight of one hundred Kalashnikovs freaked me out a bit. It started to look as if everyone had guns. I saw an old man walking towards me, swinging his long rifle, prodding the tip of the barrel into the ground like a walking stick, until he came closer and I realised he carried a long umbrella. A herd of ten fat-tailed sheep overtook me, with a teenage boy trotting behind them, his arms folded over the gun he'd laid across his shoulders until I looked again and realised it was the wooden staff all the farmers carried.

At the basketball courts, instead of teenagers shooting hoops as there usually were, at least forty soldiers milled about. I didn't look up, trying to avoid eye contact with these men in camouflage and assault rifles across their backs. I heard a big engine behind me and turned to see a troop carrier. It dropped a gear and slowed as it ascended the steep hill. As the truck drew level, I kept my head down, but I had the feeling of being watched. When I looked up, a young soldier with his upper body leaning out the open back of the troop carrier was windmilling his arms at me with a goofy expression. The rest of the young troops were grinning as if they might have dared him. These boys seemed more like kids on their way to a sports carnival than troops on their way to oppress the citizens. I wondered if they wished it the case. The antics caught me by surprise and I laughed and waved back, and the clown's friends cheered as the truck gained speed ahead of me. The moment of comedic reprieve lasted only a few minutes, until I passed more troops, this time with real rifles and serious faces.

It was hard to feel motivated for work that afternoon. Tadesse and the other staff told me how there were protests all over the country, not just in Gondar. Their mobiles rang all day with reports from their friends in different towns and cities, of protests in the streets, of people coming together to rise up in opposition to the unjust electoral process.

Doctor Tesfaye popped in on his way to the X-ray department to advise there was a new patient. On the ward, I found her chart and read the medical history: *Five-year-old female patient. Presented with fever and complete paralysis right side of body. Query cyst inside skull. Malnutrition. Stunting. Social history: lives in one room with eight family members. Parents are farmers. Parents do not produce enough food for family.*

Tadesse and I were at her bedside, about to begin assessment when Doctor Tesfaye called over to say, 'Actually, no need for physiotherapy. This patient is going home today.'

I looked down at the tiny girl and blurted, 'But she has a fever! And she is paralysed on one side of her body!'

Doctor Tesfaye was calm. 'It is against our advice. But it is harvest time. Her father will take her back to their village. There are five other children. If the father will miss the harvest there will not be food for the rest of the family.' I wondered why her father couldn't leave her here like so many other parents left their children.

'*Ayzosh, mimi*, it's okay, little one,' Tadesse said to the little girl. I tried to give her a reassuring look and struggled not to think about the inevitable outcome of her going home today, then we moved on to our next patient.

We had been to see Tigist four days in a row, and on each of those days we had reminded her grandma to change the sheet on her bed. But today, as on the other days, Tigist lay in a pool of urine. The wet sheets had soaked the gauze dressings over the pressure sores on her buttocks. Wound up from the morning's events, frustrated and bewildered by this avoidable unsanitary situation, I verged on tears. I snapped at Tadesse, 'Why doesn't her grandma listen to us? Why didn't she ask for another sheet? Or wash this one?'

Tadesse translated the old lady's reply. 'She doesn't want to leave Tigist alone. She is too worried.' The grandma looked up at us from the low bedside stool, her elbows resting on the bed. I stayed at her bedside while Tadesse found her a clean sheet. Together we turned Tigist onto her side and pulled the sodden, acrid mess out from beneath her. When I laid out the fresh sheet I saw it was torn all the way down the middle, only connected at the top and the bottom seams.

Without speaking, Tadesse and I rolled Tigist onto her stomach to relieve the pressure on her sores. Her paralysed foot caught in the tear in the sheet, and as she was too tall for her bed, we had to manoeuvre both feet through the bars to let them hang out over the edge of the mattress. Tigist's steady tears widened a dark spot on the pillow. She wiped her nose with the back of one bony hand.

By now I had become so accustomed to the filthy wards and the unwell children, I couldn't feel sad for her; instead my sadness welled into anger. I was outraged at the unnecessary suffering. I was furious we lived in a world where some hospitals couldn't afford to replace their sheets or provide their patients with the right sized beds, and there was nothing we could do to change it.

'*Ayzosh*, *mimi*, it will be okay, little one,' I said. Her back was so wounded I had to rub her shoulder instead. She remained impassive and I repeated it, trying this time with her name, '*Ayzosh*, it will be okay, Tigist.'

The name 'Tigist' translates to 'patience' and it was a common name, as regular as Sarah, or Julie. It struck me how patient people seemed to be in this hospital, about the election results, or just in general. At night I had been studying history books about previous elections in Ethiopia. In 1960 during a failed coup attempt, the emperor's son was forced by revolutionaries to read out a speech on the country's only radio station. He read: 'The people of Ethiopia have waited for the day when poverty and backwardness would cease to be, but nothing has been achieved after innumerable promises. No other nation has borne so much in patience ...' The coup was overturned in a matter of hours, and the dictator resumed power.

Today, I heard soldiers shooting in the streets and witnessed a father choose between healthcare for a terminally ill child and food for his other children. This afternoon I had lost patience amid the baking heat in the ward, the smell of vomit, curdled milk, and unwashed bodies, the moaning and crying of thirty sick children. The coup had been forty years ago. This week, the government was shooting anyone who demonstrated for a new government, anyone who demanded an end to backwardness and poverty.

The grandma leaned forward to clear Tigist's hair from her sweating forehead, then, leaning her elbows again on the bed, she put her chin in her hands and stared at the wall.

Chapter 13

To prepare: ማዘጋጀት /*mazegajet*/

That afternoon the *ferenjis* gathered on the balcony of the Circle Hotel after work as we always did on a Friday. Drinks were more expensive here than other venues and the service was never anything but surly, but the views from the sixth-floor terrace were unbeatable.

I sipped a cold beer, watching eagles circling as the sun set behind the mountain, and wondered what it might be like when the country fell apart. It had been a tense week, and I made myself more anxious every evening reading the BBC and CNN news online. In addition to the news about the election, I read about the anti-aircraft weaponry gathering along Ethiopia's border with Eritrea, and about how armed militias now patrolled the streets of every major city. On the bus and in the tearooms at work I heard so many stories, it was hard to tell what was accurate and what was exaggerated. People whispered that thousands of opposition party supporters had been arrested, or just disappeared right across the country, that hundreds of students had been arrested in the major cities. It seemed the violence was building all the time and no-one could predict when it might end. Many of the shops stayed shut, services closed down. Most of the small blue kiosks around the university remained padlocked and the university fitness centre didn't open.

Sitting on the balcony that Friday, I saw the streets were quiet. Only a few minibuses idled in the street and only one sheep bleated its discontent at being led down the hill on a string, as a single truck horn hooted.

One of the older *ferenjis* led our discussion. She was a natural leader with decisive, yet gentle, schoolteacher mannerisms. When she passed around a handwritten list of names and emergency contact details and requested we add ours, she spoke with a very formal tone

'In the event that civil unrest deteriorates and it is too dangerous to travel to Addis Ababa, we will be evacuated directly from Gondar to Kenya. If the situation subsequently improves we will return to Ethiopia to continue our university work. If not, we will be repatriated. Do you all have your go-bags packed like I asked at the last meeting?'

Around the circle, the seven other *ferenjis* nodded, so I did too. Although, just like my sixteen-year-old self when I pretended to have completed my chemistry homework, I had instead lain on my bed and read a novel. The others reported on packing themselves a bag with passport, credit card and money, change of underwear, toothbrush and contact details for next of kin, just in case. I had put a lot of effort into thinking about packing my go-bag, intending to wash clothes for it and planning how I would find my passport. I assumed the others kept their bags close to the door to grab and go if we were airlifted out in a hurry. Or if *they* were airlifted out in a hurry. I didn't work for an international organisation with safety protocols. Working for the Ethiopian government meant I had the same evacuation procedures as all the other Ethiopian university employees: none.

Each of the *ferenjis*, working for a few different organisations between them, recounted their different emergency procedures in turn while the group leader jotted them down. At my turn she said, 'Julie, we've checked already. Because you are staff of the physio department, we can include you in our agency's emergency airlift to Kenya. You can make your own way to Australia from there.'

Relieved, I made a mental note to pack my go-bag that night. It wouldn't be polite to keep them waiting since they'd offered me a lift. But then I thought of our department's Ethiopian staff: Tadesse and the other physiotherapy assistants; Mama Zenash, our department caretaker; Ruth, the department secretary. I wondered if any of them would be included in an airlift. And what about our guard Mesfin, and our neighbour Meseret and her six-year-old daughter, Hiwot? What about the Ethiopians left behind to face the Kalashnikovs and the streets lined with militia?

Having the same evacuation procedures as the Ethiopian staff was where the similarity ended. I had a plane ticket to Perth, an Australian passport, and a credit card. My hypocrisy was glaring. Before I left Australia I had been so outraged at the asylum-seeker debate. Back then I had pictured suburban automatons declaring 'Go back to where you came from' at footage of asylum seekers being rescued on Ashmore Reef. I had imagined them sitting smug on their nothing-to-pay-till-next-year couches, feeling superior to the refugees they saw on their enormous TVs. Back then I wanted to confront them, to ask: 'Why do you deserve more peace than a refugee? Are you more entitled to safety than someone born in a war zone?'

Yet it turned out I *did* have more right to peace. Being born Australian gave me more chance of safety than those who'd be left behind.

That night I retrieved my passport from where I'd hidden it in the powdered-milk tin beneath my bed, and I handwashed socks for my go-bag.

In the kitchen I looked for almonds and peanuts for go-bag sustenance. Pushing aside a bag of dried lima beans, I was overjoyed to find, left over from my preparations for election day, an unopened packet of orange Hip Hop biscuits. Although I considered an emotional eating binge, I instead manoeuvred the pack right to the bottom of my go-bag, hiding it somewhere below the burden of guilt for my privilege, but not on top of my relief at a way out.

In the midst of all this uncertainty, there was one small pleasure. Tomorrow I would get vitamin B. I couldn't remember the last time I'd eaten anything green. Since I'd arrived in Gondar, the only vegetables available at the market had been potatoes, carrots and tomatoes. Each was appealing as part of a healthy eating pyramid but lost their appeal on becoming the pyramid's entirety.

The previous week I had seen vendors sitting behind hessian sacks on the ground piled with *selata*, cos lettuce, and *gomen*, spinach, as we passed the Friday–Saturday markets on the way to work. But by the time I reached the marketplace midmorning on Saturday, the greens had sold out, dashing my dreams of stir-fry and caesar salad.

However, this morning, when I had checked from the window of the service bus, I saw spinach and lettuce at the market again.

After I finished packing, I set my alarm and put my sneakers at the door, next to my go-bag. Even if the shopping tomorrow was like the Boxing Day sales, and I had to sprint and elbow my way to nutritional variety, it would be worth the effort. The leafy greens only came into season for such a short time, and everyone said there would be no more for months.

My only competitors at 6.45 a.m. were three tan calves who, like me, tested their footing before leaping across the drainage channel behind the market. They trotted alongside me in what I thought was a congenial silence until a man yelled at them to go away.

I found a vendor squatting beside spinach and chickpeas laid out on a hessian sack. She had a traditional tattoo dotted concentrically around her neck and wore a patterned dress of bright colours which she tucked behind her knees.

'*And kilo efellegalehu. Sent new*? I'll have one kilo. How much is it?' I pointed at the spinach.

'*Ara*! *Amaregna techeyallesh*? Hey! Can you speak Amharic?' She squinted up at me against the sun.

'*Tennish tennish Amaregna bicha*. I speak a little Amharic.' Smiling, I pointed to the chickpeas. '*And techemari ezziya*. One more kilo of those.'

'*Amaregna techelallalech*! She can speak Amharic!' the old lady clucked to the ten other old ladies with bright patterned dresses and tattoos dotted around their necks.

'She's very clever,' I understood her say as she bundled my spinach, then measured out dried chickpeas with an empty tomato tin and poured them into my shopping bag.

'Yes, yes, she is,' the others all agreed, all squinting against the sun, their spectrum of smiles ranging between gap-toothed and pure gum.

I had a similar conversation with the old ladies selling lettuce at the next stall over.

It was so pleasant in the bustle of the market, being flattered by grannies in the early-morning sunshine, that I temporarily forgot about civil unrest and potential evacuation, until I headed off for the fishmongers. The minibus on the way blasted the 'Ethiooooppppiiiiiaaaa, Abyssinnnniiiiiaaaaa' song about regime change and human rights, and when I alighted near the New York Cafe, it was playing there too, and in the music shop beside the fishmongers. Even the revving engines at the truck mechanics next door couldn't drown it out.

On my way from the fish shop to the post office I ran into my friend Mulugeta and two of his friends, who often joined us for Friday beers. They were all about our age and made their living by enlisting tourists at the bus station and being their tour guides around Gondar's mountains and mediaeval buildings. We walked together towards Piazza, at the centre of town.

'*Sira endet new*? How is work?' I asked.

'No work for us,' said Mulugeta. 'Look around, do you see any tourists?'

Normally tourists in zip-off shorts with cameras crowded Piazza. But today it was deserted save for a row of child vendors sitting on the post office steps, with no customers for their sachets of tissues or chewing gum.

'What *ferenji* would be stupid enough to stay in Ethiopia while the soldiers are shooting?' Mulugeta asked.

A bus groaned up the hill with a young conductor leaning out the open door. Recognising the tour guides he yelled, '*Aman new*? Everything's cool?'

'*Aman new*! Everything's cool!' Mulugeta yelled back. '*Ferenjoch allew*? Are there any *ferenjis*?'

The conductor bellowed, '*Yellem*! None!'

At the music shop near the edge of Piazza, someone flipped the tape over and 'Ethiooooppppiiiiiaaaa, Abyssinnnnniiiiiaaaaa' played again.

'Do you know this song?' Mulugeta asked me.

I wanted to say that I knew it was important, but I'd heard it a million times, it got stuck in my head and I wished someone would change the tape.

Instead I said, 'I've heard it once or twice.'

'The singer lives in Sweden now,' Mulugeta's friend said.

'*Washet*, untrue,' said his other friend. 'He lives in France.'

A small argument ensued until they remembered that I was still there. They turned back to me without a consensus on where he lived but with an agreement about why it wasn't Ethiopia. 'Because the government wants his ass in jail,' Mulugeta said.

I laughed because the others did, but I felt ashamed for wishing the song away. It was such a luxury to take human rights and democracy for granted and to be sick of hearing songs about them. Later, at the post office, I set my bag of spinach and lettuce down on the counter while I posted a parcel to Australia, and then walked off without them. I remembered at the bottom of the steps and raced back, panicking that I might have lost the vegetables I didn't appreciate until I had to work so hard to get them.

Even as we readied ourselves for an emergency evacuation, we still needed to prepare for mid-term exams. Although the academic year would finish in July, this second semester had started late for the second and third years. The department secretary explained it was because the planned start date had coincided with exams from the previous semester. That didn't make sense to me at all but nobody else said anything. I felt sorry for our students: they would have mid-terms and then just a few weeks later would be studying for their end of semester exams.

On Monday morning I signed out textbooks for the students. Although there was a main university library with general resources, we managed our special physiotherapy texts – expensive hardcover tomes with glossy pages, donated from various universities around the world. I was proud of the students' conscientiousness and was thrilled to see so many of them lining up to borrow books.

Elias, the student I had supervised when I first arrived in Gondar, was at the front of the queue, waiting for his turn to receive *Essentials of Cardiopulmonary Physiotherapy*.

He looked so earnest I wished him good luck. My own last-minute cramming at uni came back to me in a wash of shame and I determined to reward his diligence by teaching him well.

Elias signed his name and student ID number in the logbook while I looked through the two small shelves for *Essentials of Cardiopulmonary Physiotherapy*, returned last week by a fellow student. It appeared innocuous, but it had been my nemesis in second-year uni. Back then it had cost ninety dollars, and had caused me much pain, both financial and academic. Now, its mere presence reminded me of the hours I spent memorising its contents, as well as the hours I'd spent watching *Days of Our Lives* instead of memorising its contents. I had whined about how much it cost, but bought it anyway from my summer job savings, then procrastinated from using it until the week before the exam.

Elias was lucky to use it with just four days to go before the mid-term exam. We only had one copy of *Essentials of Cardiopulmonary Physiotherapy* for all fifty students to share. Elias would get to keep it for the next two weeks, for the mid-term and end-terms, to study with it in his dorm room. Or if his eight dorm-mates were noisy, he'd try his luck in the library, although students outnumbered library seats by about five to one.

Last semester break, one of the students had let slip to one of the *ferenji* lecturers that Elias was planning to spend the semester break alone in the dorm because his family couldn't afford a bus ticket home. The lecturer had paid for his ticket and Elias, already diligent, had become even more so.

He seemed to only have two sets of clothes. Today he was wearing one set – some loose beige slacks and a cheap red t-shirt bearing a dyslexic *Abidas!*.

'Thank you, Miss Julie.' Elias waved the evil green textbook.

'You're welcome, Elias. But don't lose it!' I wanted to remind him it cost the same as what his first three months' salary would be. Just in case he took up the favoured student pastime of losing expensive textbooks, I added a silly warning. 'Remember, Elias, if you don't bring it back, I'll make sure you fail.' I hoped for a sinister undertone to make him careful but he just chuckled.

But the morning took an unusual direction. In between signing out textbooks, various lecturers listened while students confided what seemed like wild paranoias. One student said the government was supplying student factions with weapons, while another said students took turns to stay awake at night in case opponents sneaked into their dorms; another said some students have gone crazy, each group claiming the other wanted to kill them.

When the students had all gone, we lecturers turned to each other with cocked eyebrows. Could this really be happening? Having no answers, we went back to the business of preparing for exams.

Two days later I attempted to print out the cardiopulmonary written exam: fifteen pages of questions, plus a template for the practical exam. This set out space to allocate marks against the technique selected, the rationale for choosing the technique and proficiency at it.

We had no photocopier in our department; we had to use the university duplicating office, which I secretly loved. When the other lecturers' duplicates arrived still warm from the carbon copier, the smell of fresh ink flashed me back to primary school. Sister Brendan used to get the students to crank the handle of the copier to flick out pages of arithmetic questions in purple type, in a cramped airless office beside the classroom. Hot summer days in grade one flooded back. Life was so carefree then, it was just about colouring in and playing elastics at lunchtime.

I was looking forward to spending time in the carbon copier's office, enjoying the familiar smell. The secretary Ruth said it was simple to get duplicates made, that it was best to get it done the day before the exam and that I should 'just fill out a slip'.

The permission slip required three different signatures from three different offices to authorise a purple stamp verifying the document's legitimacy from a fourth office. With signed and stamped slip in hand, I took the floppy disk with the exam templates to the duplicating office. My reminiscence didn't interest the secretary at the service window. She told me in Amharic to come back at 1 p.m. before slamming the window shut.

On my return at 1 p.m., the secretary advised I should talk to the duplicating officer, whose office was inexplicably not at the duplicating office.

I walked the ten minutes to his office, but he told me the carbon machine was not working. The service bus to the university's second campus would depart in a few minutes so I ran back and got a seat.

Thirty minutes later I arrived at the second campus to discover all its senior staff were at a three-day meeting. A solo secretary remained, who dialled three different offices on the university's third campus, then apologised and told me that their carbon duplicating machine broke long ago.

I considered writing the exams by hand fifty times, but decided the written exam was too lengthy, so instead went to the head dean's office for permission to use their photocopier. The president's secretary said no and sent me to the dean of students' secretary. She got the dean of students to sign a form to authorise the head of general purchasing to sanction a memo. This gave me permission to print at the Chamber of Commerce, which had the 1982 model of carbon duplicator, still functioning. All I needed was a ream of paper from the stores department. However, the two secretaries at stores told me the Chamber of Commerce only accepted one type of duplicating paper, the entire supply of which was in the office of the duplicating officer. After a ten-minute walk to his office, I found out he had gone home for the day because his duplicator was broken.

By then it was 4 p.m. and I was frustrated and cranky and couldn't have cared less about the smell of the purple carbon copies. The secretary picking her nails in front of her screen saver outside the duplicating officer's office asked why I didn't just change the date of the exam until after the machine was fixed.

Being a *ferenji*, I was appalled. Change the date of an exam? But we had set a schedule!

Instead, I rushed around panicking myself and others, and at 4.55 p.m., due to being a pushy *ferenji*, got the head dean's secretary to use her modern photocopier to make fifty copies.

With the exams safely locked inside the cabinet at work, I walked home one happy, exhausted *ferenji*. Now it made sense how this semester's start date could have overlapped with exams from last semester.

My good mood carried over to the next morning as I carried my hard-won fifty copies of the Cardiopulmonary Physiotherapy 201 practical exam to the classroom. As usual, when I passed the paediatric ward, the two burnt sisters were at the window.

'*Ferenji*!' the littlest one called. '*Foonya allesh*? Have you got a balloon?'

When I pulled the linings from my pockets and called '*Ebde nesh*? Are you crazy?', the two girls hooted as if I'd made that joke for the first time.

As usual I waved hello to the fathers lounging beneath the blue gum outside the kids ward, and shook hands with three kids playing with sticks.

It was going to be a long day of examining students. Practical skills would be assessed in pairs, at fifteen-minute intervals. On a table at the entrance to the classroom, we set out five different case studies printed and cut into slips, turned facedown, so when the students entered the room they would randomly select a scenario on which to be examined.

When Elias appeared for his exam after morning tea, his assigned partner lay facedown on the plinth while Elias studied his question slip with a furrowed brow.

'Ready?' I prompted after giving him time to think.

'Ready, Miss Julie.' With shaking hands Elias positioned his patient on the plinth and selected a stethoscope from the tray of equipment.

'I demonstrate to you auscultation of left lower lobe of lung,' he whispered, his voice cracking as he spoke.

The stethoscope quivered as he tried to hold it steady on his model patient. He looked so nervous, I wished I could encourage him, saying, *Go on, you are doing fine!* But I stayed impersonal and professional as I was supposed to do. I jotted a score on my clipboard and leant in to check the positioning of his stethoscope. As gently as possible, I said, 'Can you explain your clinical rationale for this assessment technique?'

There was a long pause before Elias spoke and he looked like he might throw up. In a dry-mouthed whisper he said, 'Because of patient presenting with –'

The metal door of the classroom crashed open. Four students burst in, wild-eyed and shouting, 'There's firing in the dorms!'

The model patient leapt from his plinth and all the students ran from the room. Elias stopped running, turned and pointed to one of the messengers.

'Stay with Miss Julie!' he said.

The students ran out past the blue gums where the fathers sprang to their feet and ran too, and the kids ran behind until they couldn't keep up. The student who stayed with me was the student representative, Yusuf. We stood together on the doorstep, my heart pounding, my head spinning, hoping I didn't throw up. Visions of my dear students under gunfire filled my mind and I wished we hadn't underestimated the rumours of unrest in the dorms. Yusuf doubled over with his hands on his hips, gulping air to catch his breath.

It was while I was locking the door to guard against looting that we heard shots and screaming. My hands were shaking so hard I couldn't turn the key, so I passed it to Yusuf.

He had straightened up but was still panting as he said, 'There's fire, there's fire.'

'Fire or shooting?' I probed.

'Firing!' he pleaded. He grabbed my forearm and we ran up the hill towards the dorm.

Blue smoke billowed out from the five-storey building and waves of heat shimmered against the grey sky. I didn't expect to feel relief at seeing a building engulfed in flame. I let Yusuf's grammar error slip, with a mental note to revisit it at a more opportune moment.

Something small exploded inside the building, maybe a deodorant can, and it sounded like the pop of a bullet. The nervous crowd of students screamed, and I realised that must have been what we had heard earlier. My eyes stung from the smoke as we watched students and campus guards trying to salvage anything they could. Furniture came hurtling out of doorways – dressers, bookshelves, wardrobes. A man carried three foam mattresses out on his head, and two men carried out a desk, the papers flying off it, page by page, cascading behind them.

A fire engine grumbled to a stop outside the burning dorm. The firefighter sitting on the roof of the cabin jumped off while the firefighters inside piled out. Soon they had turned their hose onto the blaze, and the flames died down.

Even in the time it took to pack away the unused exams and eat my lunch in the tearoom, the rumours had multiplied: that the fire was politically motivated; it was government arsonists retaliating for students' pro-democracy protests; it was opposition arsonists warning the government of things to come; it was one ethnic group of students trying to kill another.

By the afternoon, when Marieke and I left work, past the smouldering dorms, the campus was swarming with soldiers. I counted almost one hundred skinny youths in camouflage and berets, holding their Kalashnikovs across their chests, checking ID cards of anyone entering and leaving the campus.

We could see one section of the dorms was completely razed. We guessed the students would bunk in with friends, sleeping on floors or sharing beds.

We had almost reached home when thunder started. Huge peals rolled from one side of the blackened sky to the other. A few drops of rain turned the dust at my feet into perfume. It smelt like Australia, like the first rains on the farm after summer.

Safely inside, exhausted, I retrieved the Hip Hop biscuits out of the go-bag – it was, after all, an emergency. Outside, the clouds shot charges at each other, and inside, the wind whipped the curtains against the window frame. I lay on the couch, listening to the downpour on the tin roof, hearing it splash off the concrete outside, knowing it was falling on the remains of the dorms, and wondered how to prepare for what might come next.

Chapter 14

Going home: ወደ ቤት ልሂድ /*wede bet*/

The soldiers were still at the hospital the next morning when the students took us for a tour of the campus. We squelched over mud and wet ash to where the boys dorm used to be. Labourers carted rubble in their arms and stacked sheets of seared corrugated iron while soldiers patrolled with rifles poised.

We were outside the section of boys dorm where the walls remained intact but were without a roof when the student Elias approached.

He shifted from foot to foot. 'Um, Miss Julie. I need to tell you. *Essentials of Cardio* textbook is gone. That was my dorm.'

He pointed to where two shattered windows remained in the partial wall. Inside, the doors were askew on blackened wardrobes and a pair of chequered jocks hung from a warped double-bunk.

'What else did you lose?' I asked him.

'Also some books from the library, all of my exercise books. Even my clothes and shoes.'

I knew that when Elias arrived for the semester he carried just a nylon sports bag, with only a blanket, last semester's handwritten notes and a few outfits.

'What can we do about the textbook, Miss Julie? Will you make me fail?' He bit his lip.

I bit my lip too, to stop it from trembling and fought back tears. My heart broke for all the students and the hours they'd spent transcribing lecture notes into exercise books, and their two sets of clothing in nylon bags, now melted into the ground. I put my hand on his shoulder.

When I could speak, I said, 'No, no. I think it's okay, Elias.'

No students turned up for Neurological Rehabilitation, the first class of the day, or to the second class, Anatomy, or to Community Based Rehabilitation after that. All the lecturers agreed it was unlikely the students would attend today.

'They've had a fright,' said the anatomy lecturer. 'We can just give them today to recover.'

I didn't mind because it gave me more time to prepare for Monday's Clinical Communication Skills class for the first-year students, who had one week of classes remaining before mid-term exams. Their semester had started later than the second and third years because of delays in their preferences being allocated. All the students had completed one semester of general science and then requested placement in physiotherapy, medicine, nursing, pharmacy, community health or another health science stream.

Last week in the class a student had challenged me when I explained the importance of good communication for effective treatment. He had raised his hand and stated, 'Physiotherapy is not important if medication can resolve the problem.'

I wasn't sure if he was asking me to affirm his course preference or if he was a pharmacy student in the wrong class. For his benefit and the rest of the class, I planned to show a case study about a patient where recovery would be impossible without physiotherapy. Hopefully there would be a case study in the remaining copy of *Tidy's Physiotherapy* textbook we hadn't lent to the students.

As always, that morning I was greeted at the door to the children's ward by Minte, the littlest of the burnt sisters, with her hand out.

'*Foonya allesh*? Have you got a balloon?'

As always, I flipped out the linings from my lab coat pockets and said, '*Ebde nesh*? Are you crazy?'

Giggling into her palms, she ran inside calling, 'Habtam, *ferenji timetalech*! The *ferenji* is here!'

Habtam sat up in bed and wriggled to the edge to slip on her shoes. But when her sister crouched in front, for Habtam to climb on for the usual piggyback up the hill, Habtam pushed her away.

'*Endet*? How?' I meant: how will you get to physio?

'*Ene echelalehu*! I can do it!' Her apple cheeks bunched in a smile but her face was resolute. She lurched across the ward. The stiffness from the pressure on her spinal cord remained, so that with each step she jerked upwards to pull one leg through, then the other. I stood close in case she fell.

Habtam walked independently over the gravel on the flat, pushing first me, then her sister away to insist again, '*Ene echelalehu*! I can do it!' although she accepted my hand for the steps cut into the hill.

In the therapy room, Habtam lurched up, down and sideways with each step she took, but didn't try to hold on as she sped the length of the parallel bars and back again.

'*Kes. Kes. Endezzih.* Slowly, slowly, like this.' I showed her how to walk with her hands hovering over the bars, to catch herself if she fell.

She spoke so fast and laughed so much I could only understand the essence of what she said, which was, 'I'm not going to fall.'

I wished Tadesse or a student was there to translate. The other *ferenji* therapists worked with their patients, but none of the local staff were available. Habtam was so intent on walking alone she risked falling and reversing her progress. While I was impressed with the tenacity the ten-year-old displayed, I wished I knew how to say, 'Please hold on, just in case.'

I convinced Habtam to sit in the chair at the end of the bars and took out my Lonely Planet phrasebook, by now curled and torn from taking it everywhere with me. The right word wasn't there so I selected the next most appropriate. I hesitated over the new syllables.

'*Maz-e-ga-jet.* To prepare.' I pantomimed falling and hurting myself then stood again to fall and catch myself in the bars.

The two sisters found it so hilarious Habtam doubled over in her chair, pressing her chest to her thighs to catch her breath.

I realised Habtam was the perfect case study for demonstrating to my students the synergies between medication and physio. The anti-TB drugs had shrunk the cyst on her spine, relieving the pressure on her spinal cord. But without the graded exercise regime to rebuild her leg muscles and regain her balance, she would have remained immobile. Life would be bleak in the countryside for a girl who couldn't walk. She couldn't go to school, her future would be dim. Although medication cured her TB, without physiotherapy she wouldn't be walking in the parallel bars or laughing into her knees.

Passion rose within me. *You!* I planned to tell the students in Monday morning's class. *You* are important! Physiotherapy is important for children's futures and this is why!

But we didn't have class on Monday morning. Instead, the students summoned us to a meeting. All seventy-five physio students from three year groups, and thirteen lecturers squished into the classroom. The student representative Yusuf stood in the front row and waited for the noise to subside. He had been elected at the start of semester, and had advocated fiercely about assessments and timetables, with a maturity of presence that was at odds with his youthful face.

Today, Yusuf's notes trembled in his hands. 'There is a strike of all the students from three campuses, because of political motivation of the fire. We do not know who lit the fire. We are afraid another such politically motivation act may occur. We request to finish now and return after the election results are announced. The students in every department are afraid for their safety and wish to go home.'

'What is it you are afraid of?' Marieke asked the students. 'Do you wish to tell us anonymously?'

The students murmured agreement. Marieke looked around the room, then tipped the chalk from the small box on the blackboard ledge.

'Here,' she said. 'Write down your fears and put them in this box.'

The room was silent as the students wrote on pages torn from exercise books, then moved to the front of the classroom to drop their notes into the box. They filed out of the classroom, unusually quiet. When the last student was gone we took it in turns to read out the notes:

We get threatening phone calls.
If we don't protest about the election they will kill us.
They will kill us if we go to class.
They will kill us if we study in the library.
When the election results come we don't know what will happen. We need to be in our homes.
After the election results are released the soldiers will kill us.
I fear for my life. I want to graduate but I want to live.

We shared perplexed looks. This situation had escalated so quickly and we had no way of telling if these were reasonable fears or rumours.

Back in the physio office Marieke phoned the head dean, who refused to give the students leave of absence, telling them to wait for his address the following evening.

We all had to run through the rain to get to the classroom on time for the dean's address. The lecturers said nothing to each other while we sat waiting for him to start, and I felt the hems of my jeans wet against my legs and rain seeping through from my shoes to my socks. Through the window, I watched steadily growing puddles, glowing yellow with the reflection of the campus lights.

Normally a room of seventy-five students would be noisy but this evening everyone was silent and wide-eyed. When the head dean took his place in front of the class, the only sound was the rain clashing on the tin roof.

The student representative faced the dean, then looked to the row of *ferenji* teachers at the back. 'I will make my address in English,' Yusuf said, and reiterated his statement from the day before. 'We are afraid of another such politically motivation act may occur. We request to go home and return after the election results are announced.'

The teachers listened from the back, all of us straining to hear over the downpour when the dean replied. He was a thin and wiry man, with thick, old-fashioned glasses.

'It is my opinion this fire is not politically motivated. It is students making trouble. You need not fear. And you know we cannot send students home during the academic calendar unless the government issues a decree ordering all universities to close down. The central universities board in Addis Ababa has already offered more soldiers and police on campus, to keep you safe. But the student representatives have declined.'

The dean's words were met by stony silence. At pro-democracy demonstrations at Addis Ababa University just a fortnight ago, police and soldiers killed twenty-six students and beat many others with the butts of their rifles. It was easy to see why the students mistrusted the dean's promise that things were being done 'to keep the students safe'.

The dean opened his palms towards the students. 'You are free to withdraw,' he said. 'You can go back to your homes but then you cannot re-enrol. So it is your choice.'

That seemed to end the discussion. No students raised any

further questions, and we lecturers were too stunned to offer any ideas.

Over the next week, all three campuses remained deserted. Students from every faculty refused to leave their dormitories except to hold meetings with their teachers. We visited our students and talked for hours, trying to weigh their perspectives against the dean's dismissiveness. While our students were clearly terrified, it seemed the longer they kept themselves in lockdown, the more the rumours escalated. None of us wanted to see the students throw away their education on unfounded fears, but what if we convinced them to stay and something terrible did happen?

At our next physiotherapy student meeting, seven days later, Yusuf repeated the student's request. 'We just want to go home until after the election results are released.'

Marieke addressed the students. 'We understand you want to do that. But the government has decreed that if you withdraw you will not be readmitted next year. If you go home, it is the end of your education.' Her voice was calm. 'We are sympathetic. We are not stopping you from going home if you want. We are giving you the information to help you make your choice. Do you understand?'

'After the election, the soldiers will kill us!' a student interjected from the front row. He was a good student and normally gave strong contributions in class.

Another student stood and threw his arms wide, imploring, 'If there were two paths to take in life and on one path there was a man waiting to kill you, which path would you take?'

The assembled students applauded and cheered. A student in the back row pointed an accusing finger at the teachers and insisted: he was so terrified he would get on a bus tomorrow; he didn't care at all about his education or his future. This particular student's assignments were always late and he was often belittling and obnoxious to his teachers, so his argument held less sway than it might have from someone else. However, when he finished with an agonised sweep of his finger towards the front of the room, demanding, 'So why won't you just let us go home?' the students again cheered and clapped.

Marieke looked quizzical but her voice was steady. 'If you feel in such danger, why don't you get a bus this afternoon?' The student scowled and folded his arms.

Another student, who was normally upbeat and enthusiastic, said, 'You don't understand! One cannot go without the rest. Either we all stay or we all go. And if we stay here they will kill us.'

'Who will kill you?' I probed.

'The students who want to go home!'

I was puzzled. 'But won't they have left the campus?'

'If we stay, then the town will hate us and try to kill us,' the student said.

The *ferenji* lecturers exchanged glances, confounded.

'I'm going home!' the obnoxious student called from the back. The atmosphere in the classroom ignited as other students called out they would too, and suddenly all they were all leaving the classroom, pushing chairs aside and hurrying out.

'Think carefully!' Marieke called over the din.

Elias approached me and asked if we could speak. We perched on the edge of the treatment plinth and, when the room was empty, Elias told me he'd had an anonymous phone call telling him to run for his life if the government won the election. The caller had told him there would not be time to gather his belongings, and he should just leave.

'Someone wants to kill me,' he said.

In last week's first-year Clinical Communication Skills class we'd covered reflection skills. As I spoke to Elias, my mind flailed until I remembered: *Page two: Reflection. Repeat the patient's concerns.*

'So you think someone wants to kill you?' The phrase was so surreal, I tried to be as gentle as possible.

'Yes. They said I am first on the list. To be targeted by the students who support the government.' He rubbed his eyes, as if he was very tired.

'But why would they want to ... do that?'

'You don't know their ... nature,' Elias said. He usually had a gentle manner and spoke as if he chose all his words carefully. Now he pleaded with me, animated. 'I want to stay on, but I fear for my life. I am from a poor family. I don't want to miss this opportunity to study, but I am afraid. Graduating is second to living. You don't understand the way these people think. This is the history of Ethiopia. Every time the government changes, people die.'

He was right; I didn't know enough about Ethiopia's history and I couldn't understand the way anyone was thinking at the moment. I took a deep breath. 'Do you really think someone in your dorm might hurt you?'

He pulled at the threads from the fraying vinyl of the plinth. Not looking up, he said, low but clear, 'Yes.'

I couldn't think of anything to say, except that we would tell the dean.

But the next day, when we lecturers took our concerns to the head dean again, he said, 'This concept of political pluralism is new for Ethiopia.' He stretched his legs and clasped his hands behind his head as casually as if we were planning an academic excursion. 'There is nothing to be afraid of. The students are terrified because they have no experience of democracy.' He waved his hand and his tone was blasé. 'They don't know in other parts of the world governments change all the time without bloodshed.' He pushed himself up and swivelled his chair to give us a paternal look through his Coke-bottle glasses. 'No-one is going to get hurt, and no-one is going to go home. *Ayzosh*, relax.'

The next week was another blur of meetings, with no-one turning up to class. I had difficulty focusing when I treated patients on the wards. Even the antics of the kids at the orphanage while we did physio couldn't cheer me up. We tried to reason with the students and to negotiate with the head dean, with the academic dean and at the heads of department meeting. We pleaded with the bureaucrats to consider re-enrolment if the students did leave. But both parties were resolute. The students said they were going home and the head dean said if they went, they couldn't come back.

In the last week of June, two weeks after the fire, three student representatives, one from each year, arrived at the physiotherapy office and addressed the thirteen *ferenji* teachers.

Yusuf, the third-year representative, spoke. 'Today we will all withdraw.'

When we remained silent, he said, 'Every single student. There will be no student left on campus.'

'Think carefully,' Marieke said. I knew how much she wanted the students to stay, but she managed to sound fair and impartial. 'You will fail. You will never be readmitted to university. You will ruin your chance for education.'

Yusuf replied, 'We don't want to, but this is what we must do. We cannot act as individuals. It is too dangerous.'

After the student representatives left, we sat in silence, until Marieke stood up and phoned the head dean's office. When she replaced the receiver, she faced us all.

'He says, let them go. It is better for his peace of mind. His hands are tied.'

A slight breeze played with a flier on the noticeboard, flapping it against my head. I snatched at it and saw it announced a guest lecturer for Neuro Rehab 201. It was irrelevant, suddenly belonging to an epoch now gone. I unpinned it, and was about to throw it in the bin in a dramatic gesture, but then thought better of it, in case we needed it later, so I pinned it back to the board again.

I couldn't bear to be in the physio office anymore. With a lump in my throat, I put on my white lab coat and went to the ward to collect my patients.

In the therapy room, I couldn't concentrate. Habtam walked too fast in the parallel bars, but I didn't notice until her sister told her to slow down. My mind turned the situation over and over. If all the students withdrew, they would be throwing away their past work as well as their possible future. The third-year students would walk away from two and a half years study. It was so sad that hours of transcribing notes from the blackboard, reading shared textbooks, practising hands-on techniques and writing essays would come to nothing. It seemed worse for the students from poor homes, like those I had seen during home visits from the clinic in Addis Ababa and in the countryside with Sister Almaz. One of the benefits of the socialist system in Ethiopia was that anyone could afford to go to university, even students with illiterate, destitute parents. These students had studied so hard at school to get into university, to earn a chance to change their family's trajectory. Many of the students were the first in their families even to attend high school. To have made it to university meant they surpassed anyone's dreams. A government salary as a physiotherapist was not going to be huge, but at least the graduates were guaranteed a job, unlike so many others.

When I was a physiotherapy student I'd been faced with tough choices: there were weeks when money was so tight I could afford either vegetables or beer, but not both. But I'd never been forced to decide between a livelihood and life.

Tadesse jogged to catch me up on my way home from work. He wore his soccer kit, and his Manchester United shirt outlined muscles I hadn't noticed under his white lab coat. It had been such a horrible day I was glad for his company. We fell into a rhythm and walked in silence together until I said, 'The dean doesn't mind that all the students will withdraw today. Tomorrow we have no students.'

Tadesse shrugged. 'It's his job. He must to do what the government tells him.'

'But this course is so important!' I didn't disagree with Tadesse, but I wanted him to know my sentiments. 'And these students are poor. And now they missed their chance for study. Everything is wasted.'

'Ah *ferenji*,' Tadesse shook his head as he often did, rueful for all the things *ferenjis* didn't understand. 'This is Ethiopian politic, always. It happen actually.'

He was right. The dean didn't need to care I'd made a terrific transparency about the importance of physiotherapy for my Clinical Communication Skills class. Or that our students from poor homes would lose their path out of poverty. The dean knew thousands more students would jump to take their places. This political turmoil transcended university and physiotherapy. Who were we, some silly idealistic *ferenjis*, to disregard history and politics, and demand this time it must be different? We had been so foolish. We – or at least I – had believed that if we applied reason to the situation, if we used 'I statements' and were honest about our feelings, we could resolve any conflict. We had tried with our *ferenji* ways to mend something we couldn't begin to understand.

Tadesse left me at the football stadium to join the scores of boys kicking balls. I felt a twinge of disappointment the stadium was so close to work we wouldn't get to walk together for longer, but it soon passed because, the minute I was alone, a beggar approached me. He was wrinkled and barefoot and wore oversized trousers cinched at the waist with string. Head bowed and one hand on his chest, he thrust a cupped hand in front of me, moving it up, down, up, down, begging for money.

Angrily, I brushed his arm aside. I was angry that he was poor, my students were poor and would remain poor, and I could do nothing about poor people. I was angry I got asked for money countless times a day, and angry everyone said giving money to the beggars just encouraged dependency and destitution. I didn't want to see all this deprivation I could do nothing about.

The beggar called after my back, 'Sister, sister, sister,' but I didn't turn around.

Closer to home, a bunch of preschool children ran after me yelling, 'You-you-you! Give me one pen! Give me one birr!'

I turned and shouted, '*Hid*! Go away!' This made them run closer and yell louder at me. Only when I walked stony-faced and uncaring for a dozen metres did they lose interest and chase a puppy instead.

At the turn-off to my road, two men in business suits walking past me called, 'You-you-you!' and I felt furious. A few months ago I'd been weighing up the benefits of typhoid for a quick exit from this job. But this week, the prospect of my work being cut short was devastating. Tomorrow the students would all go and everything would have been a big, fat waste of time.

Yusuf, the third-year representative, knocked on the physio office door first thing the next morning. He sat on the wooden chair with his back to the wall, his long thin face looking sad and fatigued. He seemed older than just a few weeks before. The *ferenji* teachers looked at him, waiting for him to speak.

Yusuf reported like a newsreader, with no emotion. 'Nobody withdrew until four p.m. Each student was waiting for the other to go first. At four p.m. we queued to withdraw. But the administration window is closed at four fifteen. The line was too long. So no physiotherapy student could withdraw.'

I wished I could grab Yusuf's hands and jig with him in a circle and click my heels to the side with glee, but the other lecturers remained impassive, so I kept silent.

Marieke answered a call on the department phone. 'That was the head dean. Yusuf, please collect the students. He will meet with you at ten-thirty a.m.'

When the head dean addressed the gathered student body, he roared that he would not be bullied into a political corner. No withdrawals from any other departments were accepted. No-one was going anywhere. Even though none of our students had withdrawn, the dean bellowed that anybody, from any course, who didn't turn up to class next Monday would fail.

And with that, within twenty-four hours, the political momentum on campus evaporated.

On Monday morning, notes in hand, on my way to the physio classroom to prepare for my first year Clinical Communication Skills class, I passed Habtam and her sister.

'*Wede esporte bet*? Going to exercises?' I asked.

They both shook their heads. Habtam's face was all teeth from the extent of her grin. She scuffed her little plastic shoes in the dirt. '*Wede bet*. Going home.'

I was already happy and now I was even happier. I squatted to be at her level and said, '*Hulum ken mehed ena esporte. Betam asfelagi new. Anchi betam betam betam gobez nesh.* All of the days walk and exercises. Very important. You are very, very, very clever. *Eshi*? Okay?'

'*Eshi*! Okay!' She stood up straighter and smiled harder, although I wouldn't have thought it possible.

Her sister wiped a few tears from under her eyes. Turning to her, I said, '*Anchi gobez nesh.* You are clever,' although 'clever' wasn't the right word for this fifteen-year-old girl who had cared for her sister for months, who had carried other children to the ward and the therapy room, who carted huge vats of lentil stew from the cooking shed, and ladled out dinner to the patients on the ward. I didn't know how to say she was wise beyond her years.

At the bottom of the steps they had gone by piggyback so

many times, they were ready to set off, side by side, each carrying a crinkled shopping bag of belongings.

'*Ciao lejoch*! Bye, kids,' I said.

'*Ciao*!' Habtam yelled, even though I was still standing just a few feet away. She gave me a spirited smile and waved with an arm she couldn't lift two months ago. They climbed the steps one last time, to head to the hospital entrance and catch a bus to their home, hours and hours of dusty bus ride away.

Tears threatened, but I took deep breaths and widened my eyes so they wouldn't be red and swollen when the students arrived. I had to set up the room and clean the blackboard of notes from their last class from weeks ago. That seemed a long time back, before the students' futures had been jeopardised and righted again.

From the classroom doorway, I saw the blackboard had already been cleaned. Flowers had been drawn around the perimeters in coloured chalk. In the middle, in blue chalk, was written: *To our instructors... we want to thank you for your humanity and kindness. We don't know the words to say thank you for caring so much about us. We appreciate you so much.*

This time, I couldn't hold the tears back. Through blurry eyes I switched on the overhead projector and slid on my newest transparency:

The importance of your profession: Physiotherapy

Chapter 15

No problem: ምንም ችግር የለም /*manem chigger yellem*/

The government announced the elections results would be released in three weeks. People speculated in hushed tones in the tearoom at work, in coffee shops and on the streets about the violence that might follow. As July arrived, daily life continued. But now, when the service bus picked up employees and the morning news came on, the person alighting the bus would freeze, mid-step, holding onto the rails. The others in line behind would crowd close to the bus entrance, stretching their necks to get their ears closer to the radio, to hear news from Addis Ababa.

Emails arrived from our respective embassies warning of lockdowns and power outages. They recommended stocking up on gas bottles, candles, drinking water and dry food, *in anticipation of potential civil disturbances*, which could cut electricity supplies, running water and access to groceries.

Marieke boiled and distilled drinking water while I once again dutifully purchased a month's supply of pasta, lentils and Hip Hop biscuits.

On the day the results were to be released, Marieke was in Addis Ababa and I worked from home preparing lectures on my laptop. The streets were silent all day so when I heard the theme music for the Amharic news I stepped outside to join our guard. We sat together on Mesfin's bamboo bench beside the front door and when the broadcast finished he switched off the radio.

'*Zare addis mengist*? Today the new government?' I said.

'*Awe*, yes,' he whispered.

'*Kes asfelagi new*? Quiet is important?' I thought of all the whispered conversations in the tearooms and coffee shops.

'*Awe*.' He nodded.

'*Chigger allew woym manem chigger yellem*? Problem or no problem?' I said.

He brought his fingers to his lips and whispered, '*Manem chigger yellem*. No problem.'

Manem chigger yellem is what the driver said when I had been a passenger in a minibus on remote mountain road and the engine died. He had lifted the bonnet and called it as he jumped back to avoid the geyser of steam.

Sister Almaz had reassured me with '*Manem chigger yellem*!' after I declared 'I love you' instead of 'I love this honey' to a Catholic priest.

On a road two hundred kilometres from Addis Ababa, when the rear tyre of our bus exploded and it was discovered the spare was missing, the driver called to the crowd of eighty passengers, '*Manem chigger yellem*!'

And it was only a few weeks earlier that soldiers had opened fire on demonstrators and Mesfin had said, '*Manem chigger yellem*!'

So now, *manem chigger yellem* either meant there was no problem, or a very big one.

Like so many other times, we sat together on the bench by the door. As Mesfin whispered, he waved his arms and widened his eyes. I caught the gist of his rapid Amharic: today the government announced there would duly be an announcement in four months time.

My *ferenji* sensibilities were horrified. Whoever heard of a government taking four months to declare results of an election?

'*Teru new. Salam new. Hulum salam new*. It's good. Everywhere there is peace.' He waited for me to agree and I didn't know what to say.

But Mesfin was right. There was peace everywhere. People stopped talking about the election, and although I still heard the song about regime change on a tape player every day, some other pop stars got airtime.

Life returned to normal. The fitness centre, which had remained closed during the unrest, reopened and I resumed my treadmill and fat-jiggling regimen. Most afternoons it was hard to hear the tape playing at the front over the noise of the rain on the tin roof.

The wet season had arrived, bringing daily downpours lasting for hours. The once-dry riverbed now gushed with chocolate water, opaque with topsoil from the mountains. In the evenings when I lay down to read, I heard the roaring of the river, a ten-minute walk away.

The students attended class, mostly. They handed their assignments in on time, mostly. I loved being a lecturer, mostly, except on Monday mornings. Classes and our regular visits to the wards and the local orphanage resumed.

This week, Sister Deepti greeted Tadesse and me at the orphanage, saying, 'One new patient we are having today.' She led us to six children playing on a mat, who were oblivious to the adults until a tall boy noticed me and called, '*Ferenji*!' There was a flurry of bare feet on concrete and rustling dresses as the kids ran to pull us by hand to the mat.

As I knelt on the mat the children clambered around and onto me. The patient that Sister Deepti wanted us to see was a girl about eight years old, with a shaven head, angular cheekbones and eyes shaped like almonds.

'*Semesh man new*? What's your name?' I asked.

'Selam!' a little boy answered for her, squatting beside her, his face peering in at hers.

Selam's legs crossed over at the knees, tight with spasticity. Her arms were bent and her wrists were hard against her chin, fingers splayed out in front in the characteristic posture of cerebral palsy.

'Selam, *dehna nesh*? Are you fine?' I asked. When she smiled her eyes gave an impish twinkle. '*Anchi edmesh sent new*? How old are you?'

'She doesn't talk!' the same little boy said in Amharic. It translated to 'She has no words!' but I was quite sure Selam did have some words, even if she couldn't say them.

Tadesse and I began by assessing her voluntary movement while the five other children looked on. She could turn her head and move her hands in a broad, jagged way, but beyond that, did not have control of the movements in her body.

'*Kuch bey, mitu*? Sitting up, little one?' I said.

'*Ayihonem*! Impossible for her!' the kids chorused.

'*Memoker*. Try.' I sat behind Selam and helped her into an approximation of sitting, but her body was so rigid she couldn't maintain the position. Without support, she slid down again. The little onlookers lost interest and played again on the other side of the room. I positioned my hands on Selam's hipbones to soften the spasticity and bent my knees up to support her. Once sitting up, she waved her hands at the other children.

'*Nu*! Come over here!' She had difficulty forming the word, but the children scampered back. Selam cackled and looked at me as if to say 'See what I just did?'.

With Selam, I was once again back in my therapy comfort zone. While I was now feeling more assured working with children with spinal TB, I'd had years of experience working with children with cerebral palsy. It seemed like things were back on track. Everywhere there was peace, and I was growing more confident by the day.

As the weeks passed, our two kittens grew bolder, and bigger, as did the skin lesions that appeared soon after their arrival. My torso looked like raisin bread and the chancres on my face oozed onto my pillow. Marieke's legs were patched with red. She said her lesions stopped her from concentrating, while my lesions kept me awake, itching worse than sandfly bites.

The itching, however irksome, was a consolation. The first five people I asked to compare my lesions to photos in the pathology textbook agreed they did indeed resemble early stages of leprosy. Person number six pointed out the paragraph stating leprosy did not cause itching.

This condition was the newest since my arrival in the country ten months earlier. The itemised list read:

fleas x 2
bedbugs x 1
intestinal worms from playing with Sister Almaz's puppies contrary to advice x 1
bacteria causing digestive liquidation (unquantifiable >10)
medicine's first case of itchy leprosy x 1

The list was not without benefits. Ten months of digestive upsets had led to dramatic weight loss. This allowed for guilt-free Hip Hop biscuit consumption, and with leprosy imminent, who knew how long I'd have the use of my fingers? I used them for manoeuvring cream biscuits from the packet in the meantime.

Life was good with Marieke and the kittens. We were a happy, itchy family, until Marieke discovered a diagnosis for our lesions. We both had a severe fungal infection transmitted by the kittens. The doctor said most locals would be immune to it but, as *ferenjis*, Marieke and I were highly susceptible. There were no vets in Gondar and no treatment for the kittens. They would need to go.

I had become very attached to the mewling duo. At night when I wrote in my journal, trying to make sense of my day, the white kitten sat in my lap and the tabby sat on my shoulder trying to lick my earlobes. When Marieke had been away and there were shootings in the streets the kittens had distracted and comforted me at night by paddling my stomach and purring. They seemed so teeny and vulnerable, and I revelled in nurturing them. I loved mixing up powdered milk and water for them to lap from a saucer and they appeared to love peeking out from the pocket of my jacket as I moved around the house.

On the morning we were to pass the kittens to our cleaning lady, I scratched behind each of their ears to say goodbye.

'*Menden new*? What is it?' Mesfin saw my eyes fill with tears.

Embarrassed, I said, '*Gunfan*. I have a cold.'

Tadesse met me at the hospital entrance and we took a minibus together to the orphanage, sitting in the back seat.

When Tadesse asked, 'How are your lesions?', I thought of the kittens and my eyes filled with tears again.

I closed my eyes ostensibly so Tadesse could look at the lesions on my eyelids, but really it was a good excuse to let the tears subside. I felt embarrassed about getting teary over kittens when there were much bigger things to feel sad about. I hoped Tadesse wouldn't see my tears, or that my eyes were puffy from crying. When he leaned in close to look at my eyelids, he gently rested a finger on each temple and tilted my head back, just slightly.

'Definitely leprosy,' he said.

Just then the passenger in the seat next to me, closest to the window, called, '*Waraj allew*, my stop.' She was a large lady with a generous bosom and bottom, and she clambered over me into the aisle of the minibus. I had to swing my legs towards Tadesse so she could get through. Tadesse and I had our legs jammed against each other and I felt the warmth of his thigh against mine, but then the woman was gone and Tadesse told me a joke about cats in Amharic that made us both laugh so loud the old man sitting in front turned around to look disapprovingly. By the time we reached the orphanage, my glum mood was gone.

The grandmotherly nun Sister Deepti bustled with us again to the children's ward. She wiped her hands on her gingham apron as she said, 'So glad I am you are here. Some *ferenjis* were coming this week. They bought those ... you know. What are you calling them?' She made rolling movements with her hands at her sides.

Tadesse and I shared a puzzled look.

'For the adults or children?' Tadesse asked.

'For the children. You know the ones who can't be walking. Oh, now, what are they?'

'Do you mean wheelchairs?' I said.

Sister Deepti clapped her hands together in delight. 'Yes! Those ones! Now who did those *ferenjis* bring them for?'

In the children's ward, Selam sat in a red wheelchair. Although she grinned when she saw us, she didn't look comfortable. She had slid down so far, her bottom was off the chair, her legs skewed out and her head was almost down to the seat. An older girl, maybe twelve, stood behind Selam's wheelchair. She puffed her chest as if she had the most important job in the world. She released the brake lever, moving Selam's chair a fraction, then applied the brake again, maintaining an officious air.

The wheelchair was a child's size and although second-hand and worn, it was well constructed and must have been expensive once. It looked as if it was well-used by a child of a similar age, in a richer country. A wheelchair like that in Australia would be only half of the package – the other half would include a specially made insert to sit inside the chair. This wheelchair didn't have anything to hold Selam in place and, as her body was rigid with spasticity, she just slid down and out of the chair.

'We will need a few things. Can you please bring me a sheet, some pillowcases and a pillow?' I said to Sister Deepti.

Sister Deepti sent the girl who had been applying the brakes, and she returned a few minutes later, peering over a folded sheet and a pillow.

Sister Deepti agreed I should show her how to position Selam so she might do it herself next time.

'See how Selam is sliding out of the chair? Her body is too stiff to sit upright by herself. So we need something to break that stiffness. Let's use the sheet.' I folded the sheet over on itself to form a long flat rope. Tadesse took the sheet and crouched in front of Selam with it. Standing behind her, I tilted her pelvis until she was able to bend at the waist.

'See how she can sit up with her bottom at the back of the chair? We want to keep her bottom there.' We passed the sheet-rope over her hips like a seatbelt, and, pulling it in tightly, tied the ends of the sheet behind the wheelchair. Now her upper body slumped over to the right, and her stiff arm bent over the armrest.

'*Terass eshi*? Pillow okay?' I asked our youthful assistant. I tucked the pillow in to Selam's right side, so now she was propped in the middle of the chair, not leaning at all.

The overactive muscles in her inner thighs made her knees cross and dragged her forwards, almost out of the wheelchair. I folded two pillowcases in half, rolled them into a cylinder and wedged that to keep her thighs parallel to each other rather than scissoring. Now Selam sat upright, her bottom back in the chair, her legs straight, looking almost regal.

'*Des yilal*? You like it?' I asked Selam. It was the first time I had used that phrase. I couldn't find an equivalent to it in English, being somewhere between 'I like it', 'it's fascinating' and 'looks good'.

'*Awe*! Yes!' she struggled to form the word, but with such a grin I couldn't help but smile as well.

When we returned to the orphanage the following week, Selam had none of her makeshift supports. She had twisted in her wheelchair so her knees were to the left and her bottom to the right. One arm hung over the armrest and she had slid in the seat so the back of the wheelchair pushed her chin almost onto her chest. She sobbed quietly.

When I called her name, she struggled to lift her head against the weight of gravity, but on seeing us she broke into a huge smile.

'*Adi*!' she called out, mispronouncing '*Anchi*! You!' With wet eyes and hands fisted beneath her chin, she winged her elbows out in greeting, and cackled. I was glad the sight of us could brighten her tears.

'Let's do exercises,' Tadesse called in Amharic to the kids playing on the mat. They abandoned their game and huddled around Selam's wheelchair.

'*Ene echelalehu*! Let me do it!' A girl of five strode through the crowd of miniature people. Almost tripping on the hem of her dress that reached the floor, she pushed up her sleeves with a purposeful air and gently separated Selam's spasming legs. Then she placed Selam's feet onto the wheelchair footrests and was about to reach in to do more, when Tadesse leaned in.

'It's okay, little one, we've got this,' he said in Amharic as he steered our small helper off to the side and patted her head. When he smiled, the skin around his eyes bunched and the dimple in his unshaven right cheek deepened. For a moment, I wondered how his stubble would feel against my own cheek, but then pushed the thought from my mind and turned my attention to the children.

I sat Selam on my lap and examined a pressure sore on the bony insides of her knees. The skin had broken away where her legs rubbed together all day. The sore hadn't been there before she got her wheelchair but now it seemed she spent all day sinking low in damaging angles in the chair. I asked Sister Deepti if we had any salve or gauze to treat the wounds but she shook her head. I enquired gently where the supports had gone and she said one of the orphanage workers, a local girl from the village, had put the sheets and pillows into the laundry when Selam went to bed. Sister Deepti had tried to remake the supports the next day, but couldn't get it right.

'Ooh so happy I am you are here!' she said. 'You can fix it.' She sent one of the workers to bring us another pillow, pillowcase and some sheets.

While we did exercises with Selam and I wished for something to dress her sores, the other kids played in her wheelchair. The little helping girl had hitched up her too-big dress, climbed in and was sitting tall on the ripped vinyl seat, which still had grime from its previous owner in the corners. I wondered how this donated wheelchair had reached its new home. It was causing sores for Selam but was likely once ordered for a specific child, with a custom-made insert to fit the child's needs.

After we had finished physio exercises, I repositioned Selam in her wheelchair using the sheets and pillow again. The little helping girl fussed over her, taking care to tuck Selam's dress beneath her thighs for modesty, then stepping back to admire her handiwork. I put my hand to my chin and made an exaggerated show of musing. The little girl copied me, putting her own hand beneath her chin and nodding slowly too, furrowing her brow.

'*Perfecte new*? Is it perfect?' I asked.

The small girl tilted her head to help her think. She leaned forwards to smooth Selam's red dress over her knees, straightening out any remaining rumples in the flowers and trains. She stepped back again and declared with a nod, '*Ahun. Perfecte new*. Now she is perfect.'

But the situation was far from perfect. While Tadesse and I waited for a minibus back to campus I said, 'That wheelchair isn't quite right for Selam.'

'*Teru ayidelum*. It's not good. She is all the time falling downwards,' Tadesse said.

'It's really dangerous. She might slip out and bang her head. Or if the pressure sores get infected, it will spread to her blood. She needs an insert with a strap to hold her in,' I said.

Tadesse flagged down a minibus. We climbed in over a sack of potatoes and sat across from a man with a chicken at his feet.

'Do you remember the first day we met? You said we couldn't buy wheelchairs in Gondar, but we could get them from the big clinic in Addis.'

'But very expensive,' Tadesse said.

'But now we have a wheelchair for Selam. Is there someone in Gondar to make the wheelchair inserts for us?'

'I don't know. What does the insert look like?' Tadesse asked.

In my diary I sketched a wheelchair and its insert for Selam. 'We could make it out of wood and foam, then cover it with vinyl,' I said, starting to feel excited.

Tadesse scratched his head. 'You need materials to make a small sofa?'

'Yes! Exactly! Is there a place in Gondar where we can buy a sofa?'

Tadesse organised for the orphanage car to drop Selam at the sofa shop later that week. As we approached, I heard hammering and the shrill angle grinder. Two workmen in the yard downed their saws to stare as Tadesse carried Selam from the car into her wheelchair. A group of four teenagers stopped in the street and watched, leaning on each other's shoulders. I was nervous and wondered if it had been a mistake to bring Selam here. Children in wheelchairs weren't seen often in Gondar, or even in the capital. Wheelchairs were rare, and kids with disabilities were usually kept out of sight. A *ferenji* and a kid in a red wheelchair were even more unusual.

As I struggled to push the chair over the gravel, two more women stopped to stare. I wanted to goad them to yell 'You-you-you!' but instead I glared at each of them. The passersby just stared at Selam for a while then went on their way. The workers recommenced sawing, and I rolled Selam into the yard, onto a carpet of wood shavings.

'Come in! I'm just finishing,' the carpenter called in Amharic.

In the living room he sat with a paunchy man negotiating a deal. The carpenter waved us to a seat and went back to his sums.

After a few minutes, a woman brought out glasses of sweet spiced tea while the TV blasted film clips of Ethiopian traditional music. Three songs came and went. I worried it had been a stupid idea. We didn't know the carpenter. He made sofas, not wheelchair inserts. What if he was mean to Selam? What if he tried to rip us off?

But after the customer left, the carpenter smiled at Selam and spoke in gentle tones.

'He says sorry he kept us waiting,' Tadesse translated.

The carpenter introduced himself with a handshake. Dressed in navy overalls, he had kind eyes and looked to be in his early thirties. He squatted in front of Selam's wheelchair.

'*Mitu, dehna nesh*? How are you, little one?'

When Selam tried to reply, she got a whole-body spasm. Her body jerked and her chin tucked in against her neck. She fell sideways in the chair so her left arm flopped along the wheel. I held my breath, wondering how the carpenter might react.

'*Mitu*, little one, you're falling out of your chair,' he said.

Selam returned his smile, to whisper, '*Awe*! Yes!'

Tadesse and I shared a look of relief. With Tadesse translating, we described the insert we hoped the carpenter might make. It would be made from wood, covered with foam and vinyl and would rest inside the wheelchair. It would have a seatbelt around her waist, blocks at either side to keep her hips stable and wings beneath her armpits to stop her from falling to the side.

'Do you mean like this?' The carpenter slid his hands under Selam's armpits, so she sat up straight instead of slumping over.

'Yes, exactly like that!' I said.

The carpenter made notes, and I was impressed how swiftly he seemed to know what Selam needed.

He took measurements and gave us a quote. It was very reasonable and the funds were available from the pool of donations for the physio department. As we departed the carpenter ruffled Selam's hair and said, '*Konjo lej*. Beautiful child.'

Outside, as we waited for the orphanage car to collect Selam,

I asked Tadesse when the carpenter had said the insert would be ready.

'In three weeks,' Tadesse said.

In three weeks I would be going home. Although I had a one-year plane ticket that was valid until 3 October, I had changed my ticket to return to Australia at the end of July for a family commitment.

The head dean of the university had suggested I might like to go home for a holiday and return in time for the new semester. He offered me another one-year contract, at one hundred dollars a month, with a return ticket from a special funding grant.

Although I wanted to be strong enough to teach another year, I feared if I went home, I may not be brave enough to return.

'*Anchi*! You! Why are you going home?' Sister Almaz shrieked over the phone when I called to let her know I'd changed my ticket. 'Don't go to Australia; come back and work with me in the countryside.'

Sister Almaz and I had spoken on the phone almost weekly since I left her convent in the countryside, and we spent time together whenever we were both in Addis Ababa. Despite being thirteen years my senior, a nun, and a survivor of a war that changed her nationality to Eritrean, we chatted the same way I did with my long-time friends from home. The conversation was by turns silly and serious, she would make me guffaw, then be my sounding board.

'*Anchi*, what do you think you are going to find when you get home?' Her tone somehow mixed tender derision with insight.

'I don't know. Happiness?'

She snorted. 'Happiness! Don't go home for happiness, stay here. *Ara*! Hey! You told me working with the poor was going to make you happy.'

'I thought it would, but it doesn't, Sister A. I don't know ... I'm not happy at home, where everything is comfortable, but a lot of the time, I'm not happy here, because of all the ... discomfort.'

I imagined how easy life might be back in Perth, with all its comforts, like green leafy vegetables that never ran out at Coles. I pictured myself jogging along South Perth foreshore, with no-one yelling 'You-you-you!' and a few people admiring my fashionably emaciated figure. I imagined cabernet sauvignon and double brie and beers, watching sunsets over the Indian Ocean.

But then I thought about my first-year students in my Clinical Communications Skills class – they had improved so much, and were all doing brilliantly at practice interview and history-taking in class, and I was fiercely proud of them. When I thought about giving up on therapy with the kids with disabilities at the orphanage, never getting to see Selam sitting upright with her wheelchair insert or surrounded by any of her little pals, I decided I definitely had to come back.

Then, immediately, I doubted if I had the resilience to last another year here.

Chapter 16

I'm not sure: እኔ እንጃ /*enenja*/

Everyone, from the physio assistants to my neighbours, agreed I should return to Perth with the traditional Ethiopian braided hairstyle, *shuruba*, and everyone agreed the sister of secretary Ruth was best at braiding. On the day I was to leave Gondar for Australia we set out from the office together towards Ruth's house.

'*Shurab allesh*? Have you got a jumper?' The physio department caretaker, Mama Zenash, took her caretaking duties to the extreme. She looked ancient, with skin wizened from years in the sun. She was our caretaker, our messenger and cleaning lady. It never occurred to me to ask someone if Mama was her real name or if everyone called her Mama because she fussed over us like a real, grumpy mother.

'*Awe, shurab ezzi wust.* Yes, jumper in here.' I patted my backpack.

Mama Zenash motioned at the window with her eyebrows. '*Zenabu eyemata new.* The rain is coming.' She bent down to sweep under the desk nearest the door. '*Festal allesh*? Have you got a plastic bag?'

'*Awe*, yes.' That wasn't true. *Festals* were flimsy plastic bags used in the market for vegetables or breadrolls. The first time it rained and I saw a girl wearing a plastic bag on her head I assumed it was an aberration and had been very amused. But every time it rained I noticed all the girls wore *festals* like shower caps.

There were many things I had acculturated to after ten months in Ethiopia. My Ethiopian friends told me I was good at shoulder dancing. I didn't get so bothered by all the calls of 'you-you-you' every time I went in public. I enjoyed eating with my hands instead of cutlery, and had mastered the use of a squat toilet while wearing a backpack. But I would still rather suffer wet hair than the shame of wearing a plastic bag on my head.

Ruth's family home was small and cosy, with the curtains drawn to keep out the midday heat. The family insisted I share lunch with them, and served plates of *injera* and dollops of spicy lentil stew, chickpea stew and garlicky potatoes. Ruth's teenage sister was short and slight, with hair in elaborate diagonal braids. She motioned for me to sit at her feet in front of the sofa.

'*Englizigna techeyallesh*? Can you speak English?' I asked her and she shook her head. When she enquired on my Amharic skills I responded as usual with, '*Tennish tennish*, a little.'

Ruth bade me farewell and returned to the office while her sister brushed my hair. With a full belly and dim lights, with my hair being brushed, I started to nod off. It had been almost a year since I visited the hairdresser and this was bliss. Until the braiding started. When Ruth's sister parted my hair into small sections and twisted those into rigid braids I wanted to say, 'It's too tight.' However, I didn't know the word for tight and I didn't want to seem ungrateful to Ruth's sister. I racked my vocabulary for verbs and, at a loss, I said, '*Kesabelesh*? Slowly it's possible?'

Usually my colleagues understood my language idiosyncrasies so I could say 'Slowly it's possible?' and they would understand I meant 'That's enough sugar for my coffee', or 'I prefer less chilli in my stew'. Ruth's sister, however, leant around to see my face and said, '*Yikerta*? Pardon?'

We both laughed at our mutual lack of comprehension and she continued to wind my hair into cornrows so tight it seemed my forehead was getting farther away from my nose.

At the end of ninety minutes of braiding torture, Ruth's

sister passed me a small hand mirror. My hair was braided on a diagonal down one side and an opposing diagonal on the other. The braids looked amazing; it was just me that didn't. My face looked gaunt without hair to frame it and my white *ferenji* scalp was luminescent in the spaces between my try-hard cornrows.

'*Konjo*! Beautiful!' Ruth's sister beamed.

'*Konjo*! Beautiful!' I repeated, with reference to her handiwork and not to my own *ferenji* noggin. I tried to smile back at her, but my face was already too taut. We gave polite, mute smiles to each other, then I shook her hand and said, '*Egziabher yimesgen*. Thanks to God.'

It started to rain while I waited on the side of the road for the minibus back to the hospital. Splats fell onto the dust at my feet. I popped out my umbrella while a girl also waiting for the minibus fished in her handbag and brought out two *festal* plastic bags. She and her friend slipped the bags onto their heads then huddled under the one umbrella.

Then the downpour came in sheets and the wind blew the rain sideways under the umbrella, soaking the side of my trousers, my shirt and my face within minutes. My braids snagged on a spoke when I held the umbrella too close to my head and I wished then for a plastic-bag shower cap. The thought of rain dissolving the product of my ninety minutes of beauty pain was devastating. The two girls and I leapt into the next available minibus.

When I alighted at the hospital car park, I spotted the vehicle from the orphanage with Selam inside. The orphanage workers had brought her to collect the insert for her wheelchair. The deluge splashed from the bitumen to my ankles as I held the umbrella out for the worker to lift first the wheelchair, then Selam, from the car. Raindrops landed on my exposed scalp between the cornrows.

The worker jumped back in the car and Selam and I set off for the therapy room. I attempted to hold the umbrella over both Selam's head and my braids while pushing the wheelchair up the hill. I discovered just how difficult it is to use one hand to push a wheelchair with two flat tyres, over buckled asphalt, up a hill, in the rain. Some swearwords were involved, but they were in English so Selam could not understand her therapist's profanity.

Despite the rain, the wide hospital walkway was crowded. The stream of people walking downhill from the wards to the exit stared as they passed, holding their *gabi* shoulder cloths above their heads for protection from the rain. Those with umbrellas stopped in their tracks and ogled.

It was obvious that I, a *ferenji* with cornrows, and Selam, a girl in a wheelchair, were both infrequent sights. I had never seen another wheelchair in Gondar. The beggars in Piazza were missing limbs, were blind, or had hunched backs, but none had such a visible neurological disability as Selam. These patients from the countryside might not have seen a wheelchair before, or even a child who needed one. I felt awkward from the stares, and I was just the one with the stupid hairdo.

I leant forwards to pat Selam's shoulder. '*Ayzosh, mimi, eshi*? Everything's fine, okay little one?'

But then we hit a bump in the asphalt and Selam slid down in the seat, almost falling out. The rain poured onto her legs where they stuck out in front. As I leant to apply the wheelchair brakes, an old man deviated off-course to stand in front of Selam's chair. When he peered at her as if she was a curio in a display window, Selam looked at me with a worried expression.

I wanted to protect Selam, to ask the old man to go away, to leave her alone. But instead I said, '*Yikerta*, excuse me,' and stood in between him and Selam so my back blocked his view. He left, and I squatted in front with the umbrella propped over one shoulder, trying to reposition Selam in her chair.

'Miss Julie, can I help you?' I was so grateful to see Elias holding three books over his head to keep off the rain. He passed me his textbooks and took the handlebars of the wheelchair. I held the umbrella over all of us as Elias pushed Selam over the rumpled asphalt to the therapy room.

The room was full, with four male students taking shelter from the rain. Mama Zenash stood by the door. She clicked her tongue to chide me for my lack of *festal* as I smoothed the droplets from my wet braids.

Elias carried Selam out of the wheelchair and onto the blue treatment mat. He assisted her to sit, propping her from behind so she was upright.

The carpenter had already arrived with the wheelchair insert. Tadesse put Selam's new wheelchair insert into the chair and attached it with straps around the back of the frame.

Elias carried Selam from the mat back to her chair and we positioned her in the insert. I clipped the seatbelt around her waist so she wouldn't slip forwards. I positioned her knees and ankles on either side of central foam blocks that would prevent her skin rubbing all day, causing pressure sores. With three outstretched fingers, I checked her arms didn't rub on the panels that fitted beneath her armpits. With the insert holding her upright and giving the right postural control, she looked comfortable, and much more like any of the other kids.

The four other students came over to admire Selam in her new chair.

'*Endet new, des yilal*? You like it?' I asked Selam.

'*Awe*, yes,' she whispered, but she scanned the crowd of tall boys in front of her. Her eyes were wide and uncertain, looking first to me then Tadesse.

Tadesse asked the students to leave, and when they had slunk out of the office he tapped Selam's nose affectionately. '*Ayzosh, eshi*? Everything's fine, okay?' He disappeared into the storeroom at the side of the therapy room and reappeared with stickers. He stuck a merry sun on her left hand.

This time Selam leaned her head and pointed with her eyebrows at the book of stickers.

'*Ande chemer*? Another one?' Tadesse asked.

'*Awe*! Yes!' Tadesse put a jolly cloud on her other hand and slipped the sticker pad into his shirt pocket.

The carpenter squatted with me and Tadesse behind Selam's chair to make adjustments to the insert straps.

'*Adi*! Hey you!' Selam called out.

As we stood Selam pointed with her eyebrows to Tadesse's pocket.

'*Ande chemer*? Another one?' Tadesse asked. This time, when Selam cackled, she didn't fall out of her chair like usual. Her new insert straps held her in as her legs and arms spasmed, which they always did when she laughed.

When Tadesse presented the sticker to her on the end of an outstretched finger she turned her head away. She pointed at me by poking her lips in my direction and said, '*Adi*, you.'

'*Ene*? Me?'

She gave a huge nod. With more of her artistic direction I had rainbows across my eyebrows, Tadesse had a flower on his forehead and Selam had stars on her cheeks.

I was so pleased with Selam's insert. She would be able to sit with the other children now. She would get fewer pressure sores, too. It wasn't the best insert ever made. I wasn't the most experienced of the therapists, but had helped her with a bit of expertise and locally available material. Although my shoes squelched and my shirt was slick on my back, I felt content. If I had achieved nothing else at all here, at least I'd improved the life of a smiling munchkin with stars on her cheeks.

The rain had stopped by the time the worker from the orphanage arrived. Only a few remaining drops plopped onto the doorstep from the eaves as the worker pushed Selam away. I waved her goodbye for the last time from the doorstop, realising this might be my last hour as an employee of Gondar hospital. Pressing the rainbow stickers more firmly onto my eyebrows, I headed down to the paeds ward.

I hadn't made it into the ward before Minte, the little sister with burns, came skipping down the steps and slipped her hand into mine. '*Ferenji timetalech*! The *ferenji* is here!' she yelled and five other children scampered outside too, while three small faces appeared in the open window above. I waited.

'*Foonya allesh*? Have you got a balloon?' Minte held her breath in anticipation. She had asked me nearly every day for three months now.

I put my hand into the deep pocket of the lab coat and paused. The littlest children went onto their tippy-toes to try to peer in.

'*Allegn*! I have!' I called, and this time palms flew to mouths with surprise instead of giggles as I pulled out the wad of balloons. The faces watching from the window above disappeared, then reappeared at my side. Hands were outstretched for the balloons, and immediately stretched back again as they passed the blue, red and green balloons for me to inflate.

Minte watched while her big sister Rahel blew up a yellow balloon.

I said, '*Nege, wede Australia ehedalehu*. Tomorrow I am going to Australia.'

Minte clapped her hands to her head and Rahel took the balloon out of her mouth to wail, '*Besme ab*! Oh my God!'

I wanted to clasp my head and wail with dismay too. I knew I wouldn't see these sisters again. They would be discharged by the time I returned, if indeed I did. As all the children shook my hand, I lost count of whose I'd already shaken, and they were all still outstretched so I shook those little hands all over again. I inflated more balloons, and I wondered how on earth I could leave this work and these adorable patients behind.

That night I did everything for the last time. I ate *zilzil tebs*, stretched meat, for the last time. I bopped the *Eskista* shoulder dance and drank honey wine at a traditional dancing house for the last time. I partied with colleagues for the last time in the small and sweaty Genfun nightclub we went to most weekends.

At 2 a.m., knowing my flight to Addis Ababa was in seven hours, I shouted to Tadesse over the music, 'I HAVEN'T FINISHED PACKING MY SUITCASE. I HAVE TO GO HOME!'

'*ENDEGENA*? AGAIN? I DIDN'T HEAR YOU!'

When Tadesse leant in close to offer his ear, I felt his stubble against my cheek just as I had imagined.

'I HAVE TO GO HOME!' I leaned in to shout just as the crowd on the dance floor surged, pressing our bodies against each other.

'*ESHI. ENHID*? Okay, let's go?' He led the way out of the nightclub.

There had been a downpour while we partied, but the sky had now cleared and the stars were vivid. The road was flooded in sections. Rivulets cut into the side of the road from the drain and I lost my footing on the mud. Tadesse caught my arm with both of his, keeping me upright.

'Thanks –'

'*Ayzosh*, all good.' He and I spoke at the same moment, both with faces turned so we almost collided. Tadesse kept his hands wrapped around my arm. The street was deserted and the wet road reflected golden circles from the streetlights. Two dogs barked behind a compound wall. My heartbeat roared in my ears.

'*Temeleshalesh*. Please come back,' Tadesse said, so quietly I almost didn't hear. He slid one hand down my arm until he had wrapped my hand in his own. My heart beat faster. I'd barely realised I'd been hoping for this, or that it could be something he'd hoped for too. Nervousness stirred in my stomach as we navigated puddles and mud patches hand in hand the whole way home.

When we reached my big red gate, I took my hand from his to fumble in my jacket for my keys. With a shaking hand, I got my key into the lock but before I unlatched the gate he took my hand again.

'Will you return?' he asked in Amharic.

'*Enenja*. I'm not sure.'

Tadesse slid one hand around my waist and I put my hands onto his face. I traced his stubble, the curve of his cheeks and his chin, finally feeling with my fingertips the face I'd seen every day for months. He ran a palm over my braids. Then he kissed me.

'*Temeleshalesh*. Come back.'

Chapter 17

Daisy: የመስቀል አበባ /*Yemeskel Abeba*/

On my way home, I transited through Bangkok airport and when we queued to board the final leg to Perth, the airline announced a delay but requested us to stay in line. We were stuck like that for forty-five minutes, and a couple in the queue struck up a conversation with me and a guy behind.

The couple looked just a bit younger than my parents, and both wore shorts and thongs. They told us about their beach getaway in Phuket and then asked, 'Where are you both on your way home from?'

The young guy behind me laughed in anticipation of his own anecdote. 'Contiki tour. Drank so much! Bloody just had four hours sleep each night! Who wants to sleep on a Contiki?'

'But you were away for the Eagles victory!' the older man said.

'No wuckers, mate! My old lady was texting the whole time. In the last ten minutes of the game, she called and I put the mobile up to the microphone in the bus for everyone to hear!'

The older man and his wife cracked up and looked at me expectantly. I nodded and forced a smile, when I was really thinking, what am I going home to? I don't belong there!

While her husband still chuckled, the lady asked me, 'And what about you? Have you been on holidays somewhere fun?'

'I've been working in Ethiopia, as a physiotherapist.'

The couple looked blank and the young guy asked, 'Where?'

'Ethiopia. It's in Africa. It's pretty famous for famine, in the eighties?'

There was silence until the lady inhaled deeply, and she and her husband turned to the young guy. 'So what was your favourite city? Berlin or Paris?'

For the next two months I watched as many sunsets over the Indian Ocean and had as much brie cheese and cabernet sauvignon as I could, but even the familiarity and comforts of home weren't enough to dispel my doubts about staying in Australia. I got flustered when I tried describing my experiences, ending up with phrases like 'it was indescribable'. I had nothing to say when conversations turned to real estate prices and kitchen renovations, and one evening I phoned a friend to see if she would like to hang out and she said, 'Sorry I can't. We're all going out for dinner.'

Once I was part of 'we're all', and now I was home alone, crying because I'd been to Harvey Norman to get a new charger for my video camera and there were too many things for sale.

At my temporary job, filling in for a paediatric physio's long service leave, I ordered a customised wheelchair for a boy with severe disabilities. The form from the government funding scheme asked for total cost, and I wrote in $5,000. I didn't begrudge this family the wheelchair, as that was how much a modified wheelchair cost in Australia. But the next box offered me seven lines to handwrite 'justification for expenditure' and I wondered ethically, from a global perspective, who could fill that box. It certainly wasn't me.

I'd hoped it would be wonderful to come home. I felt like I hadn't really belonged in Ethiopia and now it felt like I didn't belong at home either.

I arrived back in Ethiopia in early October 2005, not long after the festivities for the *Meskel* religious festival and *Enkutatash*,

Ethiopian New Year, just a few weeks apart. Yellow daisies dotted the roadsides and the median strips all the way from the airport to my house.

'Do you see these flowers?' the taxi driver spoke in English as he pointed out the window.

He watched for my reaction from the rear-view mirror so I nodded and said, "They are beautiful.'

'In Ethiopia we say these are the flowers for New Year. And for *Meskel.* We say the flower is the sign for new hope. When the flower comes, it is the people know the New Year is coming. It is a fresh start.'

I was a little sad to have missed the month of festivities in September, where I knew there would have been bonfires and feasting and *doro wat,* chicken stew, but I was so excited to be on the familiar road from the airport to home. The yellow *meskel* flowers grew on the roadside almost the whole way to my house in Gondar. When the taxi pulled up I was excited and exhausted from the journey, but I knew I was home.

'Julieyea!' Our guard Mesfin threw open the gate and pumped my hand, repeating my name over and over. He leant his walking stick against the wall and, still shaking my hand, he pressed his right shoulder to mine in a show of affection. '*Dehna nesh*? How are you? Are you fine?'

'*Dehna*, I'm fine.'

'*Dehna nesh*? Are you fine?' he asked again, before I had a chance to ask him.

'*Dehna*, fine,' I said.

'*Beteseb, dehna nachew*? And your family, are they fine?'

'Yes, fine, thanks be to God,' I gave the standard Amharic reply.

Before I could ask him if he was fine, he asked again, '*Dehna nesh*? Are you fine?'

'*Dehna*. I'm fine. Are you fine?' I finally got to ask.

'*Dehna, dehna*, I'm fine, I'm fine. *Gebu, gebu*, enter, please!' With his free hand he carried my backpack from the taxi to the front door and his walking stick clunked on the cement.

I was alone in the house. From the email correspondence I'd had before my arrival, I knew Marieke was due to return from her two-month vacation later that evening, and Tadesse was at Kola Diba, a remote outstation clinic. It was late afternoon and a warm breeze swept through the house as I opened all the windows. From the back door I listened to the wind in the trees and watched the afternoon shadows lengthening across the mountain, turning the fields to green velvet beneath eagles gliding in the valley. I took a deep breath and wondered why I had wanted to be anywhere else.

A few minutes later I sat on three rats. As I sat to pee, the toilet lurched forwards and there was a terrible squealing. I looked down to see two tails whipping the floor from beneath the pedestal. Then a rat darted out from the hole where the pedestal had once met the floor. I jumped onto the edge of the bathtub, knickers around my ankles, shrieking and flapping my hands like a cartoon housewife. As I retrieved my underpants, I wished I hadn't skimmed the paragraph in the Lonely Planet guide about rat bite and bubonic plague. Did it say it was a myth and there was *no risk*? Or did it say it was *no myth* and it was high risk?

I shouted, I stamped my feet on the corner of the bath and clapped. The rodent lapped the bathroom three times before it scuttled back into the sanitary waste whence it came, but two tails remained under the pedestal. I detached the shower – the length of garden hose attached to the bath nozzle – and poked at the rodents, critically aware every shower from now on would expose us to mediaeval pathologies. The two tails whipped again but remained where they were.

I racked my mind for information about the bubonic plague; surely I'd seen a documentary or read about it in school. Rats always ran squealing from fire scenes. I edged around the corner of the bath, jumped out into the hallway, slammed the door and returned with three candles and a pack of matches. From the corner of the bathtub I leaned out, holding a lit candle to each tail until it flicked under the pedestal. The rats had either gone back to luxuriate in our septic tank, or they were turning around to regroup and come out again, this time teeth-first.

Although I considered setting the bathroom alight, I settled on gathering as many tea lights as we had. I scoured the kitchen for things to plug the triple-rat-sized hole with. The only items I didn't mind exposing to septic waste and the Black Death were a wad of plastic bags and some old sandals. Engrossed as I was in my anti-rodent activities, I didn't hear Marieke arrive. She walked in to find me squatting by a toilet lit by fifteen candles with a pair of sandals sticking out of a hole.

We ate our dinner with feet up on chairs, and I stuffed towels to block the gap beneath the bedroom door before I went to bed. I didn't sleep well, with the rustling and noises from the bathroom. The rats knocked over shampoo bottles and sent toiletries clattering to the floor. But in the morning, it was silent, and I discovered a rat-sized hole gnawed in the wooden bathroom shutters. My toes curled when I saw the miniature wood shavings on the windowsill as I imagined teeth that sharp doing the same to my feet bones.

My first day back at work was nerve-racking, as if it was my first day on the job. I met seven new *ferenjis* who had arrived while I was home for the last two months. Although my Japanese and Indian colleagues from last semester were still there, we had new physiotherapists too: one from Britain, one from Holland, and two new Indian physiotherapists. I wondered what it might be like to work with this new batch of strangers. Had I done the right thing in coming back?

I was also very nervous about meeting Tadesse again. While I'd been gone we had exchanged a few emails. First we corresponded through one of the other volunteers, because Tadesse didn't have his own email address, internet being fairly new to Gondar. So our conversations were sparse, vapid even. Just, *I miss working with you, hope to see you soon!* kind of emails.

Then Tadesse set up his own email account and we corresponded a little. But neither of us had written about the kiss, before I flew out. Had it been a mistake? Maybe on that rainy night we were swept up in the emotion of departure rather than feeling a real connection.

When I arrived at the office Tadesse sat with the other two physiotherapy assistants. They all shook my hand, and we went through the same elaborate set of questions:

'How are you?'

'How's your health?'

'How's your family?'

'How's your family's health?'

'How are you? Are you fine?'

'I'm fine. Are you fine?'

Tadesse greeted me just like the other three greeted me. Like them, he shook my hand and then we pulled in close on the diagonal to touch our shoulders, somewhere midway between a hug and a handshake. There was a small flip in my stomach when he leant in and I smelt his familiar scent. I felt afraid he might have had second thoughts about me. As a physiotherapist on staff, and him a physiotherapy assistant, I wasn't sure if there were any rules about us having a relationship. There were no departmental policies about such things that I knew of and didn't want to ask anyone about it, if I didn't know where we stood. Maybe I had imagined that there was a connection between us?

I tried to keep my nerves at bay and we smiled at each other.

'How is your house?' he asked me and I told him about the rats under the toilet bowl. He laughed his deep, resonant belly laugh, with his head back and mouth open, as if I was totally hilarious. Hearing his laugh again gave me butterflies.

He said, 'Ah Julieyea. You are home.'

He offered to come with me to the hospital maintenance department for rodent advice and we walked together under the scorching morning sun.

'Come at four this afternoon,' said the maintenance man.

'You'll definitely be here?' I asked.

The maintenance man said, 'All the time,' in Amharic and leaned back in his chair. He stretched his arms wide as if to emphasise his meaning, but he wasn't there when we returned at four. A chook eyed us from his chair instead.

I had a rush of the simultaneous delight and frustration of working in these conditions again. I thought back to the job I'd had for the two months at home. There would have never been a chook sitting on the maintenance man's office chair, and if he said come at 4 p.m., he would have been there.

'What do we do?' I asked Tadesse.

'We go to Piazza, to get some poison,' Tadesse said.

We waited for a minibus at the hospital gates, and I thought maybe Tadesse might bring up us, but he didn't then, or when we got off the minibus in Piazza and he led the way down small lanes. It sort of felt like a date, until we saw the wall of a shop bearing a sign in English that read *Parasite-acide Shop*, with a large flea beside it. Inside, Tadesse ordered *ye ayit medhanit*, medicine for the rat. The shopkeeper scooped out crystals from a tub into a scrap of paper torn out of a schoolbook. The afternoon shadows were long and the air was warm as we walked from the minibus, and it could have been a date. I wondered if Tadesse might have held my hand, if I wasn't carrying a fistful of poison in someone's spelling test.

Back in our bathroom, Tadesse crushed the crystals into fine powder with a steel bar we found in the garden. He made a funnel out of the homework paper and tapped the poison onto half a tomato. I used the other half to make a salad for the three of us. We ate our dinner with our feet on chairs and decided the best thing to do was get out of the house.

The nightclub, named Lambadina after a much-loved pop song, comprised one room, smaller than our lounge room, with mirrors along one wall, a mirror ball, a cement courtyard and a booming sound system. The nightclub was full to capacity, and when 'Lambadina' came on, the crowd went wild. At the chorus, they threw their hands in the air and the DJ turned the volume off to hear the masses sing. By the fifth time it was played, and by my fifth Dashen beer, I too was waving my hands and singing. I saw friends from around town I'd missed while I was away. The street kid who always sold chewing gum and cigarettes outside the club recognised me too, and I bought two extra packets of chewies.

Marieke, Tadesse and I walked arm in arm out of the club at 1 a.m., dodging some grazing cows on the hill towards home. It had been raining and the clouds had parted after the downpour so the sky was patchy with stars. The wet road reflected the streetlights and my shoes and socks were soaked by the time we got home.

Tadesse walked us safely to our gate. I wanted to invite him in for tea, but he said he had to get a taxi home to his compound out of town before the taxis stopped for the night. We knocked on the gate and our guard Mesfin opened it sleepily. Marieke headed inside to bed. Tadesse was standing close enough to me that I could smell his aftershave. The street was absolutely still, utterly silent, no cars and no-one else around. We stood so long without saying anything I began to be aware of my cold feet. Then I couldn't handle the silence anymore and started chattering, rambling on about dancing, zipping my coat closed and then opening it again. A smile toyed at the corners of Tadesse's mouth but he didn't say anything, mainly because he couldn't get a word in edgewise. He scratched his chin and when I paused for breath I could hear his stubble bristling under his fingers. Now? I thought. Now is he going to kiss me again?

Mesfin yawned loudly, and I looked over to see him leaning against the open gate, eyebrows raised as he tried to stay awake, looking expectantly to see if he could close the gate and go back to sleep.

Tadesse said, 'See you at work, Julie.' He squeezed my forearm tenderly, and I thought I saw an apologetic smile, but I took a deep breath and smiled down at the ground instead of returning his gaze. I was too nervous, hopeful and then ashamed he might see my cheeks burning and the disappointment on my face.

As I climbed into bed that night, I was still smarting from my foolish idea that something might have happened with Tadesse, after just one simple kiss. Now we had to work together for another year, so I would have to move on past that misunderstanding. But Tadesse wasn't my only reason for coming back. I was sure I would forget my humiliation soon, because another academic year stretched out in front of me, full of exciting professional challenges. I thought about tonight, of all the friends I'd reconnected with at the nightclub and how when we walked home we heard hyenas calling to each other in the hills outside town. I thought about how I couldn't wait to get started with work on Monday. As I drifted off I thought, truly, there was no other place I wanted to be.

One hour later, I could think of many other places I would like to be: anywhere out of earshot of the prayer chants from the three Orthodox churches nearby. That night's Ge'ez prayer chants started at 2.30 a.m., and it sounded like seven different priests standing outside my window bellowing prayers. They were still going at 5 a.m. when the muezzin at the local mosque cleared his throat into the loudspeaker and commenced the morning prayer broadcast, and four other muezzins at other mosques followed suit.

Lying in the dark amongst this multi-faith cacophony, I kept shifting, trying to sleep, but my mind raced and I was so angry at myself. How did I forget about Ge'ez? How many nights had I laid awake cursing the Ge'ez prayers, then feeling guilty for cursing the Ge'ez prayers, then asking God if he wouldn't mind not smiting me for cursing prayers (and if he also wouldn't mind asking them to keep it down a bit)? What was I thinking in coming back? I'd committed myself to a year of weekend aural torture with the promise of extra on midweek holy days.

Staying for another twelve months had seemed a good idea when I boarded the plane in Perth and an even better idea earlier that evening, waving my arms in a sweaty nightclub. Now a voice on loudspeaker in my head announced this as a stupid idea. It wasn't just the night-time interruptions. Another academic year stretched ahead, full of stupid professional challenges, not to mention the personal challenges of living another year in Gondar.

But what could I achieve, even if I was tough enough to stay for another whole year? I had made the decision to come back, and in signing the one-year contract with the university, I'd made my own bed, and now I had to sleep in it, or lie awake seething in it. I had to make my time here worthwhile.

We sent our guard Mesfin to the market to buy cement for the hole in the toilet. He returned on a horse-and-cart taxi just as the hospital maintenance man arrived.

I opened the gate for him as he paid the driver.

'*Wuyi*! *Kebad new*! Oh my! It's heavy!' Mesfin whacked the cement bag onto the ground. I heard the creaking cart and horse hooves recede. The afternoon had gotten cooler since a downpour, but sweat dripped off Mesfin's brow and made splotches on the back of his t-shirt.

He spoke too fast for me to understand it all. I gathered snippets – sorry he was late, the market was really full and heaps of people were there and it was difficult to get the cement and sorry he took so long and there were many, many, many horses and carts and many, many, many people from the countryside, and it was *heavy*! His eyes bulged and he leaned on his walking stick and waved his other arm around for emphasis.

I said, '*Manem chigger yellem*! No problem!'

That was the same thing the hospital maintenance man said when I demonstrated how our toilet wobbled.

The maintenance man was a fit-looking, fortyish man strong enough to lift our toilet pedestal right into the air. He lifted it to indicate the source of the rats and to demonstrate it no longer connected to the floor – beneath it there was a cement hole in the middle of the floor, which is what most houses in Gondar had for a loo.

'*Eshi*. Okay.' I didn't know what else to say.

'*Manem chigger yellem*, no problem.' He replaced the pedestal with a genial air as if it was his pleasure to be lifting toilets up and down for the benefit of foreigners. He went outside without saying anything, and I followed. The last few drops of the afternoon downpour spotted his back as he mixed a cement paste in the mud. Cement plopped from his trowel onto the hallway floor on his way from the street into the bathroom. He trowelled the cement onto the pedestal, then walked back into the street again to top up. After many visits from bathroom to street he dusted his hands on his trousers, and announced, '*Cheresk*. Finished.'

In the bathroom, a volcano of cement plastered the pedestal to the floor and dollops of wet cement dotted the bathroom.

I was grateful for his labour but appalled at the results. Not knowing the word for 'tidy', I asked him in Amharic, 'Can you make it beautiful?'

He looked surprised. Instead of answering me, he looked around the spacious bathroom. I felt embarrassed then, in my huge *ferenji* house with five rooms for just two girls, with its sit-down toilet and bathtub with hot water. I wondered if he thought it was already beautiful enough. As a government employee, the maintenance man could likely not afford more than one or two rooms for his family, with a cold shower and a cement hole in the bathroom floor. He cleaned the splats of cement with less vigour than he had made them, but when I gave him the two hundred birr (forty dollars) unofficial 'out-of-hours fee', his enthusiasm returned. As he folded the green notes into his wallet he looked chirpy and said in Amharic, 'Don't sit on the toilet for two days.'

Later that evening, from the unique vantage point afforded while using, but not sitting upon, the toilet, I spotted a poisoned rat. The dead body was wedged between two of the huge jerry cans we kept filled with emergency drinking water. When I levered the dustpan underneath the corpse, maggots spilled out.

Holding it at a distance from my body, I handed the dustpan to Mesfin.

'*Wede koshasha*? In the rubbish please?' I thought he might take it to the rubbish collection point where he took our household garbage. I attempted to warn him, 'Careful, it's got maggots,' but what I said translated to, 'Caution, the child of the mosquito is within.'

'*Manem chigger yellem*, Julieyea, no problem.' Mesfin opened the red gate, flung the rat into the street and briskly pulled the gate shut. '*Cheresk*! Finished!' His smile had a fraternal radiance as he handed back the dustpan.

With the vermin no longer in evidence, we relaxed. That evening, Marieke and I had settled with a book each in the lounge room when the lights flared, the electricity surge protector whirred, and it went dark. Outside, rain began pelting down.

Neither of us was fazed. I fetched the candles from beside the toilet, and soon we were both comfortable again. Curled up with a candle to read by, I looked over at Marieke with her candle and book. Listening to the downpour on the tin roof, I realised I couldn't be happier.

I felt excited once more about my work, about seeing Selam in her wheelchair at the orphanage tomorrow and about supervising the students on their clinical placements. Since I had returned, Marieke and I had overcome the Black Death and arranged for a toilet that could soon be sat upon. Furthermore, we had lights that were bound to illuminate any moment, and a whole lot of hope.

I enjoyed the minibus ride to the orphanage the next morning. The van wound higher into the hills outside Gondar, where the green fields were lush after months of the wet season. *Meskel* flowers lined the roadside and grew across meadows in swathes of yellow.

The final-year student Henok waited for me at the big blue metal gates to the orphanage. He was slightly built, not very tall, with thick glasses and a neat short haircut. He beamed at me and pumped my hand as he asked, '*Dehna nesh*? Are you fine?'

When we got to the small children's ward, the four little girls playing on the mat scampered inside to retrieve four other children. I was delighted to see they all recognised me and came running for handshakes and hellos. I tried the *are you fine/I'm fine etc. etc.* but I couldn't quite get it right. Perhaps it was only an adult convention. The children seemed oblivious and just pressed me for hugs and handshakes as always. They were fine, and so was I.

But someone was missing. '*Lejoch, Selam yet allech*? Hey kids, where is Selam?' I asked.

Everyone spoke at once, with much arm-waving, nodding and pointing. The tallest child ran for Sister Deepti, the head nun.

Sister Deepti squished me in a hug and welcomed me back to Gondar. She said, 'Selam's grandmother was coming for her. But don't worry, we've kept your equipment safe.'

She beckoned us to a door marked 'storeroom'. She fished deep in her apron pocket for a ring of keys, jiggled the lock and shouldered the door open. Stepping back, she showed me Selam's red wheelchair and the black wheelchair insert made to fit the little girl's measurements.

Horrified, I said, 'Why didn't her granny take her wheelchair?'

'Oh no! Wheelchair is belonging to the sisters' home. It's not allowed to be giving it away. We must save that for the other disabled childrens.'

'But what about the black seat? Couldn't you give that to her granny?'

Sister Deepti leaned on the doorframe. 'She didn't want it. You know, these people ... they go by walking. She had Selam here,' Sister Deepti turned and mimed tying a child to her back. 'She couldn't carry Selam and the seat also.'

'Can we find her granny's home and send the insert?'

'No dear, these people are begging people. They will be going around the countryside, this way and that. It's impossible to be finding her.'

She must have seen my appalled look because she gave my shoulder a consoling pat, and said, 'Never mind, dear, we'll save it for another child.'

I didn't have the energy to explain it was custom-made, especially for Selam and her needs. It was too late now.

Henok carried another patient over for physio, and we discussed a treatment plan. Meanwhile the small children lined the edge of the mat, sitting in a line with legs outstretched, chiming '*Eski*! *Yichilal*! *Gobez*! Look! You can do it! Clever!' to our new patient.

Henok started therapy with the boy, but I found it hard to concentrate. While I was disappointed that Selam didn't use her seat for very long, I was excited for her. I assumed that being collected from an orphanage by a family member was every orphan's dream. But by the time Henok had finished the exercises and was onto passive stretches for the boy's legs, I felt sad. I thought about Selam's pressure sores and wished I could have showed her grandma how to do stretches and clean her skin to prevent the wounds deteriorating. I wished we had given Selam her very own wheelchair so she didn't need to be carried.

But Selam was gone and the new patients and their little friends giggling at Henok's jokes reminded me of the present and the future.

Monday would be exciting. It was the first day of placement for the second-years. I was looking forward to seeing my students again, graduated from first year and now ready for their first clinical placement.

I met the pair of students I would be supervising this semester. They were waiting outside the entrance to the paediatrics ward. Martha, short and slight, with dark lashes fringing her eyes, was one of the few females in the course. My other student was Solomon, who was so tall he towered above Martha, but smiled nervously from her to me. Both shook my hand, pressed their right shoulder to mine and asked me if I was fine, if my journey was fine, if my family was fine. This time I got all the right fines in all the right places.

We went inside to see our first patient for the day, and the first patient of their careers.

The paediatric ward was completely full and our patient was lying on a foam mat between two beds, like the fifteen other patients interspersed between the beds and cots and along the centre of the ward. The parents of the children in beds and cots had metal stools to sit on, but there was nowhere to sit for the caregivers of the kids on the mats. To get to our patient, we stepped over the outstretched legs of grannies, mothers and fathers, sitting on the floor, leaning against the wall. They were all from the countryside. The grannies and mums wore the same style of modest, ankle-length polyester frocks in varying shades of floral, while the fathers wore variations on the blue or khaki safari suit jacket with shorts. Only a few of the patients wore shoes, while the others had dried mud caked over their feet and spattered on their shins. We were still at the tail end of the wet season so getting to the hospital would have meant many hours of walking on muddy roads. The smell on the ward was particularly difficult to deal with today, with all our patients from the countryside, and lots of babies. The air was thick with the smell of unwashed bodies and clothes, curdled hair butter and, because there were so many babies and toddlers, the smell of milk and baby puke.

Our patient was a little boy with malnutrition and cerebral palsy. As we approached his mat, I saw the father holding the boy upright under his armpits, dangling his son's emaciated legs over the foam, trying to make him stand or take steps. The little boy's head was too big for his body; he only just managed to hold it upright. His thin arms dangled over his father's elbows.

When we arrived, the father laid the child on his back on the foam and the students took turns asking questions, practising the first of their clinical skills.

The little boy, whose father informed us was named Caleb, lay on his back, looking up at Martha as she asked questions. His big brown eyes held no fear, just curiosity. He had a small round face with skin that looked as if he'd never been outside. All his features were small – little eyes, a button nose and a little mouth. He wore the usual hairdo for countryside babies, a shaved head save for a round tuft at his forehead. I guessed his father was in his early twenties. His hair sat in big loose curls and his beard was patchy.

Caleb was four, the father told the students. Never having learnt to walk, he had spent his whole life lying on his back. He rarely lay on his tummy and couldn't sit up without support. Martha continued taking the social history – the boy's mother had died two years ago. They had a plot of land they grew crops on. It didn't yield much, but only needed to feed the two of them because they didn't have any other family. Martha pointed to the tiny leather pouch between two seashells tied on a piece of string around Caleb's little neck. 'Do you see these?' she asked.

I nodded. 'It's for local magic, isn't it?'

Martha nodded and continued with the social history from the father. 'He says he has been to many local faith healers to help his son walk. But he realised local magic was taking too long, so he brought his son to hospital.'

'How far is his home?'

'Two days by walking,' Martha said.

Caleb's father wore no socks, with the same faux shoes most of the countryside people wore. They were thin plastic shoes that looked as if they were cast in a mould, with pretend moulded seams and soles. A pair sold in the market for about two dollars. His father had no laces, just a scrap of string on each foot holding the top two lace holes together. Just like all the other shoes on the legs outstretched from mats, his shoes were encrusted in dried mud.

Less than two weeks before, I had driven into Perth city to buy hiking shoes on special for eighty-five dollars. They were good quality, which was important, as without supportive shoes I got a sore back. Like all good physiotherapists, I advised patients to choose shoes with sufficient arch support and shock absorption at the heel. I wondered if Caleb's father got back pain, carrying a child for two days wearing the world's cheapest shoes.

When Martha removed Caleb's shirt to assess his posture and muscle tone, we saw that the child's belly was distended and the delicate skin sank in between his ribs. He didn't wear trousers or a nappy, just a shirt that was long enough to be a dress.

Martha carried out a full physiotherapy assessment and when she dressed Caleb again afterwards she said, 'This shirt is very dirty.' She pointed to the milk stains and the crusted urine. 'Do you have another one?'

The father pulled a grain sack from beneath the foam mattress and took out another shirt. It was an exact miniature of his own blue drill safari shirt with white stitches. Almost all the farmers from this region wore these safari shirts. I'd seen tailors in the market stitching these on treadle sewing machines, but I'd never seen a miniature version before, let alone father and son in a matching outfit.

Martha slipped it over Caleb's head and showed the boy's father how to do an exercise to stimulate movement in Caleb's legs.

'Now you try,' she told him in Amharic. He was unsteady at first but soon got the hang of it.

'Do this one ten times,' she said to him and sat back to let the father start the exercise. The father did the exercise three times, but after counting to three he trailed off and gave an imploring look to Martha.

'*Arat ... amist ...* Four ... five ...' she prompted, and together they counted to ten as the father bent and straightened Caleb's legs.

'*Yikerta, wede temheret bet alhedkum.* Excuse me, I didn't go to school,' the father said.

'*Manem chigger yellem.* No problem,' Martha said.

We discussed Caleb's treatment plan as we squatted in a circle around the foam mat.

'What is his prognosis?' Solomon asked me, and I put the question back to the two students.

'I think he has potential to improve with therapy.' Martha used her pen to scratch between her braids.

'I'll give you five minutes to discuss a treatment plan,' I said.

While they discussed, the father tickled Caleb under his chin with a *meskel* flower, leaving dots of yellow pollen on the boy's chin. Caleb giggled and his father snatched the flower away. He hid it behind his back and slowly brought it out to tease Caleb with it again. The other parents, from their bedside stools or from their foam mats, looked on with seeming disdain, or maybe trepidation, as they observed the boy's disability, but the father remained oblivious and leant in close to tickle the little boy's dotted chin. *Meskel* flowers didn't grow on the hospital grounds; the closest spot they grew was near the sisters' orphanage, over five kilometres out of town. The boy's father must have picked and carried it, along with his son and their belongings in the grain sack.

The day before when we'd visited the orphanage, there had been two new boys with disabilities. One had been left at the gate, the other found in the street. In the countryside, people had such little knowledge about disabilities, and there was such stigma attached to a child with a disability, it often meant ostracism for the family. Yet here was this dad, unconcerned by the stares from the other parents, sharing a moment of joy over a *meskel* flower with his son.

The students devised a treatment plan, and I demonstrated correct handling at the trunk and hips for Caleb. With my hands tight around his pelvis giving him the right stability, the boy was able to take four light steps. It wasn't functional walking, but they were proper steps and it was promising to see such an increase in movement with therapeutic handling. It was both wonderful yet sad to see his potential in the first session. His development would be much further advanced if he'd had therapy long ago. Caleb wasn't concerned though, he took four more steps on the floor beside his bed-mat.

Both the students clapped. Caleb plonked himself onto Solomon's knee uninvited, and Solomon supported him to sit upright with little legs bent. The child looked up at us, and it was the first time we had seen him smile. He'd been cute before, but he was picture-book adorable when his lips curled back to reveal button teeth and his eyes crinkled. Martha cheered and Caleb turned to give a magnanimous smile for each of the students.

The father beamed and leaned forwards to slide the stem of the *meskel* flower, the symbol of a fresh start, into the little boy's hand, saying, '*Inde*. That's it.'

Chapter 18

I like it: ደስይላል /*des yilal*/

As the weeks rolled on, I got brave enough with my Amharic to go onto the wards alone. One afternoon Caleb's father saw me approach and started shaking his son awake.

'*Ayasfalligum*. Not necessary,' I said.

'*Esporte*? Exercises?' his father asked.

'*Awe*. Yes,' I could say in Amharic 'it's time to do exercises', but I couldn't say 'Don't wake him, I'll come back'. I reached down to stop him waking the child, but he shook his head with an amicable expression, saying, '*Manem chigger yellem*. No problem.'

Caleb wasn't as easygoing. He screamed and kicked as soon as he'd opened his eyes. He was still yelling and twisting when his father scooped him from the mat and cradled him like a baby. However by the time we were halfway to the therapy room, Caleb was calm and bestowing toothy grins upon passersby. His thin arms and legs bounced up and down with each of his father's steps.

Two young mothers stopped to greet Caleb's father.

'Lovely child,' one of the mothers said in Amharic, and tweaked Caleb under the chin. He raised his chin a little higher and beamed at her. This was such a difference from his arrival when the mothers on the ward were cautious and fearful of his disability.

On the mat in the therapy room, he rolled himself independently from stomach to back and held himself upright when I sat him on the smallest therapy ball we had. This was a huge improvement in just three weeks; he was making great progress. Although he was four, he was only as tall as my friend's eighteen-month-old son in Perth. But since being admitted, he had gained half a kilo with a steady diet of the high-nutrient paste Plumpy'Nut. He was now eight kilograms, about the weight of a healthy four-month-old in Australia.

I sat with my legs crossed and positioned him in front. With a great flourish, I pulled a green balloon from my pocket. Caleb stared at it and looked up at me as if waiting for the punchline.

'*Foonya*! A balloon!' His father demonstrated the level of excitement appropriate to balloons, and Caleb giggled.

I inflated the balloon and held it out to the side.

'*Wede ezzi*, this way.' I tipped Caleb to lean out to the balloon. He touched it with his tiny fingertips and straightened up again. His balance had improved so much. If we'd attempted that a few weeks ago, he would have fallen over.

'*Ezzi*. This one,' I tapped his other arm, which hung at his side. We tried it again and this time Caleb lifted both arms out to hold the balloon.

When his father said '*Gobez lej*! Clever boy!' Caleb looked at me to see if I agreed, and I nodded. He chuckled, his lips curling up to reveal his milk teeth, and his cheeks bunched.

His dad scratched the balloon to make a noise. Caleb looked up at his dad, then lifted his hand and banged the balloon to make a noise as well. For four years, Caleb had demonstrated almost no purposeful movement because he'd never had the right physical support. But now he demonstrated that he understood cause and effect, and could participate in a game. He had a lot more potential for independence than it had first appeared.

When therapy finished, his father carried him back through the garden to the ward, supporting his head with his hands, while Caleb conferred smiles from behind a green balloon on everyone we passed.

That afternoon while treating another patient in the ward, I watched as Caleb's father sat cross-legged on their foam mat bed. He propped Caleb in the crook of his legs, let the boy lean against his chest and held the balloon out for Caleb to reach for, exactly as we had in the therapy room. With his dad doing their own therapy, and good nutrition from the Plumpy'Nut nutrient paste, Caleb had the chance to make great progress.

One day, in the first week of November, everyone on the staff bus went silent when the morning news came on the radio. Then in the tearoom at work when the news played, staff stopped talking and craned their ears toward the radio. I couldn't understand the broadcast but staff shook their heads and any gaiety in the tearoom vanished.

'What's going on?' I asked an X-ray technician drinking a macchiato next to me.

'*Chigger allew*. Trouble,' was all he said.

That afternoon Mesfin called to me when he returned from the market.

'Julieyea!' He hobbled to the open lounge-room window and gesticulated with both hands, including the one holding a transistor radio. He waved it up and down, and from amongst his rapid-fire Amharic I worked out something about batteries not working ... about how it cost twenty birr for new batteries.

I rummaged in our odds-and-ends box and returned with two batteries. Leaning on the windowsill, I put the new batteries in, and we switched it on just in time for the news.

We listened together to the Amharic news bulletin although it was too fast for me to understand anything except 'Welcome to the news' and the word *motewal*. Died.

'*Motewal*? Died?' I asked Mesfin.

'*Ayzosh*, Julieyea. Relax,' Mesfin said. '*Hulet sewoch bicha.*

Polise. Only two people. Policemen.' He mimed shooting into the air and said, '*Manem chigger yellem, manem chigger yellem.* No problem, no problem.'

I knew from Tadesse that yesterday there had been protests in Addis Ababa, as the government still had not announced the results of the election six months after the event, and the opposition leaders were still in jail. Activists in Addis Ababa yesterday began a 'honk if you're unhappy' protest and the government responded by arresting anyone who honked, and the activists as well. Then the opposition party called for peaceful protests and stay-at-home strikes.

Tadesse phoned, but was calm as he told me, 'My friend just called from Addis Ababa. People are rioting in the streets about the election. People are saying crazy things. They are saying maybe a thousand people are shot, maybe war will start again.'

That sort of thing just didn't seem possible on this sunny afternoon, especially after the opposition had called for peaceful protest. I unplugged the cord from the back of the phone and plugged it into my laptop. The dial-up connection was extra slow; I assumed those with internet connections all over the country were also seeking information. I tried every ten minutes for two hours until I got online. I finally found a BBC report that police opened fire on the crowd during political protests and fifty people were shot during political protests. Another article described how tensions with Eritrea were flaring again, and each side was rebuilding their military presence along the border, where the war had finished only five years earlier. But it didn't mention active conflict so it seemed like stories were being exaggerated as they were retold. Fifty people shot was better than one thousand, but still terrible news. I remembered the refugee rights political protests I'd been to in Australia, exercising my democratic right as a civilian of a democracy. A number of us had been arrested at one protest, and spent the night in the lock-up. We felt the police were heavy-handed but at least we didn't need to worry our government might order them to start shooting us.

The next morning, I started to worry when I walked towards the main road and saw the doors to the Hip Hop barber shop were padlocked shut. Weekends, holidays, festivals, football, rain or shine, those hip-hop barbers were stylin' locals under maximum decibels from 7.30 a.m. But today the shop was silent and a ute idled in front of it while soldiers climbed on. They wore the blue camouflage of the federal militia and had bigger guns than those of the usual army. When it was full, the ute sped down the route I normally walked to work, past Fasiledes High School. I crossed the road to take an alternative road but there, in front of the fruit shop, the bread shop and the tape shop, stood men in the same blue uniforms, with legs planted wide, firearms poised.

My first instinct was to sprint, but I wondered if bursting into a run in front of militia would earn me a burst of munitions. So instead, I power-walked, well aware of its limitations as a means of escape. I didn't stop until my legs burnt and my face scorched and I was safe inside the hospital grounds.

Caleb's father had already brought him to the therapy room, and Caleb greeted me with his toothy grin. Glad for the distraction, I sat with him on the floor. Tadesse sat on a small stool in front of his patient doing leg exercises on the other treatment plinth. His patient looked much wealthier than our usual clientele. She appeared to be in her mid-thirties, with a plump face, well-moisturised skin and heavy perfume. Her spotless camel-coloured high heels sat side by side beneath the plinth. While she bent and straightened her injured leg, I inflated a purple balloon for Caleb to practise reaching. As Caleb reached up to bang the balloon, giggling at his newfound skill, the lady looked across and encouraged him, saying, '*Gobez, des yilal.* Clever, I like it.'

A mobile phone rang from inside a beige blazer hanging over the back of a chair. Tadesse passed the blazer to the lady, whose face dropped once the call started.

'*Ara*? What?' She snapped the phone shut and said, 'Excuse me,' in English, standing so fast Tadesse had to duck out of her way. 'I must go. I need to collect my children from the school.' She ran out the door, clutching her handbag against her chest, scuffing her feet into her high heels, with only one arm in her blazer.

I held the balloon out for Caleb again and he giggled. Then the gunshots started. First I heard the distant pop-pop-pop of a Kalashnikov and a deeper, more resonant boom from bigger and more powerful guns. Then distant shouting and screaming began.

The purple balloon in my hand looked ridiculously festive. I had no idea what to do. Stop working? Keep working? I looked into Caleb's father's face, but he looked impassive and I couldn't read his expression.

Tadesse's mobile rang. He took the call in a low voice then put the mobile back in his pocket.

'*Yet new*? Where is it?' Caleb's father asked, his forehead crinkling.

'Fasiledes School,' Tadesse said to Caleb's father in Amharic and then, to me, 'The young men are protesting there.'

Tadesse stood up and turned on the tape player. He turned the volume knob as high as it would go, so it drowned out some of the shots. The tape was awful synthesiser pop the students played so often I had fantasised taking to it with a mallet, but right then, I loved it. When the tape reached the end of the side, the gunshots had stopped and the silence was strange.

'Do we go home?' I asked.

'Hospital is the safest place,' Tadesse said.

Caleb's dad carried him back to the ward. I watched from the door to the therapy room as patients started arriving for X-ray next door. Two boys in school uniform, one with a bandaged head and the other with blood on his shirt, walked with arms around each other's shoulders.

Tadesse ran outside to speak to them and came back to report, 'No-one died. Just the soldiers were shooting in the air. The boys got hit with rocks.'

I was so relieved that, when more of the boys arrived with bloodstained school shirts, I didn't feel as sick as I might have done.

At 11.30 a.m. the hospital administration sent everyone home and we walked in a large group. Outside Fasiledes High School, the ground was covered in the rocks the demonstrators had thrown at the soldiers with semi-automatic weapons. Anxious parents huddled outside, waiting for their children to come out while soldiers stood to attention with guns trained on the school buildings.

The next day I went onto the ward with Henok, the final-year student. This time Caleb's father didn't shake the sleeping boy when we approached; instead he said, '*Metenyat*, sleeping.'

Caleb's little chest rose and fell with each breath, and sweat beaded on his forehead. The neckline of his safari shirt was soaked. Henok collected the medical notes from the nurses station, and together we checked the daily observation chart. His temperature had been climbing overnight and had soared that morning. He had deteriorated so quickly; yesterday he was fine and today, when I gently shook his shoulder, he remained limp. I twisted around, scanning the ward for Doctor Tesfaye, or any doctor, but the ward was empty of other professionals. The other parents in the adjacent beds peered in at us.

'*Menden new*? What is it?' his father asked.

'*Tekusat*. Fever,' Henok replied. He also looked across the ward. 'There is no doctor.' He pushed his glasses back up onto the brim of his nose and ran his hand over his hair as if that might help him think.

'*Endezzih*, like this.' Henok demonstrated to the father how to tip drinking water from his bottle onto a cloth and place it across Caleb's forehead. It would do little more than make him comfortable until we found a doctor.

Within a day of the riots at Fasiledes School, it seemed there were soldiers everywhere. On every corner there were gunmen in fatigues, standing sentry in Piazza, along the main roads, even strolling around the hospital grounds. Sometimes they were patrolling, but other times chatting, or lounging, but always with their AK-47s in hand.

In the furthest corner of the outdoor tearoom at work, where no-one could overhear, Tadesse and two of his friends, lecturers from other departments, talked in hushed tones.

They talked about their contacts at other universities, how students all over the country were protesting the election results; how there were protests across every major town, some villages and some pockets of very active resistance in Addis Ababa.

They told me the government was doing its best to shut it down.

'But how?' I asked.

'Didn't you hear last night?' one of the lecturers said.

'I heard many cars stopping. Many house gates opening and closing. What was that?'

'*Mengist*. Government.' The lecturers looked at each other.

'It's the army,' Tadesse said.

'What are they looking for?'

'Opposition,' Tadesse said and the two other staff members laughed wryly. 'I heard them beating on doors too. Putting people into cars. Now it's time to sleep in the mother's house.'

I had met his mum many times, when Tadesse had invited me and Marieke to lunch and coffee ceremonies at his house. His mum was short and round, with warm, double-clasp handshakes and an insistence we eat more *injera* and don't forget our umbrellas. I asked how his mum, as lovely as she was, would protect him from the militia.

'They'll think I'm a nice boy. They are only looking for groups of young men together. Like a political threat.' He added the last bit as an afterthought.

'What evidence do they need to decide if someone is a political threat?' I asked.

'Ah *ferenji*!' the staff laughed at me, in friendly derision.

'No evidence is needed! They are the army, they decide,' said one of Tadesse's friends.

'Can their families try to get them out of prison?'

'Prison?' he said. 'They don't take them to prison. The families don't know where they go.'

I was immediately worried about Tadesse. He was very outspoken politically and he'd made his alignment with the opposition very clear.

'*Ayzosh*!' Tadesse said. Maybe my face betrayed me. He patted my knee as he got up. 'They think I am a nice one.'

So when I woke at 3 a.m. that night, Tadesse was the first thing on my mind. Something had woken me but I couldn't work out what it was. After a few minutes of silence, the gunshots started again. Then more shots, and more frequently.

My mind raced to our lunchtime conversation – what if it was the militia? What if they had come for Tadesse and his friends?

I heard three decisive shots as if they all came from the same gun. A single siren started up and wailed through the streets.

All I could think was: Tadesse, *call me*.

I curled in a foetal position in my bed and with each shot tried to curl tighter, as if that would somehow protect me.

The phone in the lounge room rang and I ran to it so fast I banged my hip on the table and stubbed my toe.

'Julie. *Ayzosh*.' It was Tadesse. Marieke appeared in the doorway, bleary-eyed. 'There is shooting at the university. The soldiers are everywhere, to close the firing on the university dorm. But I am safe.'

I felt so sick with relief that I couldn't listen properly to what he was saying. All I heard was *soldiers*, *students* and *firing*. The soldiers were shooting at our beautiful students. I went back to bed.

'Our Father, who art in Heaven ...' With the light on, I prayed the rosary. I counted out the Lord's Prayer and the Hail Marys on my ten fingers and then went back to the start again. I tried not to think of anything else except the words, with their order and rhythm that was as familiar to me as the alphabet, while outside gunshots continued.

I woke up to a silent dawn with the light still on.

No minibuses were running the next morning but everything else on our walk to work seemed the same as always. Marieke and I walked without speaking on our usual route over stepping stones across the river, while some cows splashed past; up the embankment, past a boy beating cotton, around kids playing soccer and out onto the main road with the green patchwork hills in the distance. How could things still look the same after last night?

But at the university, everything was clearly not the same. There were even more militia than before, blue fatigues of the federal police, green fatigues of the military, khaki of the local police and green coats of some extra forces I'd never seen before. We found two of our second-year students and I ran, relieved, to ask if they were okay. What had happened last night?

One of the students said, 'There was firing in the dormitory. The soldiers were shooting into the air. They were keeping back the students who were panicking and rushing in to get their things.'

Suddenly I remembered last time, when students had burst into a practical exam, mixing up 'fire' with firing'. It seemed to be that 'fire burning' in Amharic translated to 'firing' in English.

As the students led us to the smouldering dorms, with

twisted metal bunks and curled doors hanging off doorframes, I felt such a massive wave of relief that it bordered on joy. Then I immediately felt guilty, and then embarrassed about my melodramatic nightlong prayer vigil. I hoped God would put those surplus prayers to good use where He saw fit.

I was impatient to see Tadesse in the office, to check if he was okay, if any of the militia visited his house in the chaos of the fire. But none of the physiotherapy assistants turned up to work. Only one of the others stopped in at the office to say he would be at a political meeting today instead. I tried phoning Tadesse's mobile to see if he was at the meeting too, but the mobile network was down all morning.

In the afternoon I checked in on Caleb, who was even worse. He was lying on his back, his thin legs splayed out beneath his long shirt. His chart showed his temperature was 39.5 degrees. Although the doctors had put him on antibiotics last night, phlegm rattled in his chest with every breath, and his face was pale. Henok and I discussed a treatment plan.

'What do you recommend?' I asked Henok.

'He needs to lie on his stomach, to reduce risk of chest infection; the secretions can collect at the posterior of his lungs.'

Henok and I squatted beside the mat and went to reposition Caleb to lie on his stomach with arms out in front.

His father, also squatting by the mat, lurched at us saying, '*Ara*! *Merefie allew*! Careful, he has a needle!' The father pointed to the cannula needle poking into the back of Caleb's hand.

While we reassured him, and gently repositioned the unresponsive boy, the father hovered behind us. He clutched both hands to his head, and I felt the weight of responsibility for this young man with no family at all except for his sick child.

I ran into one of the physio assistants outside the hospital on my way home from work. He was waiting for a minibus, and I casually enquired who else was at his political meeting. Had the other assistants been there?

'No, simply myself from department,' he said, just as a minibus swung in and the waiting crowd surged for the opening door. He looked regretful to cut the conversation short as he elbowed his way through the other waiting passengers for a spot on the minibus. 'See you tomorrow!' he called as he climbed in.

At home I tried phoning Tadesse again numerous times but each time I got the infuriating automated message, '*Yikerta, netework yellem*, sorry, there is no network.' With Marieke out of the house at volleyball training, I was alone with my fears. It was almost dark when there was a knock on the front door and on seeing Tadesse I burst into tears.

'I thought something happened to you!' I said and suddenly we were kissing, arms tight around each other.

I wiped my tears with my palms. Then I sank against his big chest, letting my face rest against his huge cotton hoodie that smelt like washing powder, loving the smell of his sweat under it. Loving that he was *here*.

His whiskers prickled against the top of my head. I left patches of tears on his hoodie and when he pulled back to look at me, I felt my nose running so I had to swipe at it with my sleeve.

'I heard you weren't at the political meeting in town, and I couldn't stop worrying!'

Tadesse said, 'No, I always go to political meeting at my village, Chechela. It's very active compared to town. I tried calling but *netework yellem*. No network. Why were you worrying so much about me?'

'Because ... because ...'

'Ah Julieyea,' he smiled, as he held me even tighter. 'Why we didn't ...'

Neither of us managed to finish our sentences but maybe we didn't need to.

'We wasted so much time,' I said, and we kissed again.

Henok and I checked on Caleb every day. The chart at the front of the yellow cardboard medical file showed his temperature rising. His weight went from eight kilograms to seven, then from seven to 6.6. He was losing all the weight he had gained from the Plumpy'Nut paste. Every day we visited him I expected to find him better, but instead we found him motionless on the foam mat, his sheet dampened with his sweat. His breath was rasping and although his eyes were open, he was too unwell to move even if I slipped my little finger into his hand.

'*Ayzosh*. It will be okay,' Henok said to the father each day as we left Caleb's bedside.

'*Nege emetalehu*. Tomorrow we'll return,' I said to his dad, each day, as some kind of encouragement.

But there was no improvement, even a week after his fever started. Rancid milk stains covered the front of Caleb's indigo safari shirt and sweat had hardened the fabric. Milky spew had crusted onto the corner of his mouth. He still rasped breaths and still stared past us into nothing.

Henok explained to the father he needed to clean Caleb up. His father's face showed intense concentration, and he nodded with each of Henok's points.

The mothers of the other children in the beds surrounding all pitched in.

'Clean the milk off ...'

'Change his clothes ...'

'Wash his sheets ...' they all contributed, repeating what Henok said, while appearing to do nothing about the milk stains, the clothes or sheets of their own children.

That afternoon I walked home from work with Tadesse and Doctor Tesfaye from the paediatrics ward.

'How did Caleb get so sick?' I asked Doctor Tesfaye.

'Did you see the cannula in his arm? The intern on the ward put it in, like for all the patients, but this time it had got infected. You can see the ward is not a sterile environment.' Dr Tesfaye's tone was gentle, but clinically detached.

I asked Doctor Tesfaye why the families didn't bathe their kids or wash their sheets.

'These are countryside people, they are not educated. They don't have running water in their homes so washing is not their habit. Plus there are not enough sheets in the hospital for everyone. We have no budget for hygiene.'

This seemed illogical. Couldn't the hospital budget stretch to just a few more sheets? We sometimes had running water in the basins on the paediatric ward. There were squat toilets but no showers or baths. But there was a tap outside which, at the very least, people could use to sponge down their children's faces or feet.

'Do lots of kids get this type of infection?' I asked and Doctor Tesfaye and Tadesse looked at each other.

'Many,' Doctor Tesfaye said.

'His fever is getting worse every time we see him. Do you think he might die?' I asked.

'It's a possibility.' Doctor Tesfaye said it gently, tilting his head and chewing his bottom lip. Then he looked away, straight to the green mountains ahead. 'It's happened before.'

We walked on in silence, past the basketball courts where kids shot hoops, to where the road forked. Four troop carriers groaned past us on the road out of town. The troop carrier was so old and so full we kept pace with it as it dropped a gear to get up the hill.

I looked inside the open end of the troop carrier. The troops were all young and thin, with identical shaved haircuts. They swayed as the truck moved and the barrels of their rifles knocked against their knees. The next troop carrier was also full of recruits who looked little older than eighteen.

Dr Tesfaye said, 'Did you see, Julie? The government is sending more troops in case Eritrea invades.'

'Protecting us, inside and outside. From Eritrea and from

Addis,' Tadesse said, and Tesfaye laughed as if this was a stand-up comedy gig.

I wasn't sure if I was supposed to laugh too, but instead craned my neck to follow the trucks with their teenage cargo heading off to someone else's war. It seemed crazy that the government had enough money to spend on war, but not on running water, hospital sheets or a bottle of Domestos.

We visited Caleb daily but his fever remained constant for two weeks. Then one morning in mid-November I went to the ward and saw Caleb's father sitting cross-legged with Caleb, awake, propped upright in the crook of his legs.

I beamed at him, and drew a deep breath of relief, and said, '*Des yilal*! I like it!'

The little boy gave me a wan smile and lifted his arm just a little.

The next day Tadesse brought him to the therapy room, and together we took measurements to make a corner seat to fit him, for his father to take home. We sat him in the sample corner chair we kept in the department. It was a simple and effective piece of equipment made from three pieces of wood that allowed a child to develop the skills to sit without falling over. It sat flat on the ground, with no legs, and its two sides met perpendicular at the back, giving the same effect as sitting in a corner, using the walls to stay upright.

Propped up straight in his corner chair, Caleb granted smiles to anyone who made eye contact with him. They were nothing like his toothy grins from before, but he seemed pleased to have us around. He sat in the little chair between his father and Tadesse, listening as the two men spoke. After a few minutes, Tadesse turned to me to translate, 'The father wants to take his son.'

'To go home?' I asked.

'No. He wants to take him from the hospital and leave him at the orphanage.'

My heart quickened. 'Doesn't he want him anymore?'

Tadesse asked the father, and when he replied, Caleb followed the conversation back and forward with his eyes, under a furrowed brow.

'He wants to keep him,' Tadesse said, 'but he doesn't make enough grain for him to eat. He thinks it would be better for Caleb if he was at the orphanage. Because of he is hungry.'

I was stunned. I'd seen how much the father loved Caleb; and it baffled me as to how he would consider giving up his son. It wasn't drought that made this family hungry. They were poor because antiquated laws kept farmers at subsistence level, because the government spent more on armaments than education, leaving this man with no choice except to be a poor farmer.

'Why don't you keep him and come once a month to get *tef* grain and oil from the sisters at the orphanage?' Tadesse told him in Amharic.

I'd seen the orphanage when the monthly handouts happened, when queues of countryside folk stretched almost a kilometre along the roadside outside the big blue gates.

It took very little convincing from Tadesse for the father to keep Caleb and collect subsistence rations once a month from the sisters. The father looked relieved. It was clear he'd considered giving Caleb up because he thought it would be better for the boy, not because he wanted to. We finished the measurements for the corner chair, which Tadesse would take to the carpenter. With this new chair, Caleb's independence in sitting, playing, eating and socialising would be vastly improved.

All through November, the therapy room was filled with prisoners, all young men who had been injured in the riots before they'd been arrested. One had broken his arm, another had a bullet wound, and another had a wound from the butt of a rifle. Every day prisoners turned up for therapy, handcuffed, accompanied by soldiers with rifles over their shoulders. The soldiers stood against the walls, or sat beside their patients. One morning, two weeks after Caleb's fever broke, a prisoner came into the therapy room and took a seat on the plinth. He looked to be about eighteen and supported his arm in a cotton sling. A soldier in green fatigues sat down next to him, with the strap for his rifle slung over his shoulder and the barrel pointed towards the ceiling, the butt resting on the plinth. The soldier stared straight ahead. Tadesse and I were on the other side of the therapy room, so they couldn't hear us, but I whispered anyway. 'Tadesse, why do the soldiers bring the prisoners for physiotherapy?'

'Why not?' Tadesse said. 'Government is injure them. Why not government is fix them?'

I wanted to ask so many questions: What were they charged with? Would they get trials? It seemed peculiar the government cared for the physiotherapeutic wellbeing of the citizens it arrested for dissent.

But there was no time to ask any more questions as my second-year students, Martha and Solomon, arrived with Caleb and his dad at the therapy room.

Caleb was sitting on his dad's hip, independently holding his head up. It was the first time I'd seen Caleb strong enough to do that. Both father and son looked proud. Caleb's dad knelt to sit Caleb on the therapy mat.

Tadesse sat with the prisoner, untying his cotton sling, and the guard shuffled along the plinth to make room. Martha and Solomon looked nervous when the militia man moved, but he just leaned back against the wall, stretched his legs and crossed them.

It was a big day for little Caleb. After that day's session, he and his father would go home, and take with them his very own corner chair, built for him by the same carpenter who built Selam's inserts. Martha helped Caleb to sit cross-legged in his corner chair that was painted a cute peppermint green. He had regained the weight he had lost and put more on so now his face was plump and his cheeks round like a chipmunk's.

I informed the students it was their turn to initiate treatment in this session. Martha tucked her loose hair behind both ears then leant out to hold Caleb's arm and guide his fingers to his mouth, practising the action over and over. Caleb had never fed himself because he'd never had the support to sit upright or coordination to bring his fingers to his mouth.

'*Eski*, *mamush*, little boy, watch me.' Martha bent down.

Caleb watched with big eyes as the student exaggerated the movement and brought her arm up and put her fingers into her own mouth. Caleb first looked at the group to ensure he had full audience attention, then bent his elbow and put his fingers in his mouth. His audience cheered, and, looking exultant, he repeated the action for the crowd's benefit. He moved his hand to mouth, hand to mouth, again and again as his chest wheezed up and down and he cackled like a smoker.

'Can you bring his lunch?' Martha asked Caleb's father in Amharic.

A few minutes later the father returned from the ward, puffing, holding a red plastic container. Martha lifted out a small amount of *injera* and closed Caleb's fingers over it.

'Now put it in,' she said to him in Amharic and supported his elbow, shoulder and wrist, to bend his arm and put the *injera* in his own mouth. He rubbed some across his face but the majority went in.

This time when his audience cheered again and Caleb laughed, we all saw a mouthful of mushed *injera*.

'*Ye mejemeriya gize*! It's his first time!' His father was incredulous and repeated the phrase over and over.

Caleb waved his arm in the direction of the lunchbox.

'*Lechemer*? Do you want more?' Martha held the lunchbox closer.

He paused, then flopped his hand into the container and looked up to check his audience reception. We were all laughing when the soldier leaned towards us. His Kalashnikov slipped down on his shoulder so it was pointing just above our heads. I'd forgotten he was there. We all fell silent except Caleb who continued his throaty chuckle. My back stiffened and my heart went faster.

The soldier mumbled to Martha. She replied, her face expressionless, and then nodded. The soldier straightened up, shifted the strap for his Kalashnikov back onto his shoulder and stared out the door again.

'What did he say?' I whispered to Martha. 'Are we in trouble?'

'He asked, how old is that boy, why is he sick?'

'What did you agree with him about?'

'He said *des yilal*. He likes the little boy and he hopes he gets better soon.'

Chapter 19

Thanks be to God: እግዚአብሔር ይመስገን /*Egziabher yimesgen*/

On Christmas Eve I visited Sister Almaz at her new convent in Addis Ababa, where she flung her arms around my neck and exclaimed, '*Anchi wufram nesh*! You've become fat!' It had taken me a long time to get used to this standard compliment in Ethiopia, which I assumed, or at least hoped, translated to 'you're looking healthy'.

It didn't roll off my tongue, but I tried it, '*Ena anchi wufram nesh*! And you've become fat!'

'Thanks very much, I've been trying to lose weight.' Sister Almaz whacked her belly and, with her arm around my shoulders, steered me into the lounge room.

'Shall we open the television?' Sister Almaz had already flicked to the religious channel on satellite TV.

I looked at the door to the lounge room. 'Is the head sister here? Are we allowed to open the television during the day?'

'Relax! No-one is home. This is not like the other convent in Addis you stayed in. That was a very strict place for the new sisters. This place is for grown-up sisters.' She motioned at her face to indicate her age. She poured two cups of sweet spiced tea from a thermos and I sipped mine, still feeling nervous. Sister Almaz slipped off her Homypeds and curled onto the couch, cradling her mug. A televangelist with a Texan drawl admonished his cheering crowd on the small screen while we talked about my life in Gondar, and Sister Almaz told me about her project in the countryside and the bags of *berbere* spice mix the ladies from her work had grown, dried and prepared. She had brought bags of it to the city to sell.

'My neck and shoulders became very sore.' She twisted her head to one side to show me. 'Can you fix it?'

She was already standing with arms out, her back to me before I'd said yes. It was difficult to reach her shoulder through the thick woollen jumper with the Aryan knit, so she removed that. Then I asked her to remove the acrylic zip-up cardigan beneath. Her veil got in the way so I checked if she was allowed to remove it, at which she snorted and said this wasn't mediaeval times, you know. She volunteered to remove her dress, and the polo shirt she wore beneath that. She was standing in her petticoat and bra, in the nuns' lounge room with Jesus on the cross over the mantelpiece, when the head sister and the archdeacon walked in. The head sister's jaw dropped and the elderly priest looked aghast. On the TV, the Texan televangelist bellowed something about sinners and adulterers.

I grabbed Sister Almaz's shirt and threw it at her. I expected the priest to avert his eyes or exit the room, but instead he stood immobilised, either horrified or enraptured. Clutching her shirt to her chest and suppressing a snort, Sister Almaz edged around the clergyman and out of the lounge room. I gathered her vestments and slunk out too.

In Sister Almaz's room, she snatched at her clothes as fast as I shoved them at her. The head sister knocked on the door but let herself in without waiting for an answer.

'What were you two *doing* in there?' She was an elderly sister who looked stern, and I expected the worst.

'Physio?' I offered.

I held my breath. The two sisters looked at each other, lips pressed tight, until Sister Almaz couldn't hold back her giggles any longer. They both tried to laugh without sound until the head sister had to wipe tears from under her eyes.

'Shhh!' she put her finger on her lips. 'The poor archdeacon. I think you gave him high blood pressure.'

After the head sister had left, Sister Almaz flung herself onto the bed in her petticoat and only then noticed I hadn't joined in the frivolity. '*Anchi*! You! What's wrong?'

I told Sister Almaz I did something wrong every time I went to a convent. At the first convent I'd been guilty of staying out late and carousing, nearly puking in chapel and getting fleas on the tablecloth; at the second convent in the countryside, I'd declared my love to a priest; and now I'd caused the archdeacon to see her underthings.

'I don't think I belong in a convent. Should I leave now?'

Sister Almaz said I was silly and invited me to stay for the rest of the day, until Christmas Eve dinner.

'Oh no, I couldn't,' I said, but I was secretly thrilled. I loved spending time with Sister Almaz and it gave me an excuse to cancel dinner plans with *ferenjis*. Although I had close *ferenji* friends, I didn't enjoy their big *ferenji* outings. Most of them worked in offices in the capital either for international charities or commercial ventures, and I found it hard to describe the despair I felt immersed in at the hospital. Most evenings after work, I detailed my own existential doubts in long journal entries. Reading helped a bit, and I had devoured every book I could find on history, war and famine. We had a bookshelf for the books other *ferenjis* had left behind, with novels as well as anthropology, religion and philosophy books. I hoped reading nihilist philosophy might solve the meaning of existence; however I only got two chapters into Nietzsche before abandoning him for a romantic comedy set in Mumbai.

I found it hard to converse with the Addis *ferenjis* at bars and parties, fully aware how few people wanted to talk about another book I had found on radical feminist reframing of Christianity.

And even though I longed to live an ascetic life, I was still embarrassed I couldn't afford many items on restaurant menus. My threadbare jeans and battered hiking shoes made me feel ashamed when I was with the *ferenjis* in a way they didn't when I was with Sister Almaz.

'But I didn't bring any food to contribute for dinner,' I said to Sister Almaz.

She slipped her dress on over her petticoat. '*Anchi*! How long have you been in this country for? We love to make people eat.'

At dinner Sister Almaz piled my plate with lamb stew and the head sister served two dollops of mashed potatoes, even as I insisted one was plenty. Another sister put extra chicken on my plate when I turned around to convince Sister Almaz I didn't want a third glass of Fanta. I resisted undoing the top button of my jeans until prayers after dinner were complete. Helping to clear the table with an aching belly, it was starting to feel like Christmas.

'Christmas is a busy time in *ferenji* countries, isn't it?' The head sister wrapped cling film over the lamb stew.

'Every time is busy time in *ferenji* countries!' Sister Almaz called out from the fridge where she was stacking leftovers. 'I saw that in England when I went for my operation. Imagine, everyone too busy to enjoy life.'

The head sister plunged dishes into the sink. 'Imagine! They are eating on the street! Too busy to sit down and enjoy a meal! Everyone is doing everything while they are walking: eating, drinking their coffee, talking on their mobile phone. Busy, busy, busy and life rushes past them.' She stacked clean plates into the rack and I dried.

'No-one is greeting each other; they bury their faces in their books or their newspapers.' Sister Almaz demonstrated by burying her face into my tea towel. 'I know their country is advanced, but it seems like they have no enjoyment of life. I didn't belong there. I thought: these things are for other people, not for me.'

The same was true for me about faith; it was for other people, not for me. Sister Almaz's devotion was something I aspired to. I felt disconnected from the soullessness of home, but as much as I wished for an unquestioning faith and the solace it might deliver, I still drifted spiritually. I yearned to be part of something.

But that evening at the convent, Sister Almaz's community welcomed me with such warmth I felt a glimmer of spiritual solidarity. Here was a group of women, each having taken a vow of poverty, choosing a lifestyle of service and meaning.

'What did you get for Christmas?' the head sister asked as she scraped leftovers into the cat's bowl.

'Nothing. I'm happy without presents.' I didn't feel out of place sharing that. The sisters would relate to my lack of desire for possessions.

'No presents? But you'll feel like no-one loves you!' The head sister looked shocked. She slid a bowl of scraps out the back door for the cat and disappeared out of the kitchen, returning with her hands behind her back.

'Merry Christmas, dear. Sorry we don't have any Christmas paper; we know you *ferenjis* like to wrap things.' She flung her hands out to show a yellow serviette wrapped around two Baci chocolates.

I was speechless. I hadn't even seen chocolate for three months and knew she hadn't just nipped out to get them: sweets like this weren't sold in Ethiopia.

'Where did you get these? These must be very precious for you; please, you don't need to give them to me.'

I tried to pass them back to her, but she pushed my hand away.

'Merry Christmas, dear,' she said again, as she folded me into a hug. Right then I felt like part of something: so loved and so happy, and so hungry for chocolate.

The *Timkat* festival was one of the country's most important festivals and happened three weeks after Christmas. The festival celebrated the baptism of Saint John the Baptist and took place at water sources in every town. In Gondar it was celebrated at Fasilides' Baths, a sixteenth-century construction with fortified walls and turrets. Tadesse and I stood at the front of the baths to watch the holiday parade. By now we worked together and socialised together, spending almost all our time together, although we had to keep our relationship a secret in the workplace.

First in the parade were clusters of teenage boys, brandishing sticks high as they jogged, chanting, '*Ya-ho*! *Ya-ho*!' which Tadesse said translated as 'ya-ho'. Next were groups of women in white dresses, singing and dancing; after that, circles of men danced around a central drummer. Monks paraded past, with rows and rows of men dressed in identical saffron robes. Behind them, the priests arrived, dressed like the magi of a nativity scene. Sunlight reflected off satin vestments of purple, orange and cerise dotted with gold stars and fringing. The holy men shaded themselves from the sun with umbrellas of scarlet velvet and gold tassels.

Thousands of people, singing, ululating, beating drums and blowing horns, packed the streets. I smelt the eucalyptus and pine trees and even though the dust was so thick it stung my eyes and caught in my throat, I was enraptured. I felt like I was a part, however small, of the spiritual frenzy.

That night the pilgrims lined the waterside to be first in line for a blessing at dawn. They settled down for the night under a moonless sky, curling on the ground beneath *gabi* cloths, or folding them as blankets. They were the sick, the lame, the blind and the lepers. It seemed biblical, as if it was Jesus himself they were waiting for tomorrow, and not a twenty-first century version of his baptism. I wished I knew how they held onto such faith. When I looked at these people, all I saw was gross injustice. I wanted to scream, *Don't you see all this suffering! All this deprivation! All the sick and hungry children! How can you let God get away with this?*

At 5 a.m. when we returned, it was still dark, but the moon had risen now, so it was high over Fasilides' Baths. Thousands of people prayed in unison, wrapped in white cloths with their faces lit by tapers. The praying continued while the sky turned from jet black to ink blue and the stars faded. Still the crowd prayed until twinges of orange and pink appeared on the horizon and a procession of priests emerged from the prayer tent. When the whole crowd knelt and bent their heads, I felt the power of being part of collective energy even as I wished I had as much faith as the people around me.

At the water's edge the priests formed a line of robed figures in orange, magenta, indigo and maroon. The sun glinted off the filigree swirls of their brass crosses.

It seemed the whole crowd took a breath as the priests held their crosses aloft and the high priest set a wreath of twigs and candles onto the water. The crowd clapped slowly and ululated, then the boy chosen to represent John the Baptist stepped into the baths. With the candle wreath now on his head, he scooped water into an arc to shower onlookers with the blessed water of Fasilides' Baths. Then the fun began.

People surged forward to splash themselves and others. Those at the front filled the jerry cans, water bottles and plastic jugs that were passed to them from behind, then flung the water onto the squealing crowd until everyone was saturated. My hair stuck to my head, water rolled into my eyes and down the back of my neck and into my socks. Cooled and excited, we followed the parade out of the baths where it snaked back towards Tadesse's church.

We bumped into Tadesse's friends, a married couple. Tadesse introduced me as his girlfriend, and it felt great.

'You must come to a party at our house to eat *doro wat*, chicken stew,' they said.

It was just like a party at home, with music and cold beers and friends sitting around the edges of the room, except that the house was a beauty salon by day and a home by night. Tadesse's friend and his wife slept on a bed behind a curtain next to the nail varnishes.

'Put Bob Marley on!' someone yelled at the guy loading a DVD into the player beside the TV, between the hair rollers and the trimming scissors.

'So how do you celebrate Epiphany in Australia?' Tadesse's friend Bekalu asked me.

'We don't really,' I said, leaning forwards so I wouldn't bang my head on the hood of the hair dryer that my seat was under. 'People who go to church will celebrate it there, but there is no religious feast like *Timkat*.'

'So Australia is not a Christian country then?' Bekalu looked confused.

I explained that in Australia many people practised a variety of religions but some people had no religion at all.

'But *ferenjis* love Christmas, no?'

'Well yes,' I said, then remembering rows of foil rabbits and supersized chocolate eggs, 'and Easter too.'

Now Bekalu was really confused. 'So why do *ferenjis* celebrate those church feasts and no other?'

'Those are not church feasts. Those are shopping feasts.'

Everyone laughed like I'd made a joke, but I was being serious. The conversation in Amharic was going too quickly for me to keep up so instead I pondered what I'd been thinking about at Sister Almaz's house. I looked at everyone at the party and wondered if these people were Orthodox Christians because that's what they always knew they were and would continue to be. Having the choice to define myself had left me wondering. I wondered if all these people ever grappled with existential crises, or despaired for a benevolent God. When I was younger, I assumed I yearned for a sense of meaning because I wasn't devoting my life to a meaningful purpose. I expected when I came to Ethiopia and filled my days with helping others, I would gain spiritual satiety and, with it, reprieve from the relentless questioning inside my own head. Now I just had new questions. But then the party got into full swing and there was music and dancing and *doro wat* and I put my worries aside.

It was dark outside when I left the party, with an appointment to get my hair straightened and eyebrows styled, plus the promise of a visit and coffee soon. Walking down the hill on the way back to my house, Tadesse linked his arm in mine.

'Did you enjoy?' he asked me.

'*Betam*, very,' I said.

I felt so loved and accepted and part of a community. I thought back to this morning, at the *Timkat* parade. We had followed the procession for an hour; it was midmorning so the sun was high and already scorching. My saturated clothes dried in no time and I finished my drinking water. I was so thirsty I watched enviously as a child who looked about eight emptied two small bottles of Fanta into a huge jerry can and topped it up with water from a dirty water bottle.

'Buy your squash here!' the kid yelled in Amharic, and immediately he had a patron. The little boy lugged the jerry can onto his hip to pour squash into a cup. He looked like an urchin, with skinny legs, bare feet and tattered clothes. The crowd had surged ahead, but the boy waited for his customer to finish his drink and return the cup. Then he struggled after the crowd, lugging the jerry can, so heavy he had to lean to one side.

Maybe I'd been wrong in looking for evidence of faith, for tangible miracles. Maybe the miracle was in the way people kept their faith, again and again. The way they picked up their jerry cans and kept on walking.

Chapter 20

Don't give up: ተስፋ አትቁረጥ /*tesfa atkrete*/

One morning in early February 2005, Sara arrived on the ward. Henok, our student, opened the yellow medical file and flicked to the page with the diagnosis. He read aloud, 'Tuberculosis in the chest, lymph nodes, spleen and liver, inflammation of the lining of the heart, plus chronic heart failure, plus stroke, with right side of the body paralysed.'

'How will you begin your examination of the patient?' I asked.

Henok pushed his glasses up to think. 'By examining her chest. Auscultation.'

'Good, what will you be auscultating for?'

'I will listen for phlegm on her lungs, for signs of chest infection.'

He was proving to be very competent and I felt proud of him. Together we went to see Sara. She was a thin twelve-year-old, with long eyelashes around doe eyes and hair that sprung upwards in a fuzzy mass. Her father, a slight man with a narrow face, sat next to her bed on a metal stool. He wore the olive polyester slacks only countryside people wore, and his red knitted shirt unravelled from the bottom.

'Hi there. My name is Henok, and I will be your physiotherapist,' Henok said in Amharic, with a gentle, confident manner. He took a stethoscope from his white coat pocket and positioned it on Sara's chest. 'Take a deep breath in.'

Sara looked up at Henok with eyes wide with fear.

'*Ayzosh*, relax,' Henok reassured her.

When the girl returned his smile, only the left side of her face moved.

After Henok listened to all the auscultation points on the front of her chest he knelt one knee on the bed. He helped her to sit forwards and positioned the stethoscope to listen to the back of her lungs. When she sat forwards, both emaciated arms dangled from her chest so it was impossible to distinguish the paralysed from non-paralysed side. Beneath her hospital nightie, her belly was swollen and distended.

After he had helped Sara to lie down again, Henok reported, 'She has a lot of phlegm in her chest. It's difficult to tell if this is from the TB or if it is new secretions, making her at risk of chest infection.' He thought for a while, tapping his pen against his notebook. 'I will prescribe passive movements for to keep the range of movement in her limbs. And breathing exercises for her. To stop the chest infection.' He turned. 'Miss Julie, do you think Sara, she has a good prognosis? I think she has many things wrong with her.'

I fumbled with my notebook, not sure how to answer him. 'It's hard to say.'

It wasn't really. The extremely unwell children like Sara rarely got referred for physio. We saw them lying in the beds beside our patients, and they had often gone when we returned the next day, or the next week. Their parents had either taken them home, back to their villages for holy waters or local magic, or they had passed away.

When we went on the ward the next day, Sara lay asleep, pallid and breathing in sharp rasps. Her paralysed right leg was splayed out on an angle, her bones showing through tissue-paper skin, and she had no top sheet. Her father delicately set her leg straight again, then stretched his white *gabi* shoulder cloth over her legs and swollen belly. He sat on the low stool and stroked her shin, whispering a conversation over her to the young mum and the granny in the bed on the other side.

The head nurse, an older woman with a bustling manner, approached Sara's bedside to check the girl's heart rate and temperature. Her father's brow furrowed and he leant forward as if to protect Sara. He watched the nurse keenly until she had finished her observations. When she left, his shoulders dropped and he breathed out.

When Sara stirred, Henok carried out gentle physiotherapy movements with her limbs, but she was too ill for more than that. With her composite diagnosis, and no intensive care unit at the hospital, her chances were not good.

The second-year students were to start their first external clinical placement the next day. This was to be the first time this class of students would practise their physio skills outside the hospital. One of the other *ferenji* lecturers and I were delegated to organise transport. It had been hard work to organise trips for forty-five students from the university hospital campus to treat patients at various locations around Gondar. We had scheduled them to practise at a hospice, at the army hospital, and at the community-based rehabilitation programs in communities on the outskirts of Gondar. It had required many long, frustrating meetings with the head dean and the sub-dean until they agreed to let us use the university coach to transport the students.

Mama Zenash took a coach transport request slip to the head dean and the sub-dean's offices for their authorisation signatures. She took the signed slip to a third office for a purple authorisation stamp before delivering it to the transport department.

At 8.45 a.m. on Tuesday, the students collected in small groups in the coach parking lot. Some chatted in the shade of the coach, some chewed on their pens, or reviewed notes.

By 9.15 a.m. no driver had appeared, so the student representative Dawit volunteered to go to the transport office to find one. Returning, he called across the parking lot, 'You did not submit the request slip!'

Tadesse and I hurried to the office, a plain space with a cement floor and a tin roof. The transport manager, an older man with a striped shirt and large stomach, glowered at us over his spartan desk.

'Ah, here it is!' I pointed to the completed request slip lying atop the only pile of paper in front of him.

'You did not fill the number of students going on the bus,' the manager said in Amharic without looking at the slip.

'Hm, let's see!' Fixing a fake cheerfulness, I pointed to the box where Tadesse had written the number of students. The form required only three lines of information: the time, the destination and the number of students, and we'd completed these. The manager scowled at us again saying nothing, and pointed with his chin at a woman with a scarf tied around her braids.

She took our slip and sauntered outside to the veranda overlooking the gravelled parking area. A few minutes passed while she appeared to be looking at a group of men sitting in the shade against a wall. When she eventually spotted the appointed driver, she yelled over to him, and he yelled back that he felt sick so she'd better find someone else. She strolled out of sight and twenty minutes later appeared with another driver.

We had wasted one hour, a third of this week's clinical practice time. But the students didn't seem to mind. They still chatted excitedly as they boarded the bus.

We were off to practise being physios, in the community! Within five minutes I had forgotten about the annoying transport manager, chalking up this morning's incident as a mistake.

The next morning I reached the ward before Henok arrived. Sara was propped up in bed with a pillow.

'*Ara*! Hey!' I said, surprised and thrilled to see her looking better.

Sara giggled from one side of her face and showed me a foil packet. She screwed her face to one side, using the stronger side of her face to suck from the sachet. A girl who looked about four lay propped on pillows in the next bed. She copied Sara, screwing up her face to suck from her own sachet as if that were part of the procedure.

'*Menden new*? What is it? I asked, only to make conversation. I knew it was Plumpy'Nut paste. Both girls held their packets up to show me again and both had the brown paste smeared across lips and teeth.

'*Yetafetal*? Is it delicious?' I asked, but they were giggling too much to answer. Sara's chest heaved up and down and she laughed until she got enough breath to say, '*Awe*. Yes.'

The tiny girl in the next bed squeaked as if she couldn't hold it in anymore. '*Ferenji Amaregna techelallalech*! The *ferenji* can speak Amharic!' She rolled over to bury her giggles in the pillow.

Sara flopped back in her pillow and wheezed a one-sided laugh. It was too hard not to giggle as well.

Henok arrived to start physio. 'Wow, she's better!'

When Henok pulled back Sara's bedclothes he pointed to her left leg, that was not paralysed, but looked just as thin.

'Can you move this one?'

She shrugged.

'*Mokeri, eshi*? Try, okay?' Henok said.

Sara slowly slid her left foot along the bed towards her bottom. Her whole leg quivered with the effort but she managed. With encouragement, Henok helped her to bend and straighten her leg ten times.

'Now with this one.' Henok indicated the leg affected by the stroke.

'*Embi allech*. It doesn't want to go,' Sara whispered.

Henok knelt and inched his hands beneath her paralysed leg. He cradled her heel with one hand and her thigh with another so they were just millimetres off the bed. '*Ahun*, now?' he said.

Sara screwed her face up with the effort of trying to move her leg, but it remained static.

'*Embi allech*.' Her dad's forehead creased.

'*Embi allech*,' a wizened grandma by the adjacent bed chastised Henok.

Henok inched Sara's paralysed leg, until the knee and hip were bent. Sara looked worried and lifted her head to check with her dad. He crossed his eyes and bulged his lips until she wheezed a laugh and flopped her head on the pillow and Henok straightened her leg again.

'*Endegena*? Again?' he asked, and this time she simply agreed.

The following Tuesday the students assembled in the parking lot by the coach and again the transport manager refused to assign a driver. Only this time he said, 'You didn't write the time you needed the bus.' When the student rep Dawit pointed to where Tadesse had written 9 a.m. on the slip, the manager said, 'You are going to too many destinations.' He didn't relent until after half an hour of quarrelling with Tadesse and Dawit. He finished by shouting, 'You should take all the students to one place, or order two buses!'

The following week we ordered two buses, and he refused us on the grounds of having done so, saying, 'It is permitted only to order one bus.' Dawit and Tadesse argued with him while I stood feeling furious and holding my temper, until after half an hour of arguing he relented and released a driver.

The next Monday, Tadesse dropped in to check that a driver was organised for the following day. The transport manager admonished him for coming on a Monday and told Tadesse to come back first thing the next morning.

The subsequent week Tadesse went first thing Tuesday morning and the transport manager scowled that he should have come Monday afternoon. Then he wouldn't assign a driver without an argument.

'Why does he do that?' I asked Tadesse. We were on a date, sort of. We were walking up the hill to watch the football at the Terara

Hotel bar. But I didn't feel at all romantic. 'Why does he make it so hard for us? Is he angry with the physiotherapy department or angry with *ferenjis*, or just terrible at his job? Every week for five weeks he has found a new way not to give us a bus.'

The wind howled up the street, batting papers against walls and whipping dust from the road. People in the streets grabbed at their skirts and shielded their eyes.

Tadesse waited as I puffed up the steep steps cut into the side of the hill. 'It happen actually.' I guessed he meant *these things happen*. '*Habeshas*, Ethiopians, can expect this thing. You cannot do anything about it. You just have to don't give up.' He looked at his watch. 'Hurry please, it's almost kick-off.'

It was cosy inside, with the wind kicking up at the windows, and I soon forgot about my frustrating day as I watched Ethiopian football. The hotel, built by the Italians after they invaded in the 1940s, still retained most of its lavish furnishings. Art Deco lamps cast an orange glow on the walls and a dusty electric chandelier lit the room. The curved bar was edged with brass and the glass shelves behind were lined with dusty liquor bottles.

Our grey-haired waiter hobbled to our couch and when he took our order for two beers and a menu, his lips rolled in over toothless gums.

Tadesse and I had prime seats for the match – a brown velour two-seater with curved arms. The TV itself was a huge 1960s model with its own wooden legs and a chunky dial. About ten more people sat on regal, faded armchairs facing the TV. It had the feeling of being in a very posh and cosy living room.

The waiter went back and forth, blocking our view of the TV with his hunched silhouette as he delivered beers on a small silver tray to every other patron but us. Eventually Tadesse went to the bar to remind him he'd forgotten our beers, and twenty minutes later he shuffled over. With a quivering, gnarled hand he set the bottles on the coffee table. He had his back to us by the time Tadesse said, 'And the menus?' so he didn't hear. Tadesse followed him to the bar and the waiter lumbered back with two menus, handwritten in English on one side and in a spidery Amharic on the other.

'Why not you order? You can practise your Amharic,' Tadesse said.

I was so hungry my stomach rumbled. I pointed to the top line. '*Eshi, asa cottelet efellegalehu.* Okay, I'll have the fish cutlet.'

'*Yellem*, don't have.' The waiter stood stooped, hands behind his back.

I asked for the beef cutlet instead.

'*Yellem*, don't have.'

He said the same for the lamb and chicken cutlets. When I'd exhausted the list he nodded sagely. '*Cottelet yellem.* No cutlets.'

I rolled my finger to the next section. '*Eshi, manem chigger yellem. Rost meat.* Okay, no problem. I'll take the beef roast meat.'

'*Rost meat yellem*, no beef roast meat.' He shifted his weight to the other leg.

It turned out the documented roast lamb and chicken and fish were only philosophical possibilities.

'*Men men migib allew*? Which food you have?' I asked.

'*Manem yellem*. None.' His face remained expressionless.

Puzzled and disappointed, I said to Tadesse, as if he hadn't heard, 'There's no food.'

'What is there to eat?' Tadesse asked in Amharic.

The old man blinked and paused, owl-like. '*Pasta allew. Woym sega ke injera*. There's pasta, or meat with flatbread.'

I ordered the pasta and Tadesse ordered the meat with *injera*, neither of which were on the menu. As the waiter hobbled away I whispered to Tadesse, 'Why did he give us the menu if there wasn't anything available?'

'*Essu sira*. It's his job.'

The waiter delivered our food while the picture on the TV flickered and rolled until a spectator stood up to belt the TV. The picture stabilised until he sat and then it rolled again. He banged the TV, and the picture steadied just in time to see Tadesse's team score. Everybody clapped, and the TV rolled once more.

When I said, 'Oh no!', Tadesse said again, 'You just have to don't give up.'

Sara was now medically stable and was ready to do her physio in the therapy room. Her face had become chubbier from the combination of steroids and intensive nutrition.

Every morning and afternoon, her father arranged Sara's paralysed arm into a cotton sling, rearranged her other arm to snake around his neck, and scooped her into his arms to carry her the ten-minute walk over the rocky path and up the steps cut in the hill to get to the therapy room. There he would kneel with Sara still in his arms to lower her onto the thick blue therapy mat on the floor, with sweat beading on his back.

Over the next five weeks she grew stronger. By mid-March she could unwind her arm from around her dad's neck when he carried her to the therapy room, and wave to Henok. This morning after her dad laid her on the floor mat he flopped next to her in a pantomime of exhaustion. When Sara laughed, her chest wheezed up and down and phlegm rattled.

Henok called me over to the mat. 'Julie, Sara wants to show you something.'

Sara's lips tightened as she tried to hold back a smile. The physio student and the patient grinned at each other.

'*Menden new*? What is it?' I asked.

Her father knelt beside Sara on the mat and steadied her paralysed ankle. Sara looked up at Henok again.

'Go on,' he encouraged in Amharic.

Sara closed her eyes and contorted her face with effort to lift her bottom off the mat. It was one of the simplest exercises, but it was a great sign that movement was returning to her legs.

'*Gobez lej*! Clever child!' Henok and I both cheered.

'The other side?' Henok asked in Amharic. He cupped the

heel of her paralysed leg while Sara grimaced as she bent and straightened her knee. When she opened her eyes to see me clapping and beaming at her, she looked bashful.

The next exercise for that day was to check her balance in sitting. We propped her up so she sat on the therapy mat with her legs stretched straight out in front. Henok knelt behind her, supporting her back with his thighs. Her right arm remained completely paralysed, so we had provided her with a sling to prevent it falling and permanently stretching the nerves and blood vessels of the shoulder. Though she tried to hold herself up with her non-paralysed arm, the weight of her upper body was too much. Over the months of bed rest she had lost the ability to keep her balance.

'*Dekemesh*? Are you tired?' Henok curved his head around to see her face.

'*Dekmognal*, I am tired.'

I thought of what Tadesse said, about how *you just have to don't give up*. Five weeks ago Sara was so unwell, with such a poor prognosis no-one thought she would regain much function. This young girl showed such tenacity, but I wasn't sure what potential improvements were realistic for her condition. I hoped, but wasn't confident, she would get much stronger.

The next morning when I arrived at work, Sara was already in the therapy room. She sat on the blue mat with Henok kneeling behind and her father squatting in front, tightening the ties on her floral hospital gown. She welcomed me with her lopsided smile but when she lifted her strong arm to wave she fell to the side and lay there, rasping her dry laugh until her father scooped her under her armpits to hold her upright again.

Sara's father carried her to the therapy room twice daily where she did her best to regain movement and strength every day and delight us in the process.

The following Monday morning, instead of going to the office to put my backpack down, I went straight in to see Sara in the therapy room. Her balance and leg strength had improved so much with twice-daily physio that she could now sit on the big therapy ball with Henok standing behind. He kept her steady with his knees against the ball and his hands on her shoulders. Her father stood in front, locking his knees against hers to keep her legs from sliding out.

'*Gobez, gobez, gobez.* Clever, clever, clever.' I shook my head from side to side.

Sara kept her face down as if she was embarrassed by all the fuss.

'Shall we go to the bars?' Henok asked her in Amharic, and she nodded at him.

Sara's father carried her across to the small wooden chair Henok had set inside the parallel bars. The chair faced a mirror at the other end; Sara used the mirror to check as she smoothed out her floral cotton nightie with one hand. I stood behind her chair as Henok wheeled a wooden stool in front of Sara and jammed her knees against his.

She gripped the bar with her left hand.

'You count,' Henok said.

'*And, hulet, sost.* One, two three.' She took a deep breath and stood up for the first time in seven months.

I whooped with joy.

Henok called out, 'Brava!'

'*Gobez lej*! Clever child!' I said.

Sara sat again for a rest. After a few minutes, Henok asked, '*Endegena*, again?'

I watched her lopsided grin from the mirror and she was standing almost before we had time to get our hands into position.

From behind her, I gave her the same question I asked of most of my patients, to judge their progress, '*Kebad woym kelal new*? Is it difficult, or simple?'

Her left arm quivered where she was gripping the metal bar to stay upright and her left knee wobbled. She turned to look at her dad first, then beamed at me in the mirror with one side of her face. She whispered, '*Kelal new*. It's simple.'

Chapter 21

I am happy: ደስ ብሎኛል /*des blognal*/

Now most mornings Sara beat me to work. She was usually doing her exercises inside the parallel bars when I arrived. By the start of April, two weeks after she first stood again, Sara could pull herself to stand at the bars without help. I saw her the first time she did it, shaky on her legs, but proud.

I shook my head as if in disbelief. '*Sent ken techeyallesh*? For how many days you can?'

When I had my back turned, gathering items for today's therapy session, I heard Sara chuckle.

'*Menden new*? What is it?' I asked.

Struggling to keep a straight face she said, '*Manem yellem*. Nothing.' I looked at her dad, but he only gave me a bewildered look. When I turned to get the low stool on wheels, I heard her laugh again. This time I turned fast enough to see her father making silly faces at her in the mirror.

'Today is a special day,' he said in Amharic.

'*Lemen*? Why?' I asked.

Sara whispered in Amharic, 'I walked.'

'*Ehedalehu*? I walked?' I was so surprised I used the wrong pronoun. Sara tittered but quickly caught herself. Father and daughter wore the same serene expression.

I wanted to shout, 'Aren't you excited?' But I didn't know the word for 'excited', so instead I clapped and prompted, '*Ena*? And?'

She replied with, '*Des blognal*. I am happy.'

'*Ena ene des blognal*. And I am happy,' I said.

'*Eski*? Show her?' Sara's dad walked to the other end of the parallel bars. Sara clutched the bar with her strong arm and shuffled her feet bit by bit until she had turned to face her dad.

Henok came to help when I beckoned. He stood behind Sara with his hands firm on her hips to keep her safe. '*Enhid*? Let's go?'

Sara screwed her face up with the effort and took a shaky step.

'*Gobez*! Clever!' I said. At the end of her first lap of the bars I asked her, '*Kebad woym kelal new*? Difficult or easy?'

'*Kebad*, difficult.'

That weekend Marieke went to Addis for work for two weeks, and Tadesse was working in a remote outreach clinic for a fortnight. While in Piazza getting groceries, I ran into a friend of Marieke's. We saw him most weekends at Chelada Bar, a cosy venue where our friendship group of lecturers and clinicians from the hospital met most weekends. Marieke's friend invited me for a lunch of *injera*, then we drank a macchiato together and talked about music.

'I know you like love songs,' he said.

He knew I liked love songs because at the Chelada Bar he had seen me swaying along to *Greatest Love Songs of All Time*, a compilation CD that was almost always on. It played the songs of my youth, the songs I used to listen to on Late Night Love Songs and Dedications on 94.5 FM. I used to listen with earphones in, during study time at the boarding house at Iona, when I dreamt of being somewhere different, making a difference. Sixteen-year-old Julie used to wish she had someone to phone up for, and request Johnny Logan's 'Hold Me Now' or Leo Sayer's 'More Than I Can Say'. So when these songs came on in the Chelada Bar, as they did every single night we went there, I would invariably be sitting next to Tadesse and he would slip an arm around my waist or a hand onto my knee. And I would think, I've made it. I've got a job I love, in the place I want to be, a man I adore, singing me eighties love songs. I felt so content, all the elements of my perfect life were right here.

'Do you want to make a mixtape?' Marieke's friend asked me and we walked together to the music shop his friend owned. The shop was no bigger than a department store dressing room, stacked to the ceiling with tapes of Amharic music and pirated DVDs. The three guys working there pulled out a small wooden stool for me, and the five of us squeezed in, watching eighties love-song music videos on TV at full volume with Ethiopian music also at full volume blaring from a CD player on the counter out into the street, so customers could not be mistaken about the type of shop this was. The guys kept pouring me more tea, and insisting I sit back down when I said I should be going. Customers came and went and still we sat behind the counter, compiling a love-song mix to outdo the Chelada Bar.

When the afternoon shadows grew long I caught a minibus home. That day I saw so many friends around town, I felt confident speaking in Amharic, and however malapropic it was, I was able to understand and make myself understood.

When I got home, Mesfin opened the gate to let me in, and our new guard dog Tara jumped up and panted excitedly at me. Tara had come to live with us six weeks earlier. In theory Tara was Marieke's guard dog: with Marieke away in Addis so much she decided the house needed extra security. But so far, on encountering strangers, Tara either leapt about with tail wagging or dropped a ball at their feet. She looked as if she could be part labrador, part spaniel, with big floppy ears and black fur that grew long at her stomach. When I opened the back door to drink tea on the step, Tara scampered up beside me, her nails clicking on the cement. She lay on her back with belly exposed and, when I didn't rub it, she nudged my foot with her paw. Her mouth turned up at the edges like a grin while I rubbed. Sitting on the step next to her, I sipped my tea and she rolled onto her side while I stroked her ears, looking across the valley at the low sun that painted the clouds a lemony gold, where they wisped and floated above the mountain. The smell of roasting coffee from a coffee ceremony drifted over from a neighbour's garden and I heard *Eskista* music and people singing and laughing from another garden. As the sun sank behind the mountain and the sky turned navy, Mesfin came around the corner, his walking stick clunking on the cement, whistling for Tara. She reluctantly picked herself up and clicked her way down the steps.

'You're all alone,' Mesfin said in Amharic.

And I said, '*Manem chigger yellem, des blognal.* No problem. I am happy.'

When Henok and I went to the paediatric ward the following day, Sara sat at the top of the steps, watching the other kids from the ward play in the garden. She put her finger to her lips and pointed at her dad. He was asleep with his shoulders on one bed, his feet on the other and his torso sagging between the beds.

'*Wede esporte bet enhid*? Shall we go for exercises?' I asked. When Sara nodded, another of the patients, a little girl, stopped playing. She dropped her stick, brushed her hands on the front of her dress and skipped up the three steps to stand next to Sara. Although she was younger and shorter, she was confident as she slid in at the bigger girl's side. The tiny girl held Sara tight around the waist, and supported her to walk inside together. They both were stifling giggles until they tickled Sara's dad awake.

Today was the first time I had seen Sara wear shoes. She wore purple plastic scuffs with a band across the toes. On her weak foot the scuff was fitted with a strap made from a length of clear plastic catheter tubing. It had been threaded through holes on either side of the scuff and laced behind her ankle to hold the shoe in place.

'*Gobez*! Clever!' I pointed to her new shoes and said, '*Man new*? Who?'

I was amazed she understood me, but she replied, '*Yene abate*! My dad!' She looked so proud of her dad, who was pulling on his own shoes with pillow creases still in his cheeks.

Sara's new shoes were in honour of the fact she could at last attempt the walk to the therapy room. Her dad held her tight, keeping her upright as she limped and scuffed in her purple shoes over the gravel to the steps cut into the hill.

When we reached the top, both father and daughter were puffing but Sara couldn't stop smiling.

'*Chama des yilal new*? You like the shoes?' I asked, because I didn't know the phrase for 'How do you feel?'.

Again, she seemed to understand and replied, '*Des blognal.* I am happy.'

On a Wednesday in mid-May, I got into work early for the two-hour drive to a remote outstation clinic. We lecturers alternated supervisory visits to students assigned to the university hospital outstations. Although these clinics didn't have electricity, and the water in the taps rarely ran, they were staffed by nurses and health officers and were always busy. Each fortnight, discharged patients from remote villages waited outside our therapy room for the hospital vehicle to drop them home en route to the outstations.

This morning it was Sara and her dad sitting on the wooden bench outside the physio clinic, each holding their possessions in a plastic bag. Sara wore a new purple headscarf over fresh cornrows. Yesterday I had seen her sitting on the floor while the mother of another patient braided her hair into zigzags. Her hair had barely been long enough to stand in a fuzz around her head when she was admitted three and a half months ago. Now, with her purple scuffs, her new hairdo, and most importantly, new strength and coordination, she looked like a different child.

Tadesse carried a huge box of physio supplies from the physio office, and looked around the corner of the box to Sara.

'*Yet teheje*? Where are you going?' he asked. Sara burst out as if she'd been waiting all morning for someone to ask her. '*Wede bet*. I'm going home.'

Tadesse slid the box into the back of the Land Cruiser. He shook his head in mock disappointment and said in Amharic, 'You can't leave us. You already stayed three and a half months. Stay one more month.'

'*Embi*! *Wede bet efellegalehu*! Don't want to! I want to go home!'

'*Lemen*? Why?' Tadesse teased. He counted plaster of Paris bandages into a smaller box. '*Hulum neger allew. Metwech allew*. We've got everything here. We've got toys,' he pointed inside the therapy room.

'*Embi*, I don't want!' She shook her head, trying hard not to laugh.

'*Ferenjoch allew*. We've got *ferenjis*.' He pointed to me as I stacked assessment papers onto the front seat.

'*Enat bet allech*. But my mum is at home.'

Tadesse sighed. '*Eshi, tehejalesh*. Well, okay, you'd better go.'

Sara walked independently from the wooden bench to the car, with her plastic luggage bag looped over one arm. Her other arm had regained no movement so she still wore it in a sling. Sara's father was first to climb into the rear of the Land Cruiser. Tadesse lifted the girl to the back doors of the vehicle in one swoop and her father helped her inside.

The pair were our only passengers. They faced each other on bench seats lining the rear and Tadesse and I sat on the back seat. The driver sped through the edges of town, past the busy market where the roads were crowded with vendors, children, donkeys, sheep and goats.

Soon we were onto the open roads and heading towards foothills chequered with paddocks of brown, beige, fawn and green, with the Simien Mountains etching dark shapes on the horizon. Clusters of *tukuls*, round thatched huts, dotted the hillsides with smoke spiralling skywards.

I turned in my seat to give Sara a small bag. '*Mastawesha*. Memento.'

She pulled out the small exercise book and pen I had bought on the way to work that morning.

'*Ye temheret bet*. For school,' I said.

Next Sara pulled out my favourite treat, a packet of orange Hip Hop biscuits. Although they cost just three birr (fifty cents) a packet, I assumed she wouldn't get to eat them often. Her eyes always widened with joy whenever a balloon appeared and I expected the same expression now, but instead, she turned the packet over in her hand and looked puzzled.

When she looked up at her father he whispered, '*Beskut*. *Yetafetal*. Biscuits. They are tasty.'

She didn't look convinced but as she put the biscuits back in the bag she whispered, '*Amesegenalehu*. Thank you.'

As we approached the mountains, the fields beside the road became greener and the crops thicker. We all watched the countryside for a long time without speaking. After an hour her father twisted in his seat, looking out the left window, then the right and the left again. He leant forwards to tap my shoulder.

'*Yene agare*!' He pointed to the hills visible through the windscreen. The phrase translated to 'my country' but the terms country and region were interchangeable. He hadn't been home for almost four months; I hadn't seen my country for seven months, and I knew that homesick feeling well.

The driver stopped where the road cleft. I couldn't see anything nearby, not a village or any houses, just a bare hill overlooking fields. When we got out, the wind was so fierce, Sara clutched her headscarf to stop it flying away. Chequered green-and-brown fields with a road snaking between them spread out to the horizon in one direction, and in the other spread a blue haze of mountains.

When Sara posed for a photo with her father, her face looked round and healthy, so different from her gaunt cheekbones of fourteen weeks ago.

'*Mehed ken be ken, asfelagi new, eshi*! Walking every day important, okay?' I shook her hand.

Sara told me in Amharic that she would walk to school. She put her arm around her father's waist and he supported her shoulders.

'*Enhid*? Let's go?' her father asked and they set off down the hill.

As we pulled out, I asked the driver to toot the horn. Sara turned to wave and gave a big, lopsided smile.

In the months of her hospitalisation, she never complained to any of us about being there, or having to do physio exercises, and I never saw her cry. How brave she'd been. She was clearly stronger than this *ferenji*, because a lump welled in my throat and I kept my face to the window so Tadesse couldn't see my tears.

He leant across the back seat and checked if the driver was watching, then, ever so gently, rested his hand on my forearm and said, '*Ayzosh*. It's okay.'

I swallowed the lump and kept looking out the window. I didn't remember how to say it in Amharic, so I spoke in English. 'I am happy.'

Chapter 22

I have hope: ተስፋ አለኝ/*tesfa allegn*/

On the day after Sara went home, Doctor Tesfaye stopped by the physio office with a new referral for another patient with spinal TB. There was no-one to translate for me as the physiotherapy assistants were out at clinics and the students had finished their required hours of clinical practice for the week. I wasn't too concerned as my Amharic was now passable for a therapy session.

The patient was a nine-year-old girl named Samira; both legs were paralysed from TB of the spine; the doctors had started her on steroid medication weeks earlier but she was only admitted from the remote outstation clinic today.

Samira's face was puffy and round from the side effects of the steroids and she looked uncharacteristically chubby for a child from the countryside. She had chunky loose curls, a long aquiline nose and her two front teeth were missing. She wore a countryside frock of floral cotton with short sleeves. I sat on the metal stool by her bedside.

'*Yikerta, tennish tennish Amaregna bicha.* Sorry, I speak only a little Amharic.'

Her mother shook her head to show it was fine.

'*Yet chigger*? Where is problem?' I asked Samira, and she turned to look at her mum by her bed. Her mother was striking, with the same aquiline nose. She wore a Muslim headscarf and the light from the window behind made the turquoise headcloth translucent.

'*Egeroch chigger allew*. Legs have problem.' Samira's mum spoke in simple phrases for my benefit and pulled back the blankets and Samira's long dress to reveal her thin calves and soft feet.

'*Eskemeche alhedkum*? How long you didn't walk?' I asked.

Samira's mum restraightened her daughter's dress down to her ankles before she answered quietly, '*And amet*. One year.'

When I asked Samira, '*Kuch bey techeyallesh*? Can you sit up?' she again looked to her mum to answer.

'*Bajerba bicha*. She can only lie down,' her mum said.

'*Yanchi jerba. Ayalehu*? Your spine, I can see?' I said.

I helped her to swivel her legs over the edge of the bed and wedged my knees against hers to keep her upright. Samira had what I now recognised as a classic presentation of spinal TB, where her spine had crushed in on itself, so a sharp tip pointed out from between her shoulderblades. When I asked if she could move her legs she kept her chin to her chest and said, '*Alchallem*, I can't.'

'*Tennish, tennish*? Little, little?' I said.

She nodded, but even with all her effort she could only slide one leg an inch sideways.

I laid Samira down again and assessed the movement in her hips, knees and feet. As I lifted her legs, her mum panicked and shot forwards to tuck Samira's long dress between, to maintain her modesty in this open room of twenty patients.

'*Suri yellem*? No pants?' I asked.

Samira's mum shook her head and asked in Amharic, 'Exercises are important? Every day?'

'*Lemehed, esporte betam asfelagi new*. For to walk, exercise very important,' I said.

Her mum's brow furrowed and she looked out the window. I didn't know how to convince her and hoped she wouldn't refuse physiotherapy for her daughter on the basis of modesty.

But the next day, instead of her hand-stitched countryside

dress, Samira wore a synthetic tracksuit emblazed with an enthusiastically misspelled SPROT! in large red letters beneath a soccer ball logo.

'*Addis lebs*! New clothes!' I was excited for her. Being from the countryside, getting new clothes from a packet was a huge deal.

'*Enat gezach. Ye esporte.* Mum bought them, for exercises.' Samira pointed with a flourish to her mum, who blushed. She kept her head down, pulling her headscarf in tight.

Samira seemed to have lost her reticence from yesterday. She turned from her mum to declare, '*Esporte asfelagi ayidel*? Exercises are important, aren't they?'

I tried to match her fervour and declared, '*Awe*! Yes!' Then I said, '*Ahun*? Now?' because I'd forgotten how to say 'Are you ready?'.

Samira and her mum shared a look, both pressing their lips tight, trying politely not to laugh. Samira's eyes were bright as she said, '*Enhid*! Let's go!'

As May drew to an end, I met with the second-year students Solomon and Martha for their clinical practice sessions. We convened outside the therapy room to discuss our plan for the day, and Martha said to me, 'Julie, there is one of your earlier patients inside. I think you remember that girl?'

I didn't recognise her immediately, although there was something familiar about her angular cheekbones and red dress printed with trains and flowers. It was only when she smiled and her big almond-eyes twinkled impishly, I remembered.

'Selam! *Anchi nesh*? Is it you?' I asked.

'*Awe*, yes!' She threw her head back and chortled.

Last year we had taken Selam from the orphanage to the carpenter to have a special insert made for her wheelchair. But when her grandmother retrieved Selam from the orphanage, she had left the chair and insert behind.

Selam raised her arm against involuntary writhing movements

and pointed to an old lady on a wooden chair.

'*Yanchi yenat enat*? Is this your grandma?' I didn't need to ask. The family resemblance was striking: they both had the same angular cheeks and doe eyes, although Selam's sparkled and her grandma's were sunken and dulled with age. Her grandma's few teeth were spaced along her gums with gaps between, but her two front teeth hung up over her bottom lip just like Selam's.

Selam had grown taller and more lean in the nine months since I had seen her. Her red dress had covered her knees when I last saw her but now it only reached her mid-thighs.

Her grandma said Selam wouldn't mind if the students practised physiotherapy with her. I sat cross-legged on the mat, sitting Selam in front of me to face Martha and Solomon.

'*Adi*,' she said, but I didn't understand what she meant so I asked her to repeat it.

'*Adi*.' She twisted her head and upper back to point to me with her eyes.

'Oh, you mean *anchi*. You.' I forgot this was her usual mispronunciation of 'you'.

Selam turned again towards Solomon and Martha.

'Make a note of your observations about her posture –'

Selam cut me off. '*Adi*, you.' She twisted again and pointed with her eyes at a ball on the floor.

'*Kwass tifellegiyallesh*? Do you want this ball?' I asked.

She gave big nods, so Solomon passed her the ball. Together Solomon and I tried to help her close her stiff fingers around it.

'This is a good opportunity to observe the effects of tone in the hands. You can see –'

Selam interrupted again, saying '*Adi*. You.' This time she motioned with her eyebrows to a small foam cushion.

Solomon bent Selam's stiff knees up to slide the cushion underneath her feet. I continued, 'You can see here the effect of tone on the freedom of movement in her –'

'*Adi*. You.'

'*Menden new*? What is it?' I raised my hands in mock exasperation.

She pointed with her eyes towards my wristwatch and kept pointing until I relented and I took it off and fastened it on her wrist. She was enchanted as the watch slid down to her elbow and tried hard to lift her arm into the air again to repeat the trick.

'*Ahun sira echelalehu*? Can I do some work now?' I asked.

She nodded, and I asked the students if either of them had treatment ideas. Solomon showed the grandma exercises to make the most of Selam's independent movement. They would help Selam experience different positions and develop muscle strength. I was glad to see them warming up to the little girl, learning she had plenty of potential.

When we finished the therapy session, and I retrieved my watch, the grandma bundled up Selam to take her home. The old lady was agile despite her appearance. She bent forwards to swing Selam up onto her back like a baby. Still leaning forwards, she tied a cloth under Selam's arms and wrapped it under her own armpits before securing another cloth over the top. Selam sat askew on her grandma's back with her head poking over the old lady's shoulder.

'*Ciao*! *Ciao*!' Selam's grin made it look as if she was about to launch mischief.

'*Nege*, tomorrow?' I said.

The old woman shook my hand with both of hers and used a gnarled staff for support as she hobbled out of the therapy room.

I had grown fond of Selam at the orphanage and was so disappointed she had left without her wheelchair and insert. It was wonderful to see her again and I wished we had a wheelchair to give her now, but we couldn't ask the sisters for the little red wheelchair she'd used before. Even if we gave her something, the roads were too sandy and too rocky for her frail grandmother to push her along. It was disappointing, but for now, being carried on her grandmother's back was her only option.

Selam and her grandma didn't come back for therapy again until the following week. I'd stayed up late the night before, marking student assignments, and then prayer chants through the loudspeaker from the church had woken me at 4 a.m. The call to prayer from the mosques at 5 a.m. started just as I had drifted back to sleep. I was tired and grumpy by the time I arrived at the therapy room for the second-year clinical placement at 8 o'clock.

Selam's grandma perched on the edge of a seat and when I walked in, she swivelled for me to see Selam, still tied to her back.

'*Adi*, *Adi*. You, you!' Selam called and poked her tongue at me. After checking no-one could see, I poked my tongue back at her. Her head bobbed up and down as she squawked with laughter. She poked her tongue out at me again, and again I reciprocated. My bad mood was gone by the time Solomon and Martha arrived a few minutes later.

The grandma knelt on the floor and untied the fraying strings holding Selam in place on her back, then bent sideways to slide her onto the mat. Even with Selam off her back, her grandma didn't straighten up. She looked haggard either from age or just years of grinding poverty. I wondered if her bent back ached and if she wanted physiotherapy treatment for it.

Solomon started with step one of the physiotherapy session, taking a social history to understand the home situation. He translated from the grandma that they lived in a church.

'See her hat?' He pointed to her saffron fez with a black cross stitched to the front. 'It shows she is *menekuse*, sort of like a monk. She lives in the church. Living is there for free.'

'Where do they get their food?' I asked.

'Begging. Just the neighbours are donating something to eat.'

That explained why they were both so thin. I thought I already knew the answer to the next question, but it was necessary for the students to practise a thorough physiotherapy assessment as per the textbook. I prompted Solomon, 'Can you ask how Selam accesses the toilet?'

Solomon used formal grammar to ask the grandma, and translated, 'There is no toilet. They use the river. You know, it's very rare for churches to have the toilet.'

Even though I had been in Ethiopia long enough to know it, I'd still hoped it might be different. I didn't like to think of the two of them traipsing down a muddy path to the river in the middle of the night.

The students started hands-on therapy. Martha supported Selam to sit on a firm cylindrical cushion while Solomon sat in front. He had his eyes down, watching as he stretched Selam's arm to feel the tightness in her muscles, and she leaned forwards slowly to nudge her forehead against his. He looked up in surprise to see her eyes looking right into his. She found this hilarious and straightened up again, only to repeat it the next time he looked down.

Selam seemed to enjoy each new exercise even more than the previous one. She radiated energy and revelled in the attention. She squealed with delight as Martha supported her on the therapy ball and her grandma raised her palms to heaven and gave thanks.

Solomon asked her, 'Have you done Selam's exercises we showed you last week?'

Grandma said she hadn't because she had injured herself. She showed us a deep gash between her second and third finger that looked red and swollen. Solomon inspected it and said in Amharic, 'This could get infected. Do you have medicine?'

The old woman looked puzzled but then said, 'Don't help me, help her.' She waved her uninjured hand at Selam.

I was proud to watch Solomon explain it was important we help her. 'You have to stay healthy. She needs you to look after her.'

Grandma replied in Amharic that was too detailed for me but I understood the core of her reply that she was trying her best to care for Selam, she'd tried everything. She listed off place names, ticking them off on her fingers. I looked at Solomon, who said, 'She is telling all the holy waters.'

Solomon recounted how Grandma had visited sacred springs all over the region to cure Selam of her disability. He explained the immersion and incantations as the priest poured holy water over her head six times in succession. Grandma said she had finished all her money travelling to different holy men for a cure. With sole responsibility to keep Selam safe, feed her and carry her, I imagined Grandma's despair when each ceremony failed to make Selam like other children. Maybe she hoped a cure would relieve the stigma and social exclusion, or imagined that when Selam was walking and talking they wouldn't have to beg. A cure meant she wouldn't have to worry about carrying her when Selam grew into an adult, or worse, who might carry her and keep her safe when Grandma wasn't here anymore.

When Grandma asked Solomon if they could heal Selam, I heard her use the phrase '*Tesfa allegn*, I have hope'.

I understood Solomon say, 'It's very good of you to bring her here.' He explained about cerebral palsy, how it was permanent, how we couldn't heal Selam but we could help her be more independent. Grandma raised her palms heavenwards and said, '*Egziabher yimesgen*. Thanks be to God.' Then she put her hands together beneath her nose and recited a prayer. I worried she hadn't understood Solomon's explanation and that she thought we could do more for Selam than was possible. I absolved myself from the responsibility of explaining this to her, telling myself I didn't have adequate Amharic. In reality, I was too afraid to smash her hopes. It looked as if they had little else.

I supervised the students with Selam in the therapy room every morning, and then with Samira on the ward every afternoon.

We stayed on the ward with Samira as her mum was too slight to carry her nine-year-old up the hill to the therapy room and there was no-one else to carry her.

The two little girls had such zest that I often finished their therapy sessions feeling enlivened from Selam's comedy and Samira's peppiness. The days were exceptionally busy with preparing and taking classes, marking assignments, supervising final-year students on the wards, day-long trips to remote outstation clinics to supervise students on placement there, second-year students on half-day practicals in the field, and assisting students to link in with the statistics and public health departments for their large-scale research papers. In addition to all this we were faced with the most important task – selecting the first six graduates to become the first-ever Ethiopian physiotherapy lecturers.

In early June the university recruitment committee sent a memo informing each department to submit a list of preferred graduates to join the academic staff. It dispensed special advice for the brand-new physiotherapy department to select six graduates.

Over a number of meetings, the *ferenji* staff agreed on criteria for selecting the graduates. The students hadn't yet sat their final exams or submitted their final assignments, so we chose criteria that were additional to their academic ranking. Between our team of eight lecturers we agreed to choose graduates to join the department based on:

1. Dedication
2. Good teaching skills
3. Interest in helping others
4. Sense of communal responsibility

The Ministry of Health would assign the remaining graduates to postings across the country. The semi-socialist state that provided free university education also required graduates to serve in the public health system for two years before they received their release papers. The students told me what they expected in their postings. They would earn a meagre government salary, with the lucky graduates assigned to hospitals in Addis Ababa, or other major cities. The others would see out their postings in rural clinics, living in government accommodation without proper electricity or plumbing. We knew the graduate positions at the hospital were highly sought after. Gondar had good amenities and, best of all, an academic posting here held the potential for a master's degree scholarship and opportunities for advancement. We hoped the six graduates we selected would be honoured and thrilled.

We had sat around this desk so many times before – planning clinical placements for seventy-five students in hospitals where there were few existing physiotherapy departments; determining exam schedules and now deciding on the people to run the department after we left. The future of physiotherapy in the country would depend mainly on our successors, and it seemed a momentous decision. It took three meetings and hours of discussion, and shortlisting, and re-shortlisting. So many of the students showed potential to lead and each of us *ferenji* lecturers were adamant about our chosen nominees. In the end, we agreed upon six preferred graduates – three male, three female.

Our secretary Ruth typed the names onto the recruitment office form and passed it on to the department caretaker Mama Zenash. She got the form signed in triplicate in three different offices and purple-stamped at the authorisation desk before delivering it to the recruitment office. Now we just needed to wait for the recruitment committee monthly meeting where ten of the staunchest bureaucrats would approve our selection and we would start the paperwork.

As June progressed, the weather became cooler and the wet season set in. Rainstorms started after lunch and each week they got more frequent and more intense until there were daily tropical thunderstorms lasting into the evenings.

Tadesse and I walked down to the ward with the students Solomon and Martha for their final day of clinical placements before the exam period. Tadesse introduced himself to a new patient in the bed beside Samira as she waited eagerly for the students to get set up for her own exercises. Last week she could do four-point kneeling, and support herself kneeling on the bed on all fours.

This week the students got her to progress from four-point kneeling to sitting, and then practise transitioning between kneeling on all fours to just balancing up on her knees. I watched as Martha explained to the mother that practising the transitions was the important skill, as it rebuilt her strength, balance and coordination.

I felt immensely proud, watching the students. They had come a long way from having almost no clinical skills to being able to carry out a full assessment and formulate a problem list. Now, with only one day left as student therapists, they could adequately implement a treatment progression. I felt lucky once again that I had this job, that I was a teacher. I was really going to miss them when they had gone.

Martha and Solomon helped Samira onto the side of the bed and, supporting her on either side, they counted, '*And*, *hulet*, *sost*! One, two, three!'

With good support at her hips and her knees, they helped Samira to stand for the first time in months. A radiant smile spread across her face.

Tadesse looked up from the patient he was working with in the next bed and clutched his beard with exaggerated surprise. '*Gobez*! *Yene anbessa*! Clever you! My lion!'

Thinking I'd misunderstood, I asked Tadesse, 'Did you just call her your lion?'

'This is traditional Amharic saying. It means my strong one. *Yene anbessa*, my lion.'

At this, Samira puffed her chest and looked sheepish while her mum kept her head down and smiled gently at her daughter. Both of the students called her *yene anbessa* again and Samira smiled so much she couldn't have smiled any harder.

I liked that saying very much. The lion was revered as a symbol of strength in Ethiopia. The famous black-maned lions lived in the imperial enclosure at the palace in the capital and the former Emperor Haile Selassie took the name 'Lion of Judah' upon his coronation as emperor in 1930. I'd visited Black Lion Hospital in Addis Ababa and bought tea with the same name at the markets. A lion seemed a fitting alias for a little girl displaying such tenacity.

Selam and her grandma came daily for physio and Selam showed signs of increased independent movement. Samira continued to regain movement and balance, and by the time the academic year drew to a close, Samira could sit independently over the edge of the bed and her mum could support her to transfer to sit on the metal stool beside her bed. The graduating students submitted their final research papers and sat their final written exams. In the last week of June, we examined them for their ultimate practical exam, the dreaded viva performed in front of five of their lecturers, and then the semester was over.

The physiotherapy student committee organised a farewell party for the graduates, to be held in the one physiotherapy classroom. They decorated the room with pink and blue toilet paper strung along the cornices and a tinsel party hat for the skeleton in the corner.

Normally, screwed-up uni notes littered the classroom floor but today it was swept and laid out with long grass. The smell of the fresh-cut grass mingled with the aroma of roasting coffee beans from the coffee ceremony in the corner. Two of the graduating girls roasted coffee. I was used to seeing them in jeans and t-shirts but today they wore cultural clothes of white gowns with coloured embroidery, and beads plaited into their braids. When the beans were finished roasting, they popped fresh popcorn on the charcoal burner and passed it in baskets around the room.

We used the treatment plinths as tables, and the students helped themselves to the biscuits, crisps and soft drinks we'd set out. The room was quiet at first, as the students murmured amongst themselves, until one of the boys retrieved his boom box from the dorm. 'Ethyiopiaaaaaa, Abysiinniiiaaa' at full volume resonated from the walls and tiled floors, and *now* it was a party.

Someone yelled 'Let's have a photo!' over the song on repeat for the fourth time. As we lined up for the photo outside, a bunch of student pharmacists and nurses leaned over their dorm balcony to watch.

'The first physiotherapists of Ethiopia!' called one of our students and everyone in the photo cheered. Our onlookers on their dorm balcony cheered too, and then we heard children cheering, and turned around to see little patients who'd sneaked out of the paediatric ward to watch the celebration.

There were speeches and congratulations, hugs and goodbyes, until the students trickled out. Just the lecturers and a few students remained, gathering the empty soft-drink bottles while Mama Zenash swept the floor for crisps and popcorn. We pulled down the toilet-paper streamers but we let the skeleton keep its party hat.

'Miss Julie, will you come back next year?' The student Elias passed me an empty Fanta bottle to stack in the crate.

'I'm not sure, Elias. I'm so tired, and there are already so many good lecturers here. The new graduate staff will make physiotherapy strong.'

Elias clinked two more glass bottles into the crate. 'You are right. Physiotherapy will be strong for the future. *Tesfa allegn.* I have hope.'

Over the first week of July, the roads outside the university thronged with students carrying duffle bags and backpacks. Students filled the minibuses as they travelled to the bus station for their journeys home. Then the area went quiet. The minibuses had empty seats again, and the university was dull.

It was quiet in the physio department too. Most of the *ferenji* lecturers left for vacation, or finished their contracts and had gone home for good. Only three *ferenji* physios remained with the local staff.

I passed my workdays on long therapy sessions for Selam, Samira and the other patients, and catching up on admin. One month after we submitted our list of preferred applicants to the recruitment committee, we were yet to hear anything so I volunteered to follow up.

The recruitment office was small and dim. The young secretary with elaborate braids looked up from her computer but continued to click her mouse; I was sure she was playing solitaire.

I enquired on the progress of the physiotherapy graduates and asked if the recruitment committee had approved our nominees and when could we start the paperwork?

The secretary sighed and pushed her chair back to stand. She disappeared into a side office and when she returned she said, 'No need of doing anything.' Resuming her spot at the computer, she clicked her mouse again.

When I returned a week later and asked the same thing the secretary shrugged at me but did not leave her desk. She said, 'No graduates yet selected.' As I left I heard the click, click, click of her mouse, no doubt dragging cards on top of each other.

I visited the recruitment office at 9 a.m. every Monday for the next three weeks. On each occasion, the secretary shrugged me off, sometimes even before I spoke, not moving her hand from the mouse.

It was now August, and it had taken almost two months for nothing at all to happen. We now had only seven weeks to complete all the administrative steps for the graduates to commence as lecturers in time for the next academic year.

A different secretary sat at the computer the following week. She was older than her predecessor and wore her hair in a bun rather than braids.

When I enquired after the recruitment for physiotherapy graduates, she looked uninterested and shook her head, saying in Amharic, 'I am new.'

That morning I went straight from the recruitment office to the ward. I preferred to work with the children, who were as entertaining as the secretaries were aggravating.

Today Samira was upright in bed, beaming at me across the room of twenty beds.

'*Eshi lejoch, man new mejemeriya*? Okay kids, who is first?' I asked.

Samira shot her arm up and eagerly pointed a finger down at herself. I had just helped her to sit over the edge of the bed when the sub-dean of the recruitment committee appeared in the doorway.

'Nice to see you! What are you doing on the ward? We never see you down here!' I said.

The sub-dean wore a tweed jacket and round glasses. He asked me to step outside. After helping Samira back to bed, I followed him out of the ward.

He smoothed the lapels of his jacket and flattened his hair before clearing his throat. Then he said, 'You have done nothing to recruit new graduates.'

I was speechless for a moment, indignant and confused. When I had gathered myself, I said, 'I checked with the secretary every week for the last five weeks. She told me there was nothing to do.'

'You didn't give your list of preferred applicants to the recruitment office,' the sub-dean said.

'But we did! As soon as the memo was issued!'

He passed me an envelope. 'Having heard nothing from your department, the recruitment committee have therefore finalised their decision.'

I tore open the envelope and read the graduates that had been selected without consultation. The recruitment committee had managed to pick six of the most belligerent, obtuse male students – pushy, vocal students, who spent more time demanding their exam be regraded than studying for it. This selection not only didn't match our criteria, it exemplified everything we didn't want.

My heart beat fast. 'But we gave our list to the secretary. Why didn't she pass it on?'

'Which secretary?' The sub-dean looked shocked.

'The young secretary! With the braids?'

He nodded gravely. 'She has left our employment.'

I was sure he must have noticed she only ever played solitaire instead of working so I said, 'We will resubmit our original list. The one your secretary lost.'

The sub-dean cleared his throat again and looked nervous. 'No. The recruitment committee has already submitted this list to central Ministry of Health. You are too late.'

Chapter 23

You are strong: ጠንካራ ነሽ /*tenkaranesh*/

This was disastrous. I imagined the new physiotherapy team turning up to work at 10 a.m. and going home an hour later, spending most of that time in the tearoom. The physiotherapy department would not survive. It seemed like everything had been such a waste: all the late nights preparing classes, marking assignments, arguing with students over marks, arguing with the transport manager for buses to clinical placements.

This week all the other lecturers were on holidays or at home, so I phoned a lecturer I knew on another campus, where she was one of only five Ethiopian women instructors. My fingers shook as I dialled.

'Bloody, bloody, stupid, stupid men!' my fellow lecturer shouted into the phone.

'The sub-dean says it's too late.'

'Rubbish! Just try. Write letters. Get them purple-stamped. Go to their meetings. Just don't give up. Be strong.'

The next day Samira was ready to go for exercises when I reached the ward. She was already wearing her SPROT! tracksuit and her mum had helped her to sit on the stool. Her mum sat on the edge of her bed, tucking stray hairs into her turquoise headscarf.

I called over a small boy, about four years old, with button eyes. '*Machina eski*? Show me the walking frame?'

We only had one paediatric walking frame, a foldable, child-sized frame with wheels on all four legs. The children called it the *machina*, the car. We kept it on the ward and the children who needed it took turns. It was often missing though as other, more mobile children rolled it around the ward for fun and we had to enlist their help to find it again.

My small helper wriggled on his tummy to retrieve the walking frame from beneath his bed and unfolded it to position it in front of Samira.

'*Endet techeyallesh*? What you can do?' I asked her.

Without speaking she pulled herself up into standing and took a few shaky steps with the walking frame.

'*Yene anbessa*! My lion! My strong one!' I clapped and exclaimed, '*Kehulet sament memoker, wede bet*!' which translated to 'Practising two weeks more then going home!'.

When her mother spoke, I understood her say, 'We will go home tomorrow. We finished her injections and I am tired, I need to go home.'

Samira and her mum had stayed in the hospital for three months, sharing a bed every night and sitting side by side in the ward every day. True, Samira had finished her three months of daily injections for TB, but she still had quite a way to go in her rehab. If Samira went home now, she might never walk properly again.

'*Ehet woym zemed allesh*? You have a sister or relative?' I meant to ask if anyone else could stay with Samira.

'*Manem sew yellem*. I have no-one.' Her mother tugged at loose threads on Samira's bedspread. When she lifted her head, she looked exhausted and sad. '*Amemegn*, I have pain.' She clutched her ear.

I called Doctor Tesfaye over, asking him in English to persuade them to stay. He pulled the metal stool close to Samira's mum, and they sat chatting in soft voices.

Samira walked to the end of her bed using the walking frame and I sent my little helper to bring me over two more metal stools from other bedsides. I understood fragments of what Samira's mum said.

'We have no money, how can we stay?'

I got Samira to sit on the stool and sat on another behind her to help her hands onto the foot rails looping high over the end of her old-fashioned bed. Even as I assisted her exercises, I could still hear the conversation.

'There's no-one to look after my other children ... I have pain, here ...' Samira's mum held her hand over her ear again.

Another child with TB hobbled over to watch Samira and stood with palms on his thighs. The helping boy put one miniature arm over the other's shoulders. Three other children from the ward who were not bed-bound formed a semicircle around Samira and me.

I supported Samira's knees with my hands and nodded to the children. We counted together, '*And*, *hulet*, *sost* ... one, two, three ...'

On the count of three, Samira stood up, using the bedstead for support. She lifted her fingers off the bar one by one and put her arms out to balance. For two full seconds, she stood completely unassisted for the first time since she had been in hospital.

'*Gobez*! Clever!' I called, and our diminutive audience cheered. Samira grabbed for the bar again, but she had felt herself balance and she looked elated.

Doctor Tesfaye stood up and walked back to the ward office. Samira's mum remained sitting on the edge of the bed looking out the window. She reached over to the bedside table and shook a handful of peanuts off their wrapper, a page of someone's old homework. She blew her nose into the square of spelling. Tears trickled down her face as she stared outside.

It was the first time I had seen an Ethiopian adult weep. I had seen ritual, noisy wailing at funerals but I had never witnessed an adult let silent tears fall.

Unable to comfort her, I just watched, hoping she would know

I was empathising with her. I had let tears slip a few weeks ago, when I had been returning from an expensive and painful trip to the dentist in Addis Ababa. Those had been tears of frustration and fear, because at 4.30 a.m. in the airport two soldiers yelled at me before blocking my entry because I'd tried to enter the terminal with the wrong ticket. I had run out of birr so I couldn't get a minibus or taxi to the Ethiopian Airlines office in Piazza to amend the ticket, and I couldn't call anyone because none of the payphones in the airport car park worked and the soldiers shouted at me again when I tried to use the payphones in the terminal. It was dark and I felt so tired, alone and powerless, but foolish for weeping. Those frustrations seemed so minor in comparison to the scale of obstacles and conflicted feelings this mother must have been facing.

'*Hulet hakim asfelagi new*. I need two doctors here,' I announced to all the children. The two little boys shot their arms into the air and I positioned them on either side of Samira with their arms outstretched. Samira reached out to tap the helping boy's finger, and her junior onlookers were awed.

Samira lifted her hands into the air again and called, '*Enat*! *Enat*! *Yehewlesh*! Mum! Mum! Look at me!'

Samira's mum crumpled her paper hanky in her hand and turned back from the window. She smiled through her tears. '*Yene anbessa*. My lion,' she said and resumed the never-ending job of being strong.

They went home that afternoon.

That night I lay on the couch wishing I could tell someone about my day. I had already said goodbye to Marieke. She had gone to the Netherlands when exams were over and would only come back with enough time to collect her things and move to Addis Ababa to start a new role there in the next academic year. Tadesse was working for the week at an outstation clinic and out of mobile range, and I didn't know who else to call. I felt heartbroken that Samira's treatment was cut short, but my sadness seemed silly, self-indulgent. This suffering seemed to dwarf me. I was overwhelmed by questions about what I was supposed to do with my privilege. Just as at the end of the last academic year, I was torn about whether to give up and return to Perth or renew my contract again. What could I contribute to this situation? I couldn't even persuade a mother to stay. Samira was just a patient, and I a health professional, I reminded myself. It wasn't my job to get upset over patients.

The electricity stayed on for the entire evening, a rare luxury that allowed me to listen to music and read a book to avoid thinking too much until bedtime. I knelt on my bed and opened my wooden shutters.

'*Dehna eder*. Goodnight, Mesfin!' I called out.

'Julieyea! *Battris allesh*? *Ney*? Have you got batteries? Can you come here?' Mesfin yelled.

Glad for the company, I got some spare batteries from the cupboard and went around the side of the house to his guard's hut, a one-roomed hut with dirt floor. He sat on the edge of his wooden bed, rummaging in the grain sack he stored his belongings in. I always wondered how old Mesfin was. He looked about my age, but when I asked him he said he didn't know; he had no family to tell him. I stood at the entrance to the hut, scratching Tara's ears as she sat to attention beside me. Mesfin delved into the grain sack, angling it to catch the light from the bulb hanging from the ceiling. He talked non-stop in Amharic too fast for me to catch while he took out his transistor radio, twisted the grain sack closed and slipped it under his horse-hair mattress. He installed the batteries and turned the volume to full.

Then he rolled his yellow-and-black chequered blanket into a ball. He handed me the transistor, and he carried the blanket under one arm, the other holding his walking stick. We walked together across the compound to his guard's bench by the front door, and the wooden bed next to it where he would sleep the night with Tara dozing beneath. Over the tinny music he told me a story as he rolled his tartan blanket into a ball, speaking so fast I could only make out 'lovely', 'music' and 'radio'.

'*Menden new*? What is it?' I was trying my best to understand and even harder to keep a straight face. This happened so often – Mesfin telling me elaborate stories that I could only catch the thematic essence of. The radio blared an energetic tune, Tara pranced at our feet, Mesfin talked fast, arms going everywhere and I clamped my lips together to stop from giggling.

'*Algebagnem*, don't understand,' I said and then couldn't help but burst out laughing.

'Ah, Julieyea,' he laughed too then. I laughed more, and he laughed more at me and I bent my head back and we both laughed up at the stars until my eyes filled with tears.

In the second week of August, with few patients on the wards and no classes, I had more time to spend at the orphanage with Sister Deepti. The next day, instead of going into the office, I caught a minibus straight to the orphanage, hoping the kids would cheer me up. Sister Deepti was in the nursery with a toddler I didn't recognise hiding behind her long skirts.

'Who is this?' I squatted in front of the boy.

Sister Deepti reached down and the toddler took hold of her middle finger to step forwards. He looked no older than one and a half; he still had the pudgy legs of a baby.

'*Mamush*, little boy.' I held out my hands to him.

The toddler took long, slow steps, as if taking one step at a time was all he could do. When I picked him up he leant into me with the side of his face against my chest. Impassive and morose, he stared into the distance. Patting his back, I said to Sister Deepti, 'My goodness, this is a sad little boy. What's wrong with him?'

'His mother died last night. She was in the ladies ward.'

I didn't ask the cause. Most of the young girls who came in died from undiagnosed illnesses: combinations of AIDS, TB, neglect, hunger, or worse. I imagined him crying out for his mum until he'd given up. Tears pricked my eyes, and I bent my head to look into the little one's face so Sister Deepti wouldn't see. It was absurd to get upset – I didn't know the mother and had just met the child.

'What will happen to him?' I kept my head down.

'Oh, so beautiful and such a fat little baby he is.' She rubbed his back and ran a palm over his head. 'He'll go to our main orphanage in Addis, and one nice family from abroad will be having him.' Sister Deepti gave a musical laugh as another toddler lurched towards her and grabbed her skirts. She lifted the little girl, jiggling her and tweaking her nose. How did she stay so caring and jovial without being insensitive? How did she stay strong?

On the play mat with six fat, healthy babies lying around me, I set the new toddler at my side. But he cried and stretched his arms back to me, so I cuddled him on my lap until Sister Deepti was free again; then I passed him to her.

'All the healthy babies will be adopting from Addis Ababa next week,' she said.

Next to the new toddler was another baby I'd seen every week for six months now. He was skinny and dehydrated when he first arrived, but after half a year he had developed chubby thighs and rosy cheeks. He rolled himself onto his tummy and looked proud of himself.

'Will this little one go too?'

'All the healthy babies,' Sister Deepti repeated. 'Don't you worry too much about them; they'll soon be finding very nice families to love them. Thanks be to God.'

It hurt to think I wouldn't see him anymore; I'd gotten very attached over the six months. But it was amazing to imagine the light and joy he would bring his adoptive parents somewhere overseas.

I went to collect a regular patient, Mekdes, from her cot.

'Be careful, she is having a lot of sores today.' Sister Deepti handed me a pair of latex gloves.

Though Mekdes was two years old, she wore baby clothes. She only weighed six kilos, and was about the height of a six-month-old. She had big brown eyes and long, curly lashes in a heart-shaped face. Her legs were scissored with spasticity, and her little knees were already fused bent. Her disability was so severe she had no potential to develop independent movement or speech. Today sores dotted her feet and a rash covered her head and face. Normally she loved having physio, giving us toothy grins or gurgling when we moved her or gave her attention, but today she just gave a feeble cry. When I put two gloved fingers against her forehead it was hot with fever.

'*Yasaznal*, I feel it,' I whispered to her. I'd never used that word, I didn't even know if I was pronouncing it right. Sometimes when I recounted something sad, or touching, people would reply with *Yasaznal*, which Tadesse told me translated to 'I feel it for you'.

At that moment I felt it for Mekdes. I lifted her from the cot and held her against my chest. Tears rolled from her eyes, down her cheeks, but she was silent. Again my own tears threatened.

I didn't need to ask Sister Deepti because I knew Mekdes wouldn't go to Addis Ababa and would not be adopted by a nice family abroad. Even if a family wanted to adopt her, I knew from working in the disability sector that immigration restrictions in Australia made it almost impossible to get visas for children with disabilities. Visas for other countries may have been easier, but Mekdes had little chance of being adopted when there were plenty of other babies that would one day grow to walk and talk.

Worst of all, I felt hypocritical because I would not adopt her either. Even if I decided not to renew my contract in Gondar and return to Australia, right now I only had five hundred dollars in my savings account in Perth and this month's one hundred dollars salary hidden in a powdered-milk tin under my bed. I was in no position to adopt a child with special needs. Cradling

Mekdes against my body, I stroked her arm with my gloved finger. *I felt it*. She wouldn't be adopted into a family; she would grow up in this orphanage.

My gaze fell on the wall of the nursery, at a crucifix and a painting of the Virgin Mary with hands raised to heaven. The tears made it blurry, but I gazed at it, struggling to understand how I was supposed to believe a compassionate God would let a baby who needed so much help grow up without a family.

I'd come on this trip hoping to find strength in faith, or be fulfilled with purpose, but I'd never doubted the existence of God or felt the purposelessness of existence so much as now.

'She is too sick today for physiotherapy,' I said aloud as I returned Mekdes back to her cot.

Mekdes's cry was audible now as I laid her on the starched sheet. It seemed so callous – maybe I should have just held her and comforted her all day. Stroking her prickly head where little curls had started to grow, I whispered, '*Tenkaranesh*, you are strong.'

I didn't feel *tenkaranesh* myself. I wasn't strong, I could do nothing for Mekdes and I couldn't help Samira to walk again. It seemed impossible I would be strong enough to get the university to employ our list of graduates. Our efforts seemed so pointless.

Lately I felt weepy all the time. Seeing suffering and feeling powerless to alleviate it had made me so tired. *Feeling it* made me so tired. Why couldn't I be strong instead of uselessly churning over other people's pain? I had no ability to extricate myself from what I saw and didn't have the skills to live in a world of distress without making it my own.

In the minibus from the orphanage I held back tears, but the thought kept coming: I simply wasn't strong enough. It was as if someone had ripped off my do-gooder glasses and stamped their rose-coloured lenses into smithereens.

The passenger in front of me was a man from the countryside who looked about twenty. He turned around to sit sideways in his seat and stare at me. He spent the whole journey observing me with his chin resting on his hand. I glared at him, then narrowed my eyes at him, and still he stared. I felt affronted, but remembered I was a visitor to this country. If he wanted to gape at me, for looking so weird, because he had never seen a *ferenji*, that was his right. At the hospital I alighted the minibus and when some teenage boys yelled 'You-you-you!' I wanted to scream 'Leave me alone! Stop saying that!' but instead, I caught the next minibus home so I could lie down and cry.

Chapter 24

Dark night: ጥቁር ማታ /*tikkur mata*/

When Tadesse arrived that evening Mesfin opened the gate to the compound and he let himself in the unlocked front door. I was lying on the couch with my laptop, watching an episode of *Black Adder*, bawling my eyes out.

He stopped, alarmed. 'Julie! What's wrong?'

I sat up, wiping my nose on the back of my hand and smudging my tears across my cheeks. 'I don't know.'

Tadesse eased himself onto the couch next to me and pulled a tissue from his pocket. After using it I threw the tissue down beside the three empty Hip Hop biscuit wrappers. Then I started crying again, as I had been all afternoon. The tears wouldn't stop but I didn't know where they were coming from. I felt so ashamed to let Tadesse see me like this. He peered into my face.

'Are you lonely?' Tadesse tried to guess. 'Maybe we should go out with the others; they are going to Chelada Bar in Piazza.'

With lips quivering and tears rolling down my face I said, 'I'm not lonely.'

Tadesse put another tissue into my hand. 'You want to be alone? I can going to Chelada Bar and you stay here.'

'No! Don't leave me alone!' I clutched at his arm.

'You miss your family? You want to going home to Perth?'

'No, I don't want to go to Perth.'

'Aha. You're sad because you have to go home when your contract is finished, but you want to staying in Gondar.'

I snivelled as tears pooled under my chin. 'No, I don't want to stay in Gondar.'

Tadesse sat with his arm around me. 'Did you eating your dinner?' He arranged my hair away from my sticky face and draped it into a ponytail.

After dinner we joined our friends. It was a cold night but Chelada Bar was cosy, with about thirty patrons, and muted lighting from under orange lampshades on each table. The bartender greeted us by name and asked if I would have my usual Dashen beer, but I ordered a bottle of Axum wine instead. Axum looked like red wine, but was strong like port and tasted sweet and bitter simultaneously, like sangria with too much orange peel. The alcohol went straight to my head, and soon I was flushed and my cheeks were warm.

I poured myself another glass and listened to the convivial chatter. Tonight it was just Tadesse's friends so they all spoke in Amharic. They stopped to translate patches of the conversation for me, but I preferred it when they didn't. At least then I had an excuse not to join in; everything felt too heavy. Even *Greatest Love Songs of All Time* on the CD player left me numb. By my third glass of wine I could not get rid of the overwhelming feeling I had failed. I had set myself clear expectations, but I didn't live up to them. Tears threatened again and I thought of the other *ferenji* lecturers; they all appeared so resilient. I didn't see them weeping into their Axum. I poured a fourth glass, waiting for the alcohol to numb me further.

A little later, waiting for the bartender to open the next bottle, I thought again about how I wasn't strong enough for any of this. I was feeble and useless.

Quite a lot later, after the end of that bottle, Tadesse walked me home. The streetlights threw circles of light onto the gravel road and the stars were vivid. When we got to the gate outside my compound my head swirled with alcohol, sadness and pain. The bitterness and confusion were too hard to see through and I gibed and antagonised Tadesse until we were arguing.

'Please don't start fighting, Julie,' Tadesse said. 'Tomorrow I am going for three weeks to northern part.'

'We should break up now. You'll be gone for three weeks, then I'm probably leaving anyway. There is no future for us so let's just get it over with now.' In my drunkenness I liked how I sounded in control, instead of hopeless, which was how I felt. We argued some more and then I said, without emotion, 'I don't want to be with you anymore. Go home.'

In the streetlight I could see how wounded Tadesse was.

'I made a big mistake being here with you tonight.' He spoke in a low voice, with his face set hard.

Mesfin let me into the compound. He had wrapped his chequered blanket over his head and shoulders into a cheery yellow-and-black headscarf and his transistor radio blasted incongruous merry tunes. He peered around the gate to see Tadesse walking away and turned, confused. '*Tadesse almetam*? *Hule gize essu wede wust*. Tadesse's not coming in? But he always comes inside.'

My throat tightened and my eyes pricked with tears. *Tenkaranesh*, you are strong, I told myself. I shook my head.

Once inside, I kicked my shoes off and lay on my bed. Tadesse was the most reliable man on the planet. I couldn't get through a day or an issue without him. I wondered why he did so much for me, why he treated me so well, why he cared so much about me. *Had* cared. *Had* done so much for me until I broke up with him. I cried myself to sleep, then woke up forty-five minutes later and hurled into the bucket I'd had foresight to put by my bed. I puked and cried until I was empty.

The next morning, I ate dry biscuits as I penned an email:

To: Customer Service
Subject: Return date open ticket
Date: 11 August 2006

Dear Thai Airways,

I have an open ticket from Addis Ababa Ethiopia to Bangkok, then from Bangkok to Perth, with Thai Airways.

My ticket was arranged by my employer.

I collected the ticket from the Perth office in October 2005.

My employer has advised I need to organise my return flight from Bangkok to Perth. The flight number is written as open and there is no date listed in the return portion.

Could you please advise me how I can book the return portion from Bangkok to Perth? There is no Thai Airways office in Ethiopia.

My hangover had not faded even by late afternoon, when a downpour started just as I got out of the minibus from the hospital. Within minutes the dirt roads leading to my house were like rivers. I waded home through ankle-deep water that ran so fast it roared. The rain soaked my hair and ran down the back of my jacket and I had to keep wiping my arm across my face to see where I was going. Mesfin opened the gate as usual but he looked panicked.

'Julie! *Leba allew*! *Berd lebs yellem*! There is a thief! Someone has stolen my blanket!' he shouted, and it hurt my ears. Cringing, I looked as he gestured to his guard's bench by the front door.

'*Indet*? How?'

Mesfin recounted, and I understood snatches of what he said ... how he had gone to get milk from the neighbour's cow, and when he came back the expensive wool blanket, the yellow-and-black one that Marieke gave him, was stolen. He waved his arms at the low point in the fence where he suspected the thief had jumped into our compound and escaped again.

'*Gin, Tara ezzi*? But Tara was here?'

Mesfin pointed at Tara dozing beside the guard's bed, who, on hearing her name, thumped her tail and lifted her chin momentarily.

I brought out a spare blanket to Mesfin. '*Lante. Berd zare.* For you. Cold today.'

I was worried, sleep-deprived and paranoid. How was it so easy for a thief to get in and out of our compound with its high stone walls and metal gate? I feared whoever it was might return. With Marieke on vacation in Europe until the semester started again, I was alone in the house. I reconsidered my existing hiding places.

I already hid my salary. Each month I stashed the wad of one hundred birr notes inside a powdered-milk tin into a pillowcase and I alternated hiding spots between the bottom of my wardrobe and under my bed. My passport was hidden in a pair of socks wrapped inside a t-shirt.

However, I kept my SLR camera with its big zoom lens in the bottom drawer of my dressing table, ready to grab for photo opportunities. If a wool blanket was a target, my camera would be an enormous prize. I took my camera from the bottom drawer, put it inside a pillowcase and set it under my bed. Then I put the kettle on.

While the tea was brewing, I realised any serious thief would look under the bed. I retrieved the camera and put it inside the tub we stored bags of dried beans and lentils in. But as I drank my tea, I worried weevils in the legumes might damage the film or the camera mechanism. That camera was way too valuable.

After I finished my tea I retrieved the camera and stashed it inside an unused metal water filter in the spare room. Aha! Thief- and weevil-proof! Then I barricaded my door and curled up for a deep, hungover sleep and forgot I had ever hidden my camera.

A few days later I logged on to my emails while I ate breakfast and saw a reply from the airline.

> *To: Julie Sprigg*
> *Subject: Return date open ticket*
> *Date: 14 August 2006*
>
> *Dear Julie,*
>
> *I have located your ticketing data and it appears your ticket only had a validity of 4 months. Therefore, the expiry date on the ticket was 14 FEB 06. This was the last date you could travel on that ticket.*
>
> *Kind regards,*
> *Thai Airways Customer Service*

I stopped my spoonful of rice and banana halfway to my mouth, my mind telling me things that seemed impossible: my ticket had expired six months ago; I didn't have a return ticket home, and it was my fault. Why didn't I check with the airline about the expiration date? Why had it never occurred to me that the return ticket provided with a one-year contract would only be valid for four months?

I tried to phone the head dean's office, but the telephone line had gone dead and remained dead when I tried again in ten minutes. I caught a minibus to the head dean's office, only to learn from a sleepy secretary that he was in Addis.

The sub-dean was also away, his secretary told me. From that office I ran to the office of the vice-president of academic affairs, but the secretary said to return at ten o'clock the following morning. After a restless night, I reported to the office at 10 a.m. and was told again to come tomorrow. Unsurprisingly, he wasn't there at 10 a.m. that morning either, so I telephoned the staff liaison office. The secretary told me to call back after lunch but when I did so, no-one answered the phone. I was bordering on hysteria as I replaced the handset. My heart raced and I felt dizzy.

I had no money. Earning just one hundred dollars a month for nearly two years had meant I'd dipped into my savings. The five hundred in my Australian account wouldn't even get me half a ticket home.

Forty-eight hours passed before I found someone authorised to help me. This senior member of the academic committee looked up from signing papers when I entered his office, and when I showed him the print-out of the email, he looked amused.

'What a silly mistake. But it's good for us if you have to stay in Ethiopia.'

I wondered how a grumpy whingeing *ferenji* was useful to them, but I feigned amusement.

He picked up his pen to sign the next document. With his head still down to the page, he said without emotion, 'Complete an application form and we will decide if we will buy you another ticket.'

If? I thought. What if not?

The secretary interrupted, calling out from her desk, 'Mr Temusgin is on the phone. Should I put him through, or should he call back?'

The committee member continued signing documents and called out, 'Umm ... put him through. No, take a message. No ... maybe call back?'

The interruption in our conversation was only twenty seconds, but it seemed to stretch forever, and the blood pounded in my ears.

When he finally looked up at me to see I was still there, I said, 'No, no, no. You don't understand. There is no decision to be made; you *have* to buy me a ticket home. It was in my contract. I don't have enough money for a ticket home. A ticket home costs one year's salary.'

'You know this is just bureaucracy,' he waved his hand as if it was a small matter. 'Simply write us a letter.'

The word 'simply' seemed inappropriate. Achieving even small tasks required multiple visits to far apart offices, with references to minutes for meetings of subcommittees and sub-subcommittees, memos signed in triplicate and purple-stamped. Whether it was printing exam papers, organising buses for student placements, accessing donated funds, getting textbooks into the library, or collecting my salary, everything involved maddening layers of bureaucracy.

However, I had little choice. The next day I started the process of requesting a ticket. I filled out the application and sent it with Mama Zenash to get the requisite three signatures and a purple stamp. Then I waited for my ticket home. Simply.

It wasn't until a fortnight later I noticed the spare house keys were missing from their hiding place, a bowl on the middle shelf of the lounge room cupboard. Marieke had been diligent about locking the cupboard, but while she was away I had gotten slack as it seemed unnecessary. I searched the house, looking through the lounge room, the kitchen, Marieke's room and my room, but the keys were missing. No-one else but the cleaning lady and I had been in the house.

Initially I had baulked at the idea of having someone shopping, cooking, washing up and laundering for me. How bourgeois! But then, I experienced someone shopping, cooking, washing up and laundering for me ... how convenient!

Our maid looked to be a few years younger than me, and I thought we enjoyed each other's company. I practised my Amharic with her, and she practised her English as she handwashed our clothes in plastic tubs and rinsed them under the hose. She came two days a week, and every Tuesday she cooked my favourite, *atekelt*, potatoes with garlic and carrots, and Marieke's favourite, *shiro*, chickpea stew. But now, it appeared she was the only possible culprit for the key theft. What else might she have taken?

Feeling nauseous and betrayed, I checked my valuables. First,

I looked for my salary, counting out the birr notes. None were missing, so I put the stash back at the bottom of my wardrobe. My passport was still tucked in the socks inside the t-shirt. Finally I looked for my SLR camera in the bottom drawer of my dressing table. It was not there.

I could not remember the last time I had used the camera. Had it been at the students' leaving party? I tried to remember past events where I might have taken, and left, the camera. I searched my room, Marieke's room and the lounge room, increasingly desperate and suspicious.

I sat on the back step, staring over the valley, wondering what I should do. I recalled three stories, all told by someone about a friend of somebody else, where a guard and a maid conspired to rob their employer. Our maid had visited on Tuesday, maybe she had colluded with Mesfin then? But it seemed implausible our two trusted workers would betray us, after working for us for so long. Surely if they were going to steal from us they'd have done it before now. And yet, what else could I think? I remembered Mesfin's stolen blanket. Maybe that, too, was a set-up. Maybe he'd hidden it to make me think a thief was working in the neighbourhood.

With shaking hands I tried to telephone my maid, but the phone was still dead. At the small shop around the corner I paid three birr to use the phone and asked her in Amharic to come to my house now please.

As soon as she was in the door, I demanded, '*Lela kulf yet new*? Where is other key?'

'*Alawekem*. I don't know.' She looked puzzled.

Frantic and paranoid, I shouted at her in Amharic, 'No work more for you! Coming on Tuesday don't! I find cleaning lady one more another!'

She responded in long sentences in Amharic too fast for me to understand. My thoughts were so scrambled that even had there been someone to speak English that day, I might not have understood them either.

'*Beka. Hij*. Enough. Go away.' I tried to calm down. '*Anchi alfelligem*. I don't want you.'

Then I slammed the door, and with shaking hands, I tried to phone Sister Almaz in Addis Ababa, the only person I knew who could help me think rationally. But the phone was still dead. I unplugged it from the socket, banged the receiver against my hand, belted it on the table and swore at it. Unsurprisingly, it still didn't work. It had been dead for days. I couldn't call anyone or use the dial-up internet without the phone. I caught a minibus to Piazza and went straight to the Ethio Telecom office.

Inside, I joined the long queue sitting along a wooden bench. Most people held their landline telephones with them, on their laps or in bags. I wished, not for the first time, that I had a mobile, but the only way to get a mobile was with a black-market SIM from Addis Ababa, at the cost of one month's salary.

After an hour I reached the front of the queue and the Ethio Telecom worker called me to the desk.

'My telephone doesn't work,' I said in English.

'Tell me what is the problem?' the clerk said.

'I can hear it ringing, but when I pick up the phone I can't hear any sound. It is dead.'

The clerk nodded as if agreeing. 'All of these people are having the same problem. Simply it is the problem of wet season. Moisture in the lines. Just waiting until after wet season. Probably your phone is working then.' He looked cheerful, his expression saying, *problem solved!*

'But the wet season won't finish for three months! Can't someone fix it before then? I need a telephone.'

The clerk sighed and pulled out an enormous ledger. 'If you think it is necessary I will writing in the complaint book.' He leafed through the handwritten pages until he came to the last blank line. As I watched him note my name, my address and my telephone number, I saw row upon row of people's names, all presumably with my problem.

'When will they fix my telephone?' I asked.

The clerk sighed again. 'After tomorrow.'

I was sure he meant that in the vaguest sense possible.

I left even more grumpy than before. Now all I wanted was to get home for a cup of tea and to do some work. If I could lose myself in work, everything would be fine.

The next day, on my way home from work, two men in beige overalls were leaving as I arrived at my compound. Tara's tail banged my legs as she looked up at me, waiting to play ball.

'*Man new*? Who is it?' I asked Mesfin.

Mesfin said in Amharic, 'They are from electric company. Your power is cut off.' He passed me a small paper print-out showing, typed in English: *owing 600 birr.*

It was all too much. I exploded at him in Amharic, shouting syntactically impaired versions of 'Why didn't you stop them? Why didn't you ask them to wait? Didn't you tell them it's the university's fault?' Frustrated and furious, I shouted, '*Ante teru ayidelum*! *Ante leba foto*! *Ante leba allew*! You are no good! You thiefed my camera! You are a thief!'

Mesfin looked aghast while Tara cowered behind his legs.

I had never shouted at him before, because I rarely shouted at anyone. Seeing both of them react made me feel terrible.

Embarrassed, still angry, and wound up, I went inside and slammed things around. Having our electricity bill paid was part of my contract. My salary was low but some of my living expenses were covered – in theory. Every month without fail, our electricity got cut off because the bills department of the uni didn't pay the bill on time.

When Marieke was around it had been amusing, even sometimes pleasant, as we spent the evening reading books by candlelight. But this time I was really annoyed. I was putting together a booklet of resources for the paediatric physio unit, but now that I would leave the country soon I needed to get it finished. I needed electricity for my laptop.

There was a knock on the red gate. I heard voices and Mesfin's walking stick on the concrete. When he knocked, I threw the front door open with such force it slammed into the wall behind. Tara bounded to my side for a tickle but I shouted at her to get out of the way and demanded from Mesfin, '*Lemen*? What?'

Mesfin's eyes were wide, and he said in Amharic, 'The people from the water department came. The bill is due today.'

'*Sent new*? How much is the bill?'

"They didn't say. Usually about four hundred birr, Marieke gives me the money and I bring back the change.'

I collected exactly four hundred birr, the last of my money until next payday, from inside the powdered-milk tin hidden in inside a pillowcase at the bottom of my wardrobe.

'*Zerzer sechegn. Lela birr yellem.* Bring me the change. I have no other money,' I snapped at him and thrust the cash at him, then slammed the door extra hard. I hated how I was behaving, yet I seemed unable to calm down.

When Mesfin left, I dragged his bamboo bench over to the power meter. From the bench I could reach the meter and reconnect the electricity using a tarnished Ukrainian Airlines knife and a pair of pliers. I returned the wires to their connection points with the pliers and tightened the screws with the point of the knife. I'd watched how the electrical workers reconnected the power each month so it worked. The lights came on and the meter whirred. Inside I heard the reassuring hum of the voltage regulator. I pushed the bamboo bench back into place, glad to have achieved something for the first time in days.

Inside again, I typed:

Paediatric Physiotherapy. Additional resource kit.
Contents:
- *Spinal TB*
- *Cerebral Palsy*
- *Clubfoot*

I began a list of resources:

> *Spinal TB. Refer to* Tidy's Physiotherapy, *page 8, chapters 4–12. Available from: Library.*

But then I got nervous. What if the university paid the bill today? The electric man would come back to reconnect the power and discover I'd done it myself illegally. I pictured myself in an Ethiopian jail, sleeping on the cement floor, picking lice from my torso, applying for consular assistance to secure my release.

Leaving my resource kit unfinished, I pushed the bench across the veranda again. I clambered up, disconnected the power, and heard the voltage regulator sigh and go quiet.

I boiled water for tea on the gas burner and read a book in silence. When my eyes got tired, I stared at the ceiling and reminisced, almost with nostalgia, about the times Marieke and I traipsed to and from the bills department. We asked, begged and sometimes cajoled to get our electricity bill paid. It always took a few days after that before the workmen reconnected the electricity.

I sculled the rest of my tea and, outside, I pushed the bamboo bench back across the veranda. I climbed up and brandished my airline cutlery again. This time the meter spun, whirred and went dead. I pulled the leads out and put them back in again, but the meter spun, whirred then stopped, even as I tried again and again for an hour. This time the power wouldn't reconnect. I sat on the bench with my chin in my hands, missing Marieke and wondering what I should do. Where was Mesfin?

In an effort to take my mind off things, I tidied up. Under a pile of clothes in my room I found an umbrella cover, inside which was six hundred birr I'd hidden in an empty moisturiser container. I had evidently concealed it very well, even from myself.

In my haste, I almost pushed aside the conductor as the minibus stopped outside the Ethiopian Electric Power Corporation. The doors were still open. I couldn't believe my luck, I'd made it before the office shut and there was no queue. I ran to the counter and slapped my bill down.

'No more payment today.' The young clerk looked at his watch and spoke English. 'You come back next week.'

'Next week?'

'We closed bill payments already. Why didn't you come thirty minutes earlier?'

The rain began as I left Piazza. The deluge was so heavy it coursed underneath my jacket and plastered my hair to my head.

'You-you-you!' two young guys yelled from under an awning. 'Come on!' they yelled to me in English and waved their arms to summon me to share their shelter, but I plodded home in the rain like a cliché from a sentimental memoir.

When I opened the gate to my compound, Tara came bounding to my feet. I scratched behind her chin and apologised for my behaviour, but she was already licking my thighs. I stroked her silky ears and told her I would be kind to her until Marieke returned, when I would be happier, if she could only wait that long. Mesfin was still not back. He was never gone this long and the water office was only a ten-minute walk from our house. I peered into the guard's hut. The blanket I had lent him was missing from his bed, as were the two plastic bags of clothes normally hanging from the bedpost. I looked under the bed for his grain sack of belongings but that was gone too. I lifted the corner of his horsehair mattress where he stashed his papers but there were just a few yellowing receipts.

At first I was numb. How could he do this to me? I was so stupid to have given him all that money; it was more than one month's salary for him. But how could I expect him to stay while I snarled and shouted at him?

I kept telling myself he'd return and I could repent. I tried the phone again, but the line was still dead. Anyway, I couldn't think who I could call without having to explain what a cow I had been.

On the gas stove, I boiled water for a bath. I put some potatoes to bake in the gas oven, but it wasn't until forty-five minutes later I remembered the oven was broken. Then I stepped in the puddle of water from the leaking kitchen sink and cursed my wet socks.

I tried reading by candlelight in the silence, but my aloneness was overwhelming. I thought I heard the clunk of Mesfin's walking stick on the cement, but when I flung open the door, it was just overrun from the gutter plopping onto the concrete. Missing Tadesse felt like a visceral ache. If only I could apologise, but he was thousands of kilometres away on a work assignment in the northern part of Ethiopia. He was out of mobile range, so even if my phone had worked, I couldn't call him. Regardless, I doubted he would want anything to do with me after I had been so horrible.

I was immensely grateful Mesfin had not taken Tara with him, although in reality there was little chance of that. He wouldn't be able to pay for her food on his subsistence wage, and it would be impossible for him to travel with a dog on any buses or find a new guard job, or even beg in the streets if he couldn't find a job.

At bedtime, I let Tara inside to keep me safe but, unused to being indoors, she climbed onto the bed and pawed my face, thinking we were playing a game.

I realised that if someone infiltrated my compound and made it to my room, it would be too late for Tara to protect me. I unwedged the chair from beneath the bedroom door handle and put Tara back in the garden. But then, with every sound outside, I wondered why Tara wasn't barking, and whether she was sleeping or accosting the intruder for a game of fetch.

Back in bed, with the chair re-wedged beneath the door handle, I lay rigid, vigilant. Someone had the spare keys to my house, and Mesfin had a key to the compound. He might have passed it to anyone. I had no guard in a country where everyone had guards, even the poorest people. Without lights or telephone, with an adorable but useless dog, I was vulnerable to any kind of intruder. If anything happened I wouldn't be able to switch on the light or phone for help.

A flea jumped on my foot, and I swatted at it, berating myself for bringing Tara inside. I cursed myself for shouting at Mesfin, and for my stupidity at giving him the money. The scene replayed over and over in my head, only with variations where I was nice to him and he returned with the change from the water office.

I turned out not to be the person I had hoped I would be. Loathing myself, I rolled onto my side and thought about how I used to believe in doing everything from the goodness of my heart, but now all the goodness in my heart seemed gone. I rolled to my other side and swatted at a flea as I made a plan for the rest of my life.

When I got my ticket home, I would take a job with a big salary. I would buy: an ice-cream maker; fifty-seven pairs of shoes; nineteen pairs of bathers; electric venetian blinds; and a feng shui dog kennel for my fierce and effective guard dog. Or dogs, plural.

As if I'd been born again, I planned I would shout with religious zeal to anybody who would listen: I was wrong! You were right all along! Don't worry about injustice; it *has* got nothing to do with us. Don't donate your money, buy yourself something nice!

A shadow passed on the wall from the light coming through the cracks of the shutter. My heart thudded but Tara was silent. I sat up with arms around my knees scratching at another fleabite while I prayed the rosary, reciting the Lord's Prayer and counting off Hail Marys on my fingers. I hoped the holy family wouldn't mind I only turned to them when terrified. I wasn't sure why I was praying anyway. It was hard to believe in a God who handed out rules for living but overlooked the unsolvable injustice I saw every day.

It had been so easy to rage about the world from my lounge room in Australia. I had hated my country and the US, blaming our wealth and apathy for the problems in developing countries. But things were so much more complex.

If I didn't want to stay in Ethiopia to be a do-gooder, and I didn't go home to be a consumer, I didn't know what was left for me. I thought helping the world was my religion, but I couldn't help the world; it seemed I couldn't help anyone. Not little Mekdes or Samira or so many others. My entire purpose for being was a silly waste of time. I lay down again and stiffened with every breeze, every rustle, until grey dawn slunk through the slats in my shutter.

Chapter 25

To return: መመለስ/*memeles*/

At work the next morning, with bleary eyes and a weary mind, I made a to-do list.

1. *Change lock on front door*
2. *Get electricity reconnected*
3. *Get water reconnected*
4. *Get telephone repaired*
5. *Get leaking water pipe repaired*
6. *Find new guard*
7. *Find new maid*
8. *Get university to employ preferred graduates rather than random selection of inappropriate candidates*
9. *Get university to consider employing female graduates*
10. *Get university to purchase airline ticket home to Australia*

Although reluctant to confide the details, I'd mentioned the missing keys and absent guard to my office colleagues. Their responses – panic on their faces and urgency in their voices – convinced me I required new locks and a new guard without delay. The department secretary accompanied me to be my interpreter with the university maintenance man. And when he shook his head and scoffed, I didn't really need her to translate, 'He says, no need of change the locks.'

The maintenance man was the only person who knew how to change the lock, so I had no choice.

The secretary went back to the office and I tackled the next items on my list alone. My Amharic allowed me to understand a broad overview of what people said. Sometimes I got things right, sometimes I missed nuances, and occasionally I got things wrong. I didn't want to impose further on the secretary that day, and no-one else was available to assist me.

I walked to the university finance department to see if they would pay my electricity and water, as was stipulated in my contract. The secretary there said, predictably, 'Come back tomorrow.' The same thing happened at the university plumbing repairs office, on the other side of campus, and on my way back I stopped at the recruitment office. The new secretary scowled at me before I even asked about progress on the new graduates. I walked to the head dean's office and the secretary there said there was no decision yet on a plane ticket for me. I trudged back to my office.

At least I could do my work. I would print off the next round of letters to the dean and the sub-dean, requesting permission to employ our preferred graduates. Even though I had had almost no sleep the night before, I didn't need to compose anything. The letters were waiting for me on the office computer, after many hours and many rewrites to get the tone and wording right, so I now just needed to print them. Then Mama Zenash would take them to the three requisite offices for signatures to sanction the purple university stamp from another office. If we were lucky, the recipients might read them.

In the office I switched on one of our department's two computers, the one that actually worked. The computer booted up but wouldn't open any programs. After turning it off and back on again, it remained the same so I called out for the department secretary.

She poked her head around the partition and in Amharic told me it was like that since yesterday and the computer department technician had already checked it.

'And?'

'*Ayserum*. It doesn't work.'

I couldn't think anymore so I rested my forehead on the desk, between the broken computer and the phone (also nonfunctional due to 'wet season lines'). I was so, so tired, and every aspect of my life seemed pointless. Tears welled again, involuntarily. I was aware how silly I looked, crying over domestic amenities, when the people I worked with had lived through famine and war, but I couldn't stop the tears. I kept my head down and hoped no-one would notice me.

But people who've grown up not crying over domestic inconveniences jump to terrible conclusions when they see someone crying. I heard voices:

'*Besme ab*! Oh my God!'

'Julie's crying!'

'Quick everyone, get here now!'

'What is it, Julie?'

A circle of colleagues crowded, passing me tissues and looking panicked. I blew my nose and mumbled, shamefaced, into it. I told them how I'd stayed awake all night, afraid, with no guard. Then, sniffing and trying to look composed, I passed my to-do list to the secretary.

The manager from another department pressed his mobile phone into my hand, saying, 'You have this. Until your phone is fixed.'

Another colleague set off for the electricity office, while the secretary gathered my backpack, put my papers inside and handed it to me, her head tilted in sympathy, saying, 'Going home, Julie. Sleeping please.'

It was dusk when I woke up to a rapping on the metal gate. Outside, Tara pranced at my feet as I unbolted it, calling, '*Man new*? Who is it?'

'It's me,' said Tadesse.

I couldn't open the gate fast enough. I hugged him, let him go, then hugged him again, then teared up. I buried my face into his shoulder, breathing in his familiar scent. Tara knocked into me as she jumped up to lick his thighs and then down to lick his toes and then back to his thighs.

'You're here! You're here!' I said. 'I thought you weren't coming back.'

'Of course I was coming back.' Tadesse looked incredulous.

'But why? Why would you come back? I was so mean. I was feeling so bad. I don't know why I said those things.'

He wound his arm around my waist and we walked together to the kitchen.

'I'm so sorry. I tried to call and say I was sorry but my phone ...'

'*Ayzosh*, Julieyea. It happen actually,' he said and he seemed so unflappable, and I so flighty, tears welled again.

I turned away from him, ashamed of these relentless tears. I busied myself with my head down, lighting the gas burner and putting the kettle on to boil. It was almost dark inside so I opened the back door to let the last of the afternoon light in. Tara scampered up the back steps to sit at the threshold, watching us with her chin on her paws, while the evening light filled the valley and gave her black fur a gold halo.

'Do you want biscuits?' I said, still not meeting his eyes, leaning under the table to take Hip Hops from a tub.

Tadesse clutched my arm and pulled me close and, like so many times before, I relaxed into him. It felt like Tadesse held me up all the time. With his arms around me I felt so loved, so protected. It felt like nothing mattered, it didn't matter that I was a failure or that I wasn't robust enough for this big dream I had planned my life around.

We stayed like that for ages, with the hiss of the gas burner and the lid of the kettle clattering, and Tara's tail beating on the cement.

'Next time tell me,' he said. 'If you're happy tell me. If you're feeling sad. Tell me. Your happiness is my happiness and your sadness is mine too.'

I let myself imagine a future with this man. It seemed almost tangible. I felt it the length of my body, with my thighs against his, his arms squeezing my waist, my head nuzzled into the space beneath his chin, feeling his heartbeat against my cheek. I let myself imagine a lifetime of babies and of being held and being told I was good enough, that no matter what, he loved me anyway. I breathed it in, I imagined it, I held him tight. But every other part of my future felt too bleak; that happiness seemed incongruous. So I let it go.

I turned off the stove and Tadesse reached for the light switch.

'*Mabrat yellem*, no electricity,' he said, and I saw a look of sudden realisation pass his face. 'Also, where is Mesfin?'

It seemed everyone was at Chelada Bar that night. The bar was crowded with regulars, and usual friends from town – lecturers, and doctors from the wards. I chatted with Doctor Tesfaye from the paediatrics ward and told him about my domestic plight.

He said, 'One day you will laugh about this.'

I said, 'I can't imagine when. The other thing that hurts, next door's guard told me no-one stole Mesfin's blanket. Mesfin sold it at the market because he knew I'd give him another one. So if he did that, and he ran away with my money, probably he took my camera too. It's not so much their money value ... or at least, it's not mainly their value, it's the betrayal. He was my friend, I thought.'

Doctor Tesfaye swirled his whisky. 'One day, you will tell your friends, "I had this guard, who stole my money. And maybe he stole my camera too. He was shifty."'

But Mesfin *wasn't* shifty, or he hadn't been before. I remembered how sometimes he would surprise me by bringing in the washing when it started to rain, or knocking on my window to pass me a hot corncob from his charcoal burner. It was only after he'd gone that I realised how much I relied on him. I didn't know where to get the gas bottle filled, which neighbour's door to knock on for fresh cow's milk, or which part of the river to throw our rubbish in.

While Doctor Tesfaye talked, I conjured misty-edged memories of Mesfin. We would take it in turns throwing the ball for Tara, or listen to the news together on the transistor. He guarded me and entertained me so much I sometimes forgot to be overwhelmed by life. It hurt that he had looked after me so well, yet I had treated him badly, and then he tricked me.

Tadesse returned from the bar with a round of drinks and slid onto a stool beside me. 'Try not to be upset by this bad thing. It happen actually.'

'My cousin got robbed last month,' Doctor Tesfaye said. 'They took everything. His bed, his chair, even they took his textbooks.' He snorted as he tried to keep a straight face.

'Everything?' I was incredulous.

'Even they took his toilet paper. Just they left the floor.' Doctor Tesfaye couldn't hold it in any longer. Tadesse slapped the table and everyone in our group roared.

'That's not funny! It's horrific!' I sputtered, but the group's laughter was infectious as I imagined the cousin's face when he found even his toilet paper missing. I sniggered at first, then for the first time in ages, I laughed too.

Within two days Tadesse had organised a new cleaning lady and a repairman for the leaking sink. After the weekend we got the water bill paid, and the electricity reconnected. Tadesse helped me to find and hire a new guard. Although the university paid our rent and utilities, Marieke and I had to pay for our own guard. As frustrating as that was, I was grateful that was one less thing to wade through bureaucracy for.

The first guard agreed to employment but, preferring to stay at home, sent his ten-year-old son to work instead. Firing the duo one week later, I realised I didn't know the word for 'adult'.

'*And tellek sew efellegalehu.* I want a tall person to work for me,' I said, wishing I knew I the term for 'child labour'.

The next guard came recommended, a colleague's neighbour's cousin's uncle. He shuffled rather than walked, was stooped, had only three remaining teeth and a snowy beard. His eyesight was so deteriorated he often pushed the key into the part of the gate with no keyhole. He was so aged it was hard to picture him beating an egg, let alone a thief.

So I employed another guard, a healthy eighteen-year-old with all his teeth, good vision and tall enough to see over the windowsills. While arranging employees for home, I also spent my days at work, setting up for the next academic year, seeking authorisation for the preferred graduates, and getting myself a ticket back to Australia.

As October approached, some of the other lecturers returned from leave and it took another three weeks of combined efforts – lodging new purple-stamped memos and following up on old ones. It had now been months of waiting outside the offices of the head dean, the sub-dean, the academic dean, the finance dean, the recruitment office and the contracts office.

Forget food aid. I wished Sir Bob Geldof would airlift in some self-help books:

Getting Things Done In Triplicate!™

The 7 Habits of Apathetic Bureaucrats!™

Tangible Achievements Despite Institutionalised Inertia!™

Then, one day, instead of shrugging at me, the secretary from the recruitment office passed me a sheet of university letterhead paper with the purple stamp at the bottom. It was a list of five of our preferred candidates. She went back to playing solitaire and, facing the computer, said in English, 'Approved by recruitment committee. Already we have called them. They will come after two weeks.'

Speechless, and a little dubious, I scrutinised the list again. Excitement rose, but then waned when I noticed they had missed one of our applicants. 'There are only five applicants here. You have missed one of the girls. Her name is Birke.'

'She wasn't approved by recruitment committee.' The secretary didn't look at me, just shrugged and continued to click her mouse.

'Is there anything I can do?' I asked.

The secretary shrugged again.

The other physios were on the adult wards and I was alone in the therapy room. It was a hot afternoon, and no patients had turned up. I was bored and lonely, which gave me time to wonder how we would get one solitary candidate approved. There was a knock at the door and I looked up to see a small girl peeking through.

She said, 'Julie?'

'*Abet*? I'm here?' I wondered how this child knew who I was. Then her mum put her head around the corner too, and I remembered her aquiline features and turquoise headscarf.

'Samira! *Anchi nesh*? Is it you?' I barely recognised her. Where before her face had been puffy and round from the steroid medication, it was now thin, smooth, and healthy. Samira stayed in hospital for three months and left before finishing her rehabilitation, almost two months ago now. At the time I'd worried she would never achieve independent walking, but today Samira strolled across the therapy room, balancing just fine. I exclaimed. '*Gobez nesh*! You are clever!'

Samira's mum clasped my hand and air-kissed my cheeks, three times. Samira stood on tippy-toes to slide her hand around my waist and looked up at me, beaming with pride. I slid my arm around her shoulder too.

It was so gratifying to see Samira mobile, and finally feel I had achieved something, however little it might be in the grand scheme of Ethiopian physiotherapy. I was elated she was walking again, and that she showed no sign of complete paralysis as she had when she was admitted.

'*Esporte be yanchi bet*? You did exercises in your house?' I asked her.

Samira gave big head nods. '*Awe. Ke Enat gar*! Yes. With Mum!'

Her mother blushed with her head down and gave a dismissive wave of her hand.

'*Esporte ahun tifellegiyallesh*? You want exercises now?' I hoped I didn't look as eager as I felt.

'*Gize yellem. Ketoro ke hakim gar allegn.* No time. We have an appointment with the doctor.' Samira's mum clasped my hand again, this time in both of hers, and held it close. She and Samira both spoke, and I couldn't understand everything they said but I caught the idea they had just dropped by to say hi.

I waved goodbye from the step of the therapy room as they departed for the paediatric ward.

'*Keketoro behuala temeleshe. Ye ciao bey. Yanchi bet ruk new*! Returning after your appointment, for goodbye say it! Your home far away!'

An hour later I was summoned to the finance department and handed a plane ticket. I would be leaving the country in one week.

That afternoon Tadesse and I met up at the Blue Asa Fish restaurant, one of our favourites in Merkato, the huge market area. Like always I ordered *asa dulet*, battered fish in spicy sauce and *injera*, and Tadesse ordered *asa goulash*, fish without batter in spicy sauce and *injera*. These were the only two items the restaurant served, each of them delicious as the other.

We hadn't seen each other all day, so once we'd ordered,

Tadesse lifted his Dashen beer in a toast.

'I got a chance today! I got accepted into university. I can become a physiotherapist, with a bachelor degree.'

Tadesse and the other physiotherapy assistants had waited months for approval to join the physiotherapy degree as mature-entry students. It was momentous news for him, and I felt terrible I might later spoil his happy day with my update. I congratulated him and hugged him, telling him I knew he'd do very well and I was proud of him.

I couldn't bring myself to tell Tadesse until our dishes were served. When we'd had a few fortifying bites, I took a deep breath.

'Tadesse, I got my ticket home. I'm leaving in a week.'

'Will you return?' he asked.

'I can't.' I hoped he knew it was because I didn't feel strong enough, not because I didn't want to be with him.

'*Eshi*, okay, Julieyea. You need to doing what makes you happy.'

There was a silence until I said, 'But it's so great you got into university!'

'Maybe when I finish university I can come to Australia to work as a physiotherapist?' That would be in three years. 'I can be your boss,' Tadesse said.

As we laughed, I looked down, pretending to wipe condensation off the label of my beer, but really I didn't want Tadesse to see my wet eyes. I tried to imagine a life together back in Perth. Even if we waited three years, he wouldn't get work as a physio in Australia. His three-year bachelor's degree would not be recognised – the *ferenji* lecturers had already investigated the possibilities of international recognition.

I remembered the Ethiopian family who lived on my street in Perth, who had taught me the rudiments of Amharic before I departed on this adventure. In Australia, the university-educated husband of the family had a job stacking frozen chickens.

'All of the people working in that chicken factory are Ethiopian,' he told me. When I asked him if it was a nice job, he said it was fine, because they spoke Amharic at work, but he felt sad because he didn't know any Australians. 'Simply Ethiopian friends,' he said with a sigh.

I imagined Tadesse studying for three years to end up as a factory worker.

Here, even as a physiotherapy assistant, he was already recognised as an expert in the Ponseti Method of clubfoot treatment. The orthopaedic surgeons on campus organised their clubfoot operation schedule around Tadesse's availability to perform rehabilitation. His eyes lit up when he worked with the kids from the villages, correcting their foot positioning so they could walk, and teaching their families to overcome stigma.

I imagined him putting it all aside to pack chicken nuggets, bewildered in a new land, just like I was, only with everything flipped and this time the responsibility on me for his happiness.

'Okay, maybe?' I said. 'Come after you finish uni. See you in three years.'

'I'll visit you.' We both pretended it was funny, but neither of us had thousands of dollars for a ticket or the extra thousands the government demanded as a bond against absconding. We finished our dinner, chatting as we usually did. Tadesse still corrected my Amharic grammar as if I might need it after a week.

When dinner was over, we went outside to wash our hands under a tap set in a water tank. From the cramped balcony we had a view out over the market below us. The minaret of a mosque stood above the fuzzy silhouette of the hills against a smoky dusk. In the street below, vendors packed away their wares, moving amid dust motes swirling in the thick afternoon light. I watched as two goats ate tomatoes in the street while another nibbled at tufts of cotton from a hessian sack. The evening star twinkled in a sky the colour of gunmetal.

When I said, 'It's the first star, make a wish,' Tadesse looked up too.

I made a wish it were possible to be in two places at once. If only I didn't have to leave this wonderful man and the work I loved, while also being at home in Australia near my family. Those were nonsensical wishes, I realised. So instead I just wished for happiness for us both.

My final week was spent packing up the house. It had come furnished with manchester, cutlery and crockery, so I had to make sure those were in reasonable shape for the new tenants. Two more *ferenji* physiotherapy lecturers from a European volunteer agency would move in to our house in a fortnight. I arranged Marieke's things, already boxed and ready to be moved, against the wall in her room. I piled things the new tenants might need on the bed in the spare room and wondered what I should do with the extra water filter in the corner. It was already propped against the wall, so I didn't move it. Instead I stacked blankets, clean sheets and spare jerry cans around it. I gave the guard enough food for Tara for the next two weeks.

At work I tidied up loose ends and said goodbye to the children on the wards. At my last session with Selam, I gave her three of my good shirts to keep. Her grandma slipped a long-sleeved t-shirt over Selam's red train dress, and rolled the sleeves up. The shirt reached Selam's knees but I figured she would grow into it soon enough. It seemed like a lifetime ago that Sister Starling had told me not to give clothes to patients as it just encouraged dependency. If only Sister could see me now. I slipped a one hundred birr note into Grandma's hand when I handed her the bag of shirts. She spoke to Selam in rapid Amharic and Selam started a theatrical bawling. It was so immediate and so exaggerated that I wondered if this was a begging trick, and if Grandma was using Selam to boost her begging profits. I wondered then if I had done the wrong thing giving them clothes and money, but

I couldn't bear the thought of them both going hungry. I was so tired of wondering and second-guessing myself. I just wanted to go home, where I wasn't confronted with moral ambiguity every day.

While we waited for the taxi, Tadesse and I stood like we had last time I had left the country. He wrapped his arms around me and I ran my hands along his jaw as if my fingertips could prolong the memory. We were silent, holding each other until the cab beeped outside. He smoothed my hair from my eyes, saying, '*Temeleshe*, please come back.'

I swallowed the lump in my throat and wished I was a stronger person, strong enough to stay, or come back, or be anything other than who I was.

'*Aymelesum*, I won't return.' Then I said in English, 'I'm sorry.'

He kissed me for the last time and I stood beside the taxi watching Tadesse walking away over the gravel until he turned the corner. I felt if I breathed in, my heart might crack.

When I boarded the plane for Addis Ababa, I couldn't work out if the tears were for relief or sadness. I was crying for Tadesse, not knowing if I would ever see him again. There were tears of confusion. I had loved my life in Ethiopia but hated it too, had adored and abhorred my workplace and the challenges of daily life. I leaned my head against the window as we gained altitude over the foothills of Gondar, where the circular thatched huts peppered the landscape like mushrooms. I watched the green hills and the Simien Mountains recede until we were immersed in grey clouds and lightning sparked in front of the plane.

I met Sister Almaz in a cafe before going to the international airport in Addis Ababa.

'*Temeleshalesh*? Will you return?' she asked while we waited for our drinks.

'*Aymelesum*. I won't return. I have to give up because I feel too much anger, and too much sadness. There is too much suffering.'

The young waitress set two cups of sweet spiced tea onto the table.

'*Anchi*, you, this means you have been close to God. It says in the Bible when you have experienced their sadness and their anger, then you have felt the poor. You are feeling their pain.' Sister Almaz spoke gently, and took a sip of tea.

'But I don't want to feel pain if I can't do anything about it. I want to stop it. How can we stop people from being poor?'

I'm not sure if I meant it as a rhetorical question, but Sister Almaz scoffed and pushed her cup and saucer away.

'*Anchi*! You! You can't. No way. That's why we have to stay here and be with them. We need to suffer with them.'

She spoke so confidently but it made little sense to me. I just nodded and said, '*Eshi*. Okay.'

'So you're definitely not returning?'

'No, Sister A, definitely *aymelesum*, I won't return.'

'Oh.' She looked disappointed. 'I was going to ask you to bring me some ugg boots.'

When we hugged goodbye, I saw tears in her eyes. She squeezed my hand hard and gave me a gentle push towards the waiting blue and white taxi.

'Never forget your Sister Almaz!' she called while I slammed the door.

'Never!' I yelled out the window as the taxi pulled out.

The clerk at the check-in counter at Addis Ababa airport asked me in English, 'When will you return?'

I replied, '*Aymelesum*. Won't return.'

'*Amaregna techeyallesh*? Can you speak Amharic?' he asked, surprised.

'*Tennish*, *tennish*, a little.'

He entered my details into the computer and looked up. He

asked me in Amharic, 'Would you like to travel in business class?'

I was speechless for a moment before I burst out, '*Awe*! *Betam*! Yes! Very!' I might have even shouted, I was in such a hurry to agree in case he retracted his offer.

In the business lounge I poured a huge glass of Baileys and found a leather armchair, the most comfortable seat I had sat in all year, or maybe all my life. I took a gulp of Baileys, and it was the most delicious thing I had tasted all year, or ever.

Everything was done. I'd enjoyed a long wash in the huge, sparkling bathroom of the lounge, and I'd found a place to settle near the bar and complimentary snacks. It was only when I looked at my watch and saw it was almost midnight that I registered how exhausted I was.

I couldn't believe only the day before I had still been working for University of Gondar. Yesterday morning I had attended a meeting of the academic committee and presented to ten heads of department. The meeting took place at 11 a.m., just one hour before I had to leave for the airport.

Standing tall and trying to sound authoritative but polite, I'd said, 'I would like to request you to authorise the recruitment committee to appoint our nominee, Birke. Of our nominees, three male students but only two female students were appointed. As a final-year student, Birke showed an aptitude for teaching. She is strong academically and she will be a good role model for female students. In this coming year, there are only ten females out of fifty physiotherapy students. They need strong role models.'

I scanned the meeting room where the ten men in suits and ties looked unconvinced. There was silence until the head of the radiology department spoke.

'We must support the education of women. I motion that the academic commission approve this request.'

The men around the room discussed in murmurs until the head dean spoke. 'All in favour?'

Every member of the academic commission raised their hand.

The head dean faced me with a smile. 'Are you satisfied with this outcome?'

'*Betam*! *Betam*! Very! Very! *Amesegenalehu*! Thank you!' I beamed like I'd won an Oscar as I left the meeting room and ran to get a minibus home.

In the business-class lounge, I considered the gourmet treats arrayed in the bain-marie. One last thing remained to be done: my stomach rumbling, I piled a plate with two sausage rolls, a party pie and a mini quiche. It was hours since I'd eaten anything today, and a year since I'd seen these sorts of treats.

A year had seemed like an eternity when I had returned to Ethiopia. Back then I couldn't imagine how I would get through it. But I had, and I'd fulfilled my obligation to the university. But more importantly, I had fulfilled an obligation to myself. I'd wanted to stick it out, to do some good, to feel I could achieve something.

I stacked a cupcake on top of a slice of vanilla Madeira cake on my saucer and reflected that these last two years were more emotionally challenging than I ever expected. Sometimes I had hated being here, then I hated myself for hating it. I had spent so much time being angry at the situation, at the apathy of the bureaucrats, the doctors and the nurses. And now a part of me felt heartbroken to be leaving.

I topped up my Baileys while I waited for the man in front of me to finish filling his plate. By the time I reached the final table in the buffet and collected two mini-packets of peanuts, I felt calm. Relief, that's what it was. Almost two years ago to the day Sister Starling had collected me from this airport. Back then, I'd been shocked to see a young skinny guard with a Kalashnikov picking his teeth with a stick. Today as I checked in, another young skinny guard sat with a Kalashnikov across his lap, daydreaming into the sky. When I first arrived, I was so full of dreams, of the idea that the world was brimming with potential. When I discovered how much suffering the world was full of, I'd been enraged, baffled, and intent on trying to alleviate it. All I had learned since then was that it was impossible to make sense of. Suffering is pointless, arbitrary and defies explanation. Had I lessened any of it? I thought maybe, an infinitesimal amount. Maybe.

And maybe, having found a way to do my best, I could find a way of living without feeling so overwhelmed by the world's unfairness and injustices.

A *ferenji* in a business suit sank into the armchair next to me. He crossed his arms and huffed, 'Goddamn, I hate waiting. Can you believe my plane is delayed?' ,

I took a huge bite of the Madeira cake.

He continued although I hadn't replied. 'Don't you hate these delays? I'm going to Washington. Where are you going?'

I leaned back in the chair and put my feet up on my hand luggage. I raised my glass to him, and said through a mouthful of cake, 'Home.'

Epilogue: Here by your thought

One: እንድ /and/

To: Julie
Subject: Hi from Gondar!
Date: 3 December 2006

Hi Julie,

How are you? Thanks for leaving your house in such a nice way for us to move in to. We like living in Gondar. Tara had puppies! I am expecting them to open their eyes any day now.

I found a Canon camera inside the water filter in the spare room. It is a big camera with long lens. Is it yours? Tadesse told me you were missing a camera. Anyway, let me know if you need me to send it to you!

Take care,
Katarina

Two: ሁለት/hulet/

To: Julie
Subject: Update from Gondar
Date: 23 June 2007

I've been meaning to send you an email for ages, to let you know how things are going with your former maid. We got one of the students to translate your letter to her and explained about the situation with the camera.

She was really pleased to have your gift. She used it to pay for cookery lessons and joined a women's cooperative. They have set up a small shop. I'm not really sure of the details, but we're going to visit her shop soon and I'll give more info then.

Bye for now,
Katarina

To: Julie
Subject: Mesfin in Addis Ababa
Date: 5 April 2008

Hi Julie,

Quick email. Guess who I bumped into today? Mesfin! I saw him in Piazza in Addis Ababa. He is living in a big house with other people with disabilities near Merkato. I asked him if he wanted to work for me again, but he says he is very happy. He earns good money begging. I explained to him about your camera in the water filter.

More later,
Liefs,
Marieke.

Three: ሦስት/sost/

To: Julie
Subject: Exams finished!
Date: 13 July 2009

Hi my dear,

We finished our exam and now we will graduate from bachelor degree on July 18.

I know you are here by your thought,

I miss you,
Tadesse

To: Julie
Subject: News for you :)
Date: 26 June 2014

Dear Julie,

I am almost finished my thesis. I will graduate my Master of Physiotherapy after one month. Next month I am to give training to physiotherapists about clubfoot. It's a collaboration with a big international hospital.

Give my hi to all your family. I hope we will talk soon.

Miss you betam, very.
Tadesse

Four: አራት /arat/

Since 2006, more than five hundred physiotherapists have graduated from the Bachelor of Physiotherapy at University of Gondar. A Master of Physiotherapy program commenced there in 2010. Physiotherapy is available in clinics and hospitals all over the country.

Julie visited Ethiopia in 2010 for Marieke's wedding, and again in 2013 for work. These days she uses her Amharic for ordering in Ethiopian restaurants and chatting with Ethiopian taxi drivers about where to find good Ethiopian restaurants. Despite occasional lapses into despair, Julie has salvaged her idealism and continues do-gooding where possible. She encourages anyone who feels it's a waste of time making the world into a better place to try anyway.

Afterword

A word to Ethiopian readers: '*Yikerta, tennish tennish Amaregna bicha*. Excuse me, I only speak a little Amharic.' It's a privilege to use your language to tell my story and I hope you'll forgive any mistranslations, grammatical errors and inaccuracies. *Betam amesegenalehu*, thank you for making me feel welcome in your country.

A word to *ferenji* readers: '*Yikerta, tennish tennish Amaregna bicha*. Excuse me, I only speak a little Amharic.' My Amharic translations were confirmed by Tadesse Teshager Woreta, with backup from *Lonely Planet Ethiopian Amharic Phrasebook*. Transliterations were corrected by Gizachew Tessema. Some variations in spelling may occur as there is no official transliteration from the Amharic fidel alphabet to English, and Amharic contains additional vowels and consonants that do not occur in English. Any errors in translation or spelling are mine.

A further note to *ferenji* readers: Ethiopia's history extends over three thousand years of dynasties, kingdoms, emperors, empresses, conquests and resistance to colonisation. However, in the West, the story of Ethiopia is often conflated with famine and poverty, and the length of its history overshadowed by the last sixty years. My story is set while Ethiopia was recovering from a war that had ended five years earlier, and is framed by the narrator's own expectations and mental health. While writing this book I felt the tension between contributing to stereotypical representations of Ethiopia while detailing what the unfair distribution of our planet's wealth looks like up close.

In the fifteen years between my experiences and this book being published, Ethiopia has undergone tremendous change.

There have been changes in government, and the border conflict with Eritrea is over. New roads, hospitals, supermarkets and restaurants have been built while internet, mobile phones and social media are now widely accessible.

Poverty still persists, but that isn't the only story to tell about Ethiopia. Any conversations about addressing the imbalance of resources between developed and developing countries need to move beyond generalisations, and the idea there's a single narrative to be told about a nation.

Just as my fledgling vocabulary won't convey the lyricism and complexity of Amharic, this work won't convey the range of lives across the country, which has as many stories as it has people. Ethiopia has the full range of people who are rich, poor, or in-between. There are people who attend art galleries and go out for ice-cream, people who work in downtown offices and have picnics on weekends, as well as families in similar circumstances to those I wrote about.

In my book there wasn't space to write the full spectrum of each of the children's stories, beyond being a physiotherapy patient. How at home, they sang songs and made-believe, kicked footballs, collected rocks and picked daisies. How they were busy being amazed by life while some of us worried ourselves sick over it. This story is a snapshot of a particular place in time, from someone taking small steps to find her place in the world.

Acknowledgements

My sincere thanks go to the following people: Georgia Richter, my publisher at Fremantle Press, for recognising my vision for the story and shaping it with such warmth, humour and patience. Gillian Kendall, my early editor and mentor, for guiding me to trust my voice and bring this book into being. Tadesse Teshager, for Amharic translations and agreeing to play a starring role. Gizachew Tessema, for finalising the translations and providing a consistent transliteration from the Amharic fidel into English. Sally Couboules, Andrew Fox, Ahona Guha, Andrew Hately, Maciej Napieraj, Belinda Nechwatal and Brooke Underwood Murray for their meticulous critique and suggestions. Martin Lyndsay and members of the Perth Writers Forum critique group for feedback. Anna Solding from MidnightSun Publishing for a mentorship, and Katharine Susannah Prichard Writers' Centre for coordinating the opportunity. Maria de Vicente Capua and Kate Lomas Glendenning for edits to Amharic spelling. Claire Miller, Jen Bowden and Chloe Walton for marketing support. The judges of the 2018 City of Fremantle Hungerford Award, Delys Bird, Catherine Noske and Richard Rossiter, for shortlisting my manuscript. Marieke Boersma and the real Sister Almaz for agreeing to appear in the book. I would also like to thank Natasha Clement, Emma Field and Melanie Gallagher for critiques, workshopping and decades of support. Chris Schlusser for refusing to let me leave the computer until I sent the submission to the Hungerford Award, for always agreeing to recheck sections, and for everything. Nigel and Renee Sprigg, Michelle Sprigg, Anita and Andrew Skelton for holding me afloat. Mum and Dad for making us watch *Four Corners* while everyone else at school was watching *A Country Practice*, and encouraging us to dream up a lifetime of adventures.

First published 2020 by
FREMANTLE PRESS

Fremantle Press Inc. trading as Fremantle Press
25 Quarry Street, Fremantle WA 6160
(PO Box 158, North Fremantle WA 6159)
www.fremantlepress.com.au

Cover photograph by Joel Carillet, 'African children and shoes outside church on Lake Tana, Ethiopia': iStock, 182862111.
Cover design: Nada Backovic, nadabackovic.com
Author photo: Leigh Miller
Printed by McPherson's Printing Group, Victoria, Australia.

ISBN 9781925815603 (paperback)
ISBN 9781925815610 (ebook)

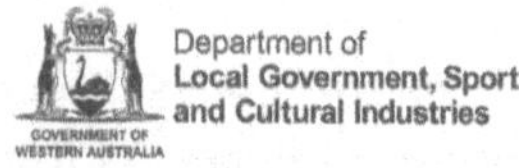

Fremantle Press is supported by the State Government through the Department of Local Government, Sport and Cultural Industries.

Publication of this title was assisted by the Commonwealth Government through the Australia Council, its arts funding and advisory body.